FIELD HOSPITAL

FIELD HOSPITAL

The Church's Engagement with a Wounded World

WILLIAM T. CAVANAUGH

WILLIAM B. EERDMANS PUBLISHING COMPANY
Grand Rapids, Michigan / Cambridge, U.K.

Published 2016 by
WM. B. EERDMANS PUBLISHING CO.
2140 Oak Industrial Drive N.E., Grand Rapids, Michigan 49505 /
P.O. Box 163, Cambridge CB3 9PU U.K.

Printed in the United States of America

22 21 20 19 18 17 16   7 6 5 4 3 2 1

Library of Congress Cataloging-in-Publication Data

Names: Cavanaugh, William T., 1962-
Title: Field hospital: the church's engagement with a wounded world /
William T. Cavanaugh.
Description: Grand Rapids, Michigan : Eerdmans Publishing Company, 2016.
Identifiers: LCCN 2015038501 | ISBN 9780802872975 (pbk.: alk. paper)
Subjects: LCSH: Mission of the church. | Catholic Church — Doctrines.
Classification: LCC BV601.8 .C38 2016 | DDC 261.8 — dc23
LC record available at http://lccn.loc.gov/2015038501

www.eerdmans.com

For my parents, Bill and Marian Cavanaugh

CONTENTS

ACKNOWLEDGMENTS

WRITING A BOOK is always a communal effort. Much as they might come to regret it after reading these pages, a number of people have encouraged me and helped me to develop the thoughts in this book. All the chapters in this book were written at the invitation of others. I would like to thank Paul Allen (Concordia University, Canada), Maria Clara Bingemer and Paulo Fernando Carneiro de Andrade (Pontifical Catholic University of Rio de Janeiro), Michael Budde and Peter Casarella (DePaul), Monserrat Herrero (University of Navarra, Spain), George Kalantzis and Gregory Lee (Wheaton), John McCormack (Notre Dame), James Murphy (Dartmouth), and Charlie Pinches (Scranton) for invitations to present some of the material in this book at their universities. Thanks also to Christian Amondson, David Cunningham, Tim Furry, Peter Hampson, Craig Hovey, Eugene Korn, Robert Jenson, David Matzko McCarthy, Beth Phillips, John Roth, and Christopher Vogt for their invitations to write and their careful editorial work.

Additional thanks go to my colleagues and friends at DePaul and St. Thomas for being excellent conversation partners. As always, my wife Tracy and my sons — Finnian, Declan, and Eamon — are my constant source of support and joy. This book is dedicated to my parents, Bill and Marian Cavanaugh, who showed me how to be faithful.

INTRODUCTION

WHAT KIND OF church do you dream of?"
This was the question to which Pope Francis was responding when he famously likened the church — at least the church
he would like to see — to a field hospital. "I see clearly," Francis said,
"that the thing the church needs most today is the ability to heal wounds
and to warm the hearts of the faithful; it needs nearness, proximity. I
see the church as a field hospital after battle. It is useless to ask a seriously injured person if he has high cholesterol and about the level of
his blood sugars! You have to heal his wounds. Then we can talk about
everything else. Heal the wounds, heal the wounds. And you have to
start from the ground up."[1]

The pope could have answered the question about his dream church
with an idealized portrait of the institution, but immediately he turned
to the overwhelming reality of suffering; the ideal church is a wounded
church, one where wounds are acknowledged first, and the acknowl-
edgment itself begins the healing. Nearness, proximity to wounds —
that is where the church needs to be found. The battle rages — all is
not well with the world. But rather than condemn the evils of the world
from a position of superiority, the church needs to be on the battlefield,
not as a participant in the bloodletting but as the medical corps that
risks its safety and its very life to bind up the wounds inflicted in the
battle.

It is possible that the pope meant the metaphor of battle in a purely
spiritual sense. He goes on to explain the reference to cholesterol and
blood sugars in terms of "small things," "small-minded rules" that have
to do primarily with the Catholic Church hierarchy's emphasis on a few
sexual issues to the neglect of more central matters.[2] By way of con-

---

1. Francis, "A Big Heart Open to God," interview with Antonio Spadaro, S.J., *America,*
September 30, 2013; http://americamagazine.org/pope-interview.

2. "We cannot insist only on issues related to abortion, gay marriage and the use of
contraceptive methods. This is not possible. I have not spoken much about these things,
and I was reprimanded for that. But when we speak about these issues, we have to talk

1

trast, the pope offers that "The most important thing is the first proclamation: Jesus Christ has saved you."[3] Salvation, however, is not just
something for the spirit; we are bodily creatures, and Pope Francis has
put those who are materially poor at the center of his ministry. When
he says that the church needs to heal wounds and warm hearts, he is
addressing both the body and the soul, the exterior and the interior,
of the human person, and addressing both those who suffer material
deprivation and those who suffer spiritual deprivation. The two are inherently related. As Francis has made clear in his fierce denunciations
of the "economy [that] kills,"[4] the exclusion of a billion people from
access to a dignified subsistence is directly related to the sickness of
spirit that worships at the altar of capital. The "idolatry of money"[5] is
both a material and a spiritual wound.

My purpose in this introduction is not so much to explain Pope Francis's thought as to explain why I have borrowed his metaphor of the
church as field hospital for the title of this book. The chapters of this
book, like much of my earlier work, examine the intersection of theology with economics, politics, and violence. The church that I dream
of in the following pages is one that helps heal wounds both spiritual
and material, a church that does not remain confined to the ambit of
"religion" but, as in Pope Francis's metaphor, goes out on to the field

---

about them in a context. The teaching of the church, for that matter, is clear and I am a
son of the church, but it is not necessary to talk about these issues all the time.

"The dogmatic and moral teachings of the church are not all equivalent. The church's
pastoral ministry cannot be obsessed with the transmission of a disjointed multitude of
doctrines to be imposed insistently. Proclamation in a missionary style focuses on the
essentials, on the necessary things: this is also what fascinates and attracts more, what
makes the heart burn, as it did for the disciples at Emmaus. We have to find a new balance; otherwise even the moral edifice of the church is likely to fall like a house of cards,
losing the freshness and fragrance of the Gospel. The proposal of the Gospel must be
more simple, profound, radiant. It is from this proposition that the moral consequences
then flow." Francis, "A Big Heart Open to God." Francis is not saying that sexual issues
are unimportant, but that the church's stance on them needs to come out of our more
central convictions about salvation through Jesus Christ.

3. Francis, "A Big Heart Open to God."

4. Francis, *Evangelii Gaudium,* §53; http://w2.vatican.va/content/francesco/en/
apost_exhortations/documents/papa-francesco_esortazione-ap_20131124_evangelii
-gaudium.html. "Such an economy kills. How can it be that it is not a news item when
an elderly homeless person dies of exposure, but it is news when the stock market loses
two points?"

5. Francis, *Evangelii Gaudium,* §55.

of battle, not to kill and maim but to bind up wounds. The church in this image is a hospital, an organization of people for a specific healing purpose. Francis dreams not merely of individual Christians going out into the world to help; "it would be wrong to see [the church's mission] as a heroic individual undertaking, for it is first and foremost the Lord's work, surpassing anything which we can see and understand."[6] The church is not a collection of individuals, not even just an organization, but an organism. The church is in fact not an "it" but a "we," a living subject, united to Christ our head, a body of people that brings many individual persons together, binding wounds precisely in binding people to one another in mutual care and love. For the same reason, the church is not the hierarchy but all of us. You have to start, as Francis says, from the ground up. And like any good hospital, the church attempts to heal all those looking for healing, Christian or not.

The church, though, is not just a hospital but a *field* hospital. Unlike a stationary institution that occupies a certain territory and defends it against encroachment, a field hospital is mobile, an event more than an institution. A field hospital is unconcerned about defending its own prerogatives, and instead goes outside of itself to respond to an emergency. As a body, it is visible, but it does not claim its own territory; its event-like character creates spaces of healing. It neither withdraws from the world, sect-like, nor resigns itself to the world as it is. It is not confined to working within the given political and economic structures of the world, nor is it concerned primarily with gaining influence among the powerful in order to change the world from above. The approach is from below. As Francis has written in *Evangelii Gaudium*, "An evangelizing community gets involved by word and deed in people's daily lives; it bridges distances, it is willing to abase itself if necessary, and it embraces human life, touching the suffering flesh of Christ in others."[7] This church is not a "player" in the game of the powerful. "I prefer a Church which is bruised, hurting and dirty because it has been out on the streets, rather than a Church which is unhealthy from being confined and from clinging to its own security. I do not want a Church concerned with being at the centre and which then ends by being caught up in a web of obsessions and procedures."[8]

6. Francis, *Evangelii Gaudium*, §12.
7. Francis, *Evangelii Gaudium*, §24.
8. Francis, *Evangelii Gaudium*, §49.

The image of the church as field hospital is important because it is dynamic and helps therefore to confound one of the standard dualities used to discuss the church's social engagement: the church either engages with "culture" and "the world," or withdraws from them. The image of the church as field hospital makes clear that the church cannot retreat into enclaves but must go out and heal wounds. Real sectarians, however, are much rarer than the charge of sectarianism, which is often used to dismiss even deeply committed activists like Dorothy Day and her followers because their critique of the state goes deeper than merely trying to manage its ill effects. Those who make the charge of sectarianism regard the refusal to do violence on behalf of the nation-state as a form of irresponsible withdrawal. The image of field hospital, on the other hand, puts the burden of proof on those who would inflict wounds rather than heal them. It also opens the possibility that the church's action on the social and political field of battle could be something more creative than simply lending its support to one or the other of the combatants. In the United States, the church's political imagination is often limited to throwing its dwindling weight behind Democratic or Republican initiatives, in pursuit of a liberal or conservative legislative agenda. Absent is any deeper critique of social, political, and economic institutions, and the attempt to imagine and enact new and more humane types of social, political, and economic practices. The image of field hospital pictures the church not simply lobbying but taking risks, refusing to accept "the political system" or "the economy" as is, but rather creating new mobile and improvised spaces where different kinds of politics or economic practices can take root.

Many of the chapters of this book have taken shape in response to critiques of my work and oversimplifications of Catholic social thought more generally. I am often lumped in with a variously defined group of "radical" Christian thinkers who, though prophetic and inspiring, fail to appreciate the goodness of nature and so turn their backs on participation in the world's given structures, preferring to huddle together in small, perfectionist sects of like-minded Christians.[9] This book is

9. Benjamin Peters has argued that the critique of more radical Catholic movements is often based on an unwitting reproduction of pre–Vatican II two-tiered ideas of the self-sufficiency of nature. The newer correlational approach embraces the world as already graced and seeks to work within natural institutions like the state to thematize the grace already located there. This "sacramental" approach, as it is sometimes called, sees the sacred as the secular brought to fullness. The problem, as Peters says, is that "human

in part an attempt to change the terms of this debate. In the second chapter, for example, I take on Charles Curran's reading of American Catholic social movements and argue that the choice before us is considerably more complex than the rejection or embrace of "the world," given that Catholic social thought uses the term "world" in at least four different senses. In chapters 2 and 3, I argue that there is no "the economy" to either embrace or shun, but rather a plurality of economies that express deeply embedded theological commitments. Chapters 5 through 7, I hope, make clear that refusing to accept that the dreary choice between two corporate-sponsored political parties is all that is meant by "politics" is not thereby to refuse participation in politics, nor is it a rejection of democracy. Indeed, I advocate Christian experiments in forms of democracy that involve a much more significant commitment to politics than punching a few chads every four years. In chapters 8 and 13, I take issue with the idea that dreaming of a more interesting and healing church necessarily involves fantasizing about a purified and perfectionist church. To this end, in chapter 8 I critique John Howard Yoder's reading of church history after Constantine as wholesale apostasy interrupted by only a few "faithful remnant" communities of the pure. In the thirteenth and final chapter of the book, I show that, for Dorothy Day, Christian nonviolence was based not in a sense of separation from — and superiority to — the common run of human sinners, but rather in a deeply penitential awareness of the solidarity of all human beings in sin.

Solidarity has both the first and the last word in this book. The kind of church I dream of goes out into the world and helps to bind wounds by taking on the suffering of others into the suffering body of Christ. All people, Christian or not, are members or potential members of the body of Christ, as Dorothy Day liked to say. To see all humans as made in the image of God — which Colossians (1:15) identifies with Christ — is to see the deep solidarity of all human beings.

---

nature is understood to be sufficient 'as is' due to the always-already present, albeit unthematized, illumination of grace." This move prevents any deeper transformation of human institutions because it ignores the traditional view — stemming from Thomas Aquinas — of "the necessity of *gratia elevans* to bring about the perfection of human nature beyond that which is sinful. As a result, an always-already-graced human nature ends up looking a lot like one which is self-contained." Benjamin Peters, " 'Apocalyptic Sectarianism': The Theology at Work in Critiques of Catholic Radicals," *Horizons* 32, no. 9 (Fall 2012): 220-21.

The three parts of the book deal with three kinds of wounds: economic wounds, political wounds, and the wounds of violence. The first chapter establishes the reality of solidarity in terms of corporate personhood. I examine the reaction against the *Citizens United* ruling by the U.S. Supreme Court, which gave business corporations and unions the same free speech rights as individual persons. Contrary to the reaction that stressed that only individual humans are persons, I argue that the reality of corporate personhood is deeply embedded in Christian thought and practice. Nevertheless, I argue on a different basis that the *Citizens United* ruling was disastrous, because it privileged class-based business corporations over genuine corporate persons that instantiate solidarity among rich and poor.

The second chapter illustrates how Christians can enact economic solidarity rather than simply viewing "the economy" as an abstract and unintelligible given best left to the management of experts. I take the example of a small Catholic town in 1950s Iowa to argue that the stereotype of pre–Vatican II Catholic enclaves as separated from the world is only half right at best. Through an elaborate system of cooperative economic arrangements, the residents of Westphalia, Iowa, wove together their faith with their economy in ways that involved them deeply in "the world." Though such Catholic enclaves cannot and should not be re-created, they can provide inspiration today for the creative intertwining of faith and economic practice.

The third chapter offers more reasons why economic practice and theory should not be abandoned to the control of experts. I examine debates about the status of economics as a science and its place in the university. In many prestigious universities, econometrics — the use of statistics and mathematical theories to reduce economic behaviors to empirically-observable and predictable systems — is considered "orthodox" economics, scientific and far superior to "heterodox" economics that relies less on quantification and more on analysis of history, social structure, and so on. I argue in this chapter that the borrowing of theological language of orthodox and heterodox is telling; far from value-neutral, economics is about *doxa,* "belief." I examine economics as theology and argue for the importance of theological analysis in economic matters.

In the fourth and final chapter of the first part, I give one example of how theology and economic analysis can work together. In this chapter I place the discernment of vocation in the contemporary world in the

wider context of economic changes that have occurred since the early
modern period. The idea of choosing one's life came about as the result
of subsistence farmers being pushed off their land and into wage labor
in the course of the enclosure of common lands, the Industrial Revolution, and the colonization of non-European lands. The economy of
choice that was created, often by coercion, has its benefits but also its
drawbacks, what psychologist Barry Schwartz has called "the tyranny of
choice." Not only can we not always get what we want, but it is hard to
know what we want. I provide some theological resources for discerning our true desires and learning to narrate the choices we have made
as part of God's story.

In the second part of the book, I turn from economic to political
practices, though the two are of course not neatly separable. Chapters
5 through 7 are explorations in grassroots democracy from a theological point of view. Chapter 5 considers the peculiar anxiety of some
"postsecular" thinkers to guard against the incursion of theology into
political theology. There is a large body of political theology that draws
on Carl Schmitt and others to see political theology as an analysis of the
operative fictions and myths behind our political institutions. Though
thus blurring the lines between theology and politics, such thinkers
nevertheless insist that political theology is a "secular," not "religious,"
endeavor to which theologians like me, who actually take God seriously, are not invited. In this chapter, I argue that the kind of liberating
and democratic political practice these thinkers seek is best served not
by policing the border between transcendence and immanence, but
rather by opening political space to an incarnational and sacramental
practice. I call on Catholic thinkers Henri de Lubac and Ivan Illich to
give flesh to this idea.

Chapter 6 continues the exploration of grassroots political (and
economic) practices through an examination of Pope Benedict XVI's
encyclical *Caritas in Veritate*. Though not without its ambiguities, the
document encourages a "dispersed political authority" and attempts to
go beyond the stifling binary of state and market. I analyze two different interpretations of the idea of subsidiarity in Catholic social thought,
and I locate *Caritas in Veritate* in the more radical strand. In so doing, I
locate the encyclical within a longer tradition of Catholic advocacy for
more complex and decentralized social, political, and economic spaces.

In chapter 7 I explore some possibilities in Saint Augustine's thought
for advancing the idea of "dispersed political authority." To do so, I

read Augustine's *City of God* alongside some aspects of the thought of contemporary "radical democracy" theorist Sheldon Wolin. I make no claim that the two very different figures are up to the same thing, but in both their diagnoses of empires and their positive comments on the necessity of "pilgrim" or "fugitive" communities, they have much in common to offer a Christian practice of the political. Both advocate a kind of politics of multiplicity, though they differ on the ultimate end of politics.

The final chapter of part II, chapter 8, follows the discussion on Augustine with a consideration of Constantine and the broader question of how to narrate the history of the church and its entanglement with political power. Here I try to make plain that advocacy of a kind of anti-imperial grassroots political practice does not necessarily entail the repudiation of the long Christian experience of Christendom as the "fall" of the church, that is, wholesale unfaithfulness and apostasy from the purity of the gospel. I consider Peter Leithart's book on Constantine and its critique of the work of John Howard Yoder. I argue against the kind of moral reading of church history that both Leithart (in approval) and Yoder (in disapproval) impose on Constantinianism, and argue instead for a kind of pedagogical reading of church history that does not too easily separate the pure from the impure. I then go on to consider Leithart's treatment of violence, and argue that his defense of Christian wielding of the sword cannot be justified on christological grounds.

This discussion of the sword provides a segue into the third part of the book, on violence and "religion." For the church to be a healing presence on modern battlefields, it must both challenge the common notion that "religion" is inherently violent and challenge Christians to rethink their willingness to support killing for "secular" things like "our American way of life." Chapter 9 carries forward the discussion of my book *The Myth of Religious Violence* (Oxford University Press, 2009). I first recap the argument of the book, which in brief is that people are just as likely to kill for "secular" reasons as for "religious" reasons, because there is no essential difference between "religious" and "secular" ideologies and institutions to begin with. The religious/secular distinction is a recent Western invention, not simply part of the ways things are and always have been. After briefly laying out the argument, I respond to the discussion that the book has generated. I respond to critiques of the book and attempt to clear up misreadings of the argument. In particular, I try to dispel the idea that my book is a defense of "religion," either claiming that violence is really political and not religious or claiming that there is no such thing as religion. My historicization of the religious/secular distinction is meant to level the playing field, and show that people kill for all sorts of things: gods, yes, but also flags, kings, freedom, oil, the workers' revolution, the free market, and so on. The point is not just to defend Christianity from the charge of being inherently violent, but to pry Christians' loyalty loose from the things we actually, today, kill for, especially economic and political ideologies.

Chapter 10 takes on another variation of the argument that religion promotes violence that I did not address in my book. Here I address Mark Lilla's influential argument in his book *The Stillborn God* that Western civilization has produced a "Great Separation" between politics and theology, a fragile achievement that is now threatened by people (like me) who are stubbornly unwilling to let human politics rest on a purely human foundation. In a detailed examination of his narrative, I argue against Lilla not only on normative but also on descriptive grounds. Based on my work on the genealogy of the religious/secular distinction, I argue that there are no grounds for supposing that "secular" politics are more inherently peaceful than theological politics. And I argue that there never was in fact any Great Separation. What we have seen instead is political theology in a different guise. The sacred has migrated from the church to the "secular" nation-state, which in the West enjoys a near monopoly on violence. We need not the separation of politics from theology, but the separation of politics from bad theology.

In chapter 11 I extend the argument about religious violence into more explicitly theological territory. I argue that my claim that there is no *essential* difference between "religious" and "secular" ideologies and institutions is nothing more startling than the biblical critique of idolatry, which sees clearly that people are spontaneously worshiping creatures who treat all sorts of things as if they were gods. I show that the biblical critique of idolatry goes well beyond the explicit worship of other gods to the displacement of loyalty to the one true God onto things like military might and money. To critique idolatry is not necessarily to retreat to a pre–Vatican II church more comfortable throwing anathemas at the world outside the church, however. If we take Paul's treatment of Athenian idolatry in Acts 17 as a guide, we can, like Paul, both decry false worship in ourselves and others, and sympathetically see in it the inchoate groping of people toward the true God.

Chapter 12 takes my deconstruction of the category of "religion" to the context of present debates over religious freedom in the United States. Various Christian groups — none so vigorously as the U.S. Catholic bishops — have claimed the banner of religious liberty in response to various government encroachments against church autonomy. While I think that government interference needs to be resisted, I am ambivalent about doing so under the aegis of "religious freedom." I use the experience of Pueblo tribes in the 1920s to illustrate that defining oneself as a "religion" can have unintended side effects, including the individualization of the group and the assimilation of the group to American culture to an unhealthy degree.

As I try to make clear in chapter 13, however, the goal of the church is not to stand apart from the rest of the culture for the sake of being different. I examine Dorothy Day's nonviolence in the light of her claims that "we are to blame for the war in Europe." Day did not advocate nonviolence as a way of separating a perfectionist elite from the sinful world. On the contrary, her nonviolence stemmed from a deep sense of solidarity with all of humanity, united in the mystical body of Christ. This solidarity not only made it unthinkable to attack a member of one's own body. It also meant that the guilt for the sin that drove the violence was spread throughout the body and shared by all. Dorothy Day refused the temptation to use violence not from a sense of purity but from a sense that we are not good enough to use violence well.

The chapters of this book were written for various occasions over the last few years. Together, however, I intend them to make a coherent argument for a merciful church with the courage to be eccentric, that is, "to go forth from our own comfort zone in order to reach all the 'peripheries' in need of the light of the Gospel."[10]

---

10. Francis, *Evangelii Gaudium*, §20.

I

MARKETS AND BODIES

CHAPTER ONE

ARE CORPORATIONS PEOPLE?

THE CORPORATE FORM AND

THE BODY OF CHRIST

I N JANUARY OF 2010, the United States Supreme Court handed down its landmark 5-4 decision in *Citizens United v. Federal Election Commission,* which overturned limits on political expenditures by corporations and unions. The Court was asked to rule on the narrow question of whether or not the advocacy group Citizens United could advertise for and air a film critical of Hillary Clinton close to the Democratic primary, but the Court decided to broaden the case out to rule on the constitutionality of campaign finance laws. In doing so, they struck down significant parts of the McCain-Feingold Act of 2002. Although corporations and unions are still barred from making direct contributions to political candidates in order to avoid *quid pro quo* corruption or the appearance thereof, they can now spend freely on electioneering communications that attack or advocate for candidates within sixty days of a general election or thirty days of a primary, without the inconvenience of having to set up a separate PAC, or political action committee, to do their speaking for them.[1]

The decision was immediately hailed and decried as a major turning point in U.S. law, not simply because of the decision reached but also because of the way the majority argued. Corporations and unions were clearly regarded as the subjects of speech; they could speak like human beings, and therefore their free speech rights should not be "chilled."

---

1. *Citizens United v. Federal Election Commission,* 558 US 310 (2010). The McCain-Feingold Act is more formally known as the Bipartisan Campaign Reform Act of 2002 (BCRA).

Although the Supreme Court had long given some First Amendment protections to corporations, the majority in *Citizens United* argued against the law's ability to make any sort of distinction among speakers in First Amendment cases. Reaction against the decision by the 80 percent of Americans who oppose it[2] has tended to echo the conviction of Justice John Paul Stevens's furious dissenting opinion: the speakers in this case "are not natural persons, much less members of our political community."[3] "Corporations are not people" is the refrain of politicians, books, Web sites, and blogs dedicated to overturning *Citizens United*.[4] Only individual human beings are people, and therefore only individual human beings should be the subjects of a democracy.

In this chapter I take issue with that type of criticism from a theological point of view. The fact is that corporate personhood is central to Christianity; the people of God and the body of Christ are corporate persons, recognition of which should prevent Christians from thinking that only individuals are actors in the world. Corporate personhood is at the basis of a Christian practice of solidarity. At the same time, however, I think that *Citizens United* is a disastrous and distorting decision, not because it recognizes corporate persons as such, but because of the kind of corporate person it privileges, the business corporation. To critique *Citizens United* we must go deeper than trying to privilege the individual actor in the marketplace of ideas and critique the integration of politics and markets that stands underneath the distortion of any ideas of citizen participation.

I will begin with a brief look at bodies politic in the ancient world, compared and contrasted with biblical views of corporate personhood. Then I will discuss the simultaneous rise in modernity of states and corporations, and why they fall short of a truly participatory politics.

---

2. According to an ABC–*Washington Post* poll conducted February 4-8, 2010; see Dan Eggen, "Poll: Large Majority Opposes Supreme Court's Decision on Campaign Financing," *Washington Post,* February 17, 2010; http://www.washingtonpost.com/wp-dyn/content/article/2010/02/17/AR2010021701151.html?sid=ST2010021702073.

3. *Citizens United,* Opinion of Stevens, J., p. 32.

4. For example, Ari Berman, "Elizabeth Warren to Romney: 'Corporations Are Not People,'" *Nation,* September 5, 2012; http://www.thenation.com/blog/169773/elizabeth-warren-romney-corporations-are-not-people; Jeffrey D. Clements, *Corporations Are Not People: Why They Have More Rights Than You Do and What You Can Do about It* (San Francisco: Berrett-Koehler, 2012); corporationsarenotpeople.com; Thom Hartmann, *Unequal Protection: How Corporations Became "People" and How You Can Fight Back* (San Francisco: Berrett-Koehler, 2010).

I will examine the *Citizens United* decision in more detail, and argue that although the idea of a corporate person is coherent and important, the privileging of the business corporation is a distortion of the kind of communal body that the church is called to promote and enact.

I. Bodies Politic in the Ancient World

The idea of a corporate person can be found in the ancient Greek analogy of a body politic. Here the *polis* was construed on the analogy of an individual human body. Plato begins the *Republic* by treating society on analogy with the human body, which can be either feverish or healthy. Aristotle develops the idea further: "the state has a natural priority over the household and over any individual among us. For the whole must be prior to the part. Separate hand or foot from the whole body, and they will no longer be hand or foot except in name."[5] The *polis* is therefore not a human creation but reflects the order of nature; it is "both natural and prior to the individual."[6] The individual receives life by participation in the larger whole; the whole is not constructed of preexisting parts. The individual, then, attains fulfillment by participation in the *polis,* but that participation for Aristotle was not on an equal basis. The body analogy allowed for a hierarchical relationship; just as the head governed the body, so certain people were naturally fit for rule. Citizenship was limited to propertied men; women, children, slaves, resident foreigners, and many laborers were excluded. Aristotle was not a democrat in the modern sense because he did not think that the *demos* had either the leisure to commit to informed decision making or the means to hire someone else to represent it.[7] Democracy in the ancient world excluded the working class; it was taken for granted that to be a citizen one could not be dependent on others for employment. In other words, contrary to what we have been taught to think today, one could not have democracy in a class-divided society.[8]

Corporate personhood is inflected differently in the biblical tradi-

5. Aristotle, *Politics,* trans. T. A. Sinclair and Trevor J. Saunders (London: Penguin, 1981), p. 60 (1253a18).

6. Aristotle, *Politics,* p. 60 (1253a18).

7. Aristotle, *Politics,* pp. 254-55 (1292b21-34), pp. 368-72 (1318b6-1319b27).

8. C. B. MacPherson, *The Life and Times of Liberal Democracy* (Oxford: Oxford University Press, 1977), pp. 12-13.

tion, beginning with the creation of all human beings in the image of God. It is not the case that only individuals are made in the image and likeness of God. The image of God in Genesis 1:27 seems to apply to the whole human race: "in the image of God he created him [*adam*, singular]; male and female he created them [plural],"[9] which is why many versions of the Bible translate *adam* with a corporate noun like "humankind." Indeed, the concept of corporate personhood is a dominant theme throughout the Bible. Israel is regarded as God's son (e.g., Exod. 4:22-23; Hos. 11:1). The Suffering Servant in Isaiah (52:13–53:12) is Israel as corporate person and/or the Messiah who takes the collective sins of all onto his own body. This sense of corporate personhood is crucial to Paul's soteriology. According to Paul, Christ is able to undo Adam's sin because Christ, like Adam, incorporates the whole human race. "Therefore, just as sin came into the world through one man, and death came through sin, and so death spread to all because all have sinned — sin was indeed in the world before the law, but sin is not reckoned when there is no law. Yet death exercised dominion from Adam to Moses, even over those whose sins were not like the transgression of Adam, who is a type of the one who was to come. But the free gift is not like the trespass. For if the many died through the one man's trespass, much more surely have the grace of God and the free gift in the grace of the one man, Jesus Christ, abounded for the many" (Rom. 5:12-15). Here the concept of *type* illustrates the essential unity of the human race.

The reality of corporate personhood is fundamental to the thought of the patristic writers. As Henri de Lubac explains, "the unity of the Mystical Body of Christ, a supernatural unity, supposes a previous natural unity, the unity of the human race. So the Fathers of the Church, in their treatment of grace and salvation, kept constantly before them this Body of Christ, and in dealing with the creation were not content only to mention the formation of individuals, the first man and the first woman, but delighted to contemplate God creating humanity as a whole."[10] De Lubac writes that when pagans like Celsus and Porphyry jeered at the Christian idea that the whole human race could be united in the same faith, Christians could reply that it was simply

---

9. Unless otherwise indicated, biblical quotations in this book come from the New Revised Standard Version.

10. Henri de Lubac, *Catholicism: Christ and the Common Destiny of Man*, trans. Lancelot Sheppard and Elizabeth Englund (San Francisco: Ignatius, 1988), p. 25.

the reuniting of all people who are made in the image of the one God.[11]
This "monogenism" was at the core of the reality of the body of Christ;
Christ comes to restore the original unity of humanity by gathering all
into his body. His incarnation was not just a *corporatio,* a corporation,
but a *concorporatio,* as Saint Hilary says. "Christ the Redeemer does
not offer salvation merely to each one; he effects it, he is himself the
salvation of the whole, and for each one salvation consists in a personal
ratification of his original 'belonging' to Christ, so that he be not cast
out, cut off from the Whole."[12] There is thus a "horizontal" as well as
a "vertical" dimension to salvation; we are reconciled with each other
as we are reconciled to God. Augustine famously describes this as the
formation of a different kind of city — what Aristotle would call a *polis*
— the city of God, which is formed by the unity of people around the
altar, in the becoming of the body of Christ.[13]

Gerhard Lohfink has shown how biblical soteriology in both the Old
and New Testaments is founded on this idea that unity is not only an
effect of salvation, but *is* salvation, the restoring of the primordial harmony of a creation torn apart by sin. This is why *gathering* is a fundamental theme in both the Old and New Testaments.[14] When the early
church borrowed the Greek word *ekklesia* for itself, it took on some of
the resonances of the Greek body politic, in which the *ekklesia* was the
gathering of all those who had the rights of citizens in the city-state, as
opposed to the smaller group of elected officials that made up the council *(boule).*[15] The church thus claimed to be more than a club organized
around private interests; it claimed to be a fully "public" gathering concerned with the whole of life. At the same time, it was not the earthly
polis, but an anticipation of the eschatological gathering of the people
of God. According to Lohfink, the origin of *ekklesia* was ultimately not
the Greek city-state but the "day of the assembly" at Mount Sinai when
the Israelites received the Decalogue (Deut. 5:22).[16]

11. De Lubac, *Catholicism,* pp. 30-31.

12. De Lubac, *Catholicism,* p. 39.

13. Augustine, *City of God,* trans. Henry Bettenson (Harmondsworth: Penguin, 1972),
10.6.

14. Gerhard Lohfink, *Does God Need the Church? Toward a Theology of the People of
God* (Collegeville, Minn.: Michael Glazier, 1999), pp. 51-60, 218-36.

15. Robert L. Wilken, *The Christians as the Romans Saw Them* (New Haven: Yale University Press, 1984), pp. 32-34.

16. Lohfink, *Does God Need the Church?* p. 219.

Paul's strong identification of the *ekklesia* as the very body of Christ is no doubt indebted to Greek concepts of corporate personhood in the body politic, but at the same time it is a radical departure from Greek ideas of citizenship and class. The wholeness of the human race in biblical thought, rooted in the essential equality of all and coparticipation of all in the image of God, is recapitulated and redeemed in the one man Jesus Christ. Christ's crucified and resurrected body thus becomes the whole of humanity, restored to the primordial unity in which it was created. The distinctions with which Greek concepts of citizenship operated simply disappear: "There is no longer Jew or Greek, there is no longer slave or free, there is no longer male and female; for all of you are one in Christ Jesus" (Gal. 3:28). As the image of the body makes clear, there remains differentiation among the members; some are eyes, some are hands, some are feet, and so on. But this means that equality is not a mere formal equality, in which all are treated as the same before the law. In fact, differentiation produces a kind of attraction among the members, for, as Paul tells the Corinthians, the eye realizes that, because it is not the hand, it needs the hand, and the head realizes that it needs the feet (I Cor. 12:19-21). What holds the body together is not mutual interests or rights or fear of external enemies but *agape,* love (I Cor. 13:1-13). This love is the fruit of the Spirit (Gal. 5:22), in whom all were baptized into the one body of Christ (I Cor. 12:4-13). Not only are the weakest members not excluded from citizenship or membership in the body, but there is a preferential option for the weakest in the body: "the members of the body that seem to be weaker are indispensable, and those members of the body that we think less honorable we clothe with greater honor" (I Cor. 12:22-23). Paul takes the body analogy even further by implying that a kind of nervous system connects all the members, for "if one member suffers, all suffer together with it; if one member is honored, all rejoice together with it" (I Cor. 12:26).

The corporate nature of the church is further intensified beyond the Greek model by the Eucharist, which serves to bind the members together into the body of Christ by an act of bodily consumption. In a move that must have seemed exceedingly odd and even perverse to the Greeks, the body of Christ was identified with both the corporate person of the church and the food upon which the members of the church fed. "The cup of blessing that we bless, is it not a sharing in the blood of Christ? The bread that we break, is it not a sharing in the body of Christ? Because there is one bread, we who are many are one body, for we all partake of the one bread" (I Cor. 10:16-17). By eating the Lord's body, we become assimilated to the Lord's body, consumed by what we consume. We do not thereby eat ourselves, because there is no self, properly understood, before we enter into communion with God and with one another. As the work of John Zizioulas has made clear, the patristic anthropology is not one in which preexisting individuals subsequently enter into communion with each other. It is instead the case that we become who we really are only by entering into that communion. Being is not a mere biological fact, but an ecclesial reality. In pagan Greek thought, "person," or *prosopon,* referred to the mask that actors would wear on the stage. The substance *(hypostasis)* of the human being was a given reality unrelated to the person. The human actor could don a mask and fight with the gods and his fate on stage, but ultimately there is no true freedom for him; his person is nothing but a mask, with no ontological bearing on his substance. Once the biblical writers had traced human freedom back to God's free act of creating from nothing, however, the ontology of the human being could be unified with his or her person. The person is called out of nothing and into freedom by participation in God.[17] This act is realized in the re-creation of the person in Christ, the summit of which is the becoming-Christ of the Eucharist. We do not first have our being and then subsequently enter into communion with Christ and others; being is communion. This is why Zizioulas makes the provocative claim that the Eucharist *"is the reality which makes it possible for us to exist at all."*[18]

What the body of Christ inaugurates therefore is a new type of sociality, one that is bodily but simultaneously eschatological; its being is received from another, God, and so it is aware of the other in its midst, the stranger and poor one who is the personification of Christ (Matt. 25:31-46). There was nothing new about forming associations of like-minded people based on common interests. By the time of Jesus, associations in the pagan world were common. There were social clubs based on a particular trade — fruit merchants, for example — or funerary societies to ensure each member a decent burial, or societies based on the cult of a particular deity. They shared meals together and

17. John Zizioulas, *Being as Communion: Studies in Personhood and the Church* (Crestwood, N.Y.: St. Vladimir's Seminary Press, 1993), pp. 27-41.
18. John Zizioulas, quoted in Paul McPartlan, *The Eucharist Makes the Church: Henri de Lubac and John Zizioulas in Dialogue* (Edinburgh: T. & T. Clark, 1993), p. 270.

achieved a sense of belonging, even brotherly love.[19] What made the church different, however, was not only its choice of an explicitly public and political term like *ekklesia* — as opposed to terms like *koinon* and *collegium* that designated associations — but its transgression of ordinary social boundaries to include women, men, children, slaves, Jews, Greeks, rich, and poor all within the same gathering. There was originally meant to be only one church, presided over by a bishop, in each city, instead of many parishes into which people could self-separate. The eucharistic assembly, therefore, gathered people from across all kinds of natural and social divisions. The church came to be seen as a third race, a *tertium quid*, that not only was neither Jew nor Greek, but also superseded all kinds of divisions of class, gender, age, etc. The Acts of the Apostles makes clear that economic relationships were not exempt from this breaking down of barriers. The early Christians are said to have had no private ownership, but rather shared all things in common, taking special care of any in need (Acts 2:44-45; 4:32). Such was the ideal, anyway. The account is no doubt somewhat romanticized. As Paul's scolding of the Corinthians in I Corinthians 11:17-34 makes clear, the ideal in practice was not always so. But the type of corporate person that the body of Christ called into being was clearly a challenge to existing social, economic, and political stratification.

II. Corporate Bodies in a Market Society

In the medieval period, the body of Christ continued to be a powerful image of the corporate nature of human relations. The body of Christ produced a relation of *agape* among the members that differed from the Greek and Roman body politic, and suffused the body with a mystical sense quite alien to the classical world. The body of Christ also radically divided the political loyalties of Christians. Among the Greeks there could be no doubting one's membership in the body politic; although one could question this law or that tyranny, one's membership in the *polis* was a necessary condition for one's development as a human person. The Christian, on the other hand, could have doubts about political participation because she belonged to another type of body, a body that

---

19. Wilken, *Christians as the Romans Saw Them,* pp. 35-40.

was already a colony of heaven.[20] According to Sheldon Wolin, when participation had been stifled in the later Roman Empire by centralized power, Christianity revivified political life by projecting a new type of body politic whose full citizenship was in heaven.[21]

Christian ideals and Christian realities were not the same things, however, and the corporate nature of the Christian community was recruited into use for a more hierarchical and uniform vision of society. John of Salisbury's *Policraticus* in the twelfth century, for example, draws on Plutarch, not Paul, to establish the image of the political community on the analogy of a human body, with the king as the head, the priests as the soul, the soldiers as the hands, the treasury as the stomach, and the peasants as the feet.[22] Marie de France similarly draws on Livy and Aesop in her "Fable of a Man, His Belly, and His Limbs," which justifies taxation, collected by the belly, because the belly provides strength for the limbs.[23] As Henri de Lubac famously documented, beginning in the eleventh century, the *corpus verum,* the true body of Christ, increasingly referred to the eucharistic elements on the altar, not to the church. The *corpus mysticum* came to refer to the church, but the sacramental and eschatological elements of the image were muted as the church became increasingly bureaucratized. The term *corpus mysticum* was more and more used in a legal context to refer to the church's structure, which was seen as less of an effect of the Eucharist and more on analogy with human bodies. It became possible then to refer not to the mystical body of Christ but to the mystical body of the church.[24] As Ernst Kantorowicz writes, "Undeniably the former liturgical concept of *corpus mysticum* faded away only to be transformed into a relatively colorless sociological, organological, or juristic notion."[25] Of even greater importance was the migration of the concept of mystical body to the nascent state

20. Sheldon Wolin, *Politics and Vision: Continuity and Innovation in Western Political Thought,* expanded ed. (Princeton: Princeton University Press, 2004), p. 92.

21. Wolin, *Politics and Vision,* pp. 86-87.

22. John of Salisbury, "Metalogicon and Policraticus," in *Medieval Political Theory — a Reader: The Quest for the Body Politic, 1100-1400,* ed. Cary J. Neederman and Kate Langdon Forhan (London: Routledge, 1993), pp. 37-53.

23. Marie de France, "The Fable of a Man, His Belly, and His Limbs," in *Medieval Political Theory,* p. 25.

24. Ernst H. Kantorowicz, *The King's Two Bodies: A Study in Medieval Political Theology* (Princeton: Princeton University Press, 1957), pp. 200-206.

25. Kantorowicz, *The King's Two Bodies,* p. 202.

in the late medieval and early modern periods. Building on de Lubac's work, Kantorowicz's famed study *The King's Two Bodies* showed how the state borrowed theological body language to take on the trappings of divinity. By the fifteenth century, theologians like Jean Gerson and jurists like Jean de Terre Rouge were referring to the "mystical body of France."[26] What Wolin had found so politically promising about Christianity is also what he found so dangerous. Classical thought had conceived of political solidarity in a body politic, but never as a mystical body. "Christianity helped father the idea of a community as a non-rational, non-utilitarian body bound by a meta-rational faith, infused by a mysterious spirit taken into the members."[27] This mysticism would gradually be transferred to the nation-state, spawning nationalism and all its ills.

In previous work I have looked at the story of the nation-state as a kind of mystical body.[28] What I want to do now is look at the business corporation as another kind of body, one that arose in conjunction with the state and one whose power has now come to rival and, in many cases, to merge with the state. What we see in the modern era is a new type of corporate person, the business corporation, which has taken on powers of speech. The rise of a market economy along with the modern state is often depicted in terms of the rise of the individual over against more communal forms of living that are associated with the medieval period. The organic metaphor of the body was largely replaced by social contract theory, in which preexisting individuals band together to form a state and society based on mutual interests and mutual fears. Hobbes's *Leviathan* bridges these two traditions by depicting the state as an artificial body constructed of many individuals. In later political theory the body analogy, for the most part, disappears. At the same time that the body analogy is dropping out of political theory, however, and the new science of economics is fixating on the encounters of individuals in markets, each pursuing his or her own interests, the primary use of collective body language outside of the church becomes that of the business corporation. The idea of individuals coming together in a legally recognized body with rights and liabilities that transcend any

---

26. Kantorowicz, *The King's Two Bodies*, pp. 218-20.
27. Wolin, *Politics and Vision*, p. 119.
28. See my book *Migrations of the Holy: God, State, and the Political Meaning of the Church* (Grand Rapids: Eerdmans, 2011).

of those individuals dates back to the Roman *collegia*. What was new about modern corporations like the Dutch East India Company and the British East India Company, chartered in the seventeenth century, was their incorporation for the pursuit of profit on behalf of private shareholders.

The rise of the corporation was predicated on the creation of the capitalist and of the wage laborer, a creation that was in turn predicated on the liberation of the individual from the confines of the traditional social group. Medieval feudal arrangements, towns, guilds, clans, and other bearers of local custom were swept away by the rise of the sovereign state with one centralized political center and legal structure. The rise of market economies depended on the state and the establishment of standardized systems of law, currency, and taxation. All individuals were now, in theory, equal before the law, and all were "liberated" to sell their labor or purchase the labor of others, to deal with each other on the basis of contract, in other words, rather than as members of a social body. This process of freeing wage labor included dispossessing masses of individuals from control over their means of production, through the enclosure of common lands and other coercive means.[29]

We are accustomed to telling the story of the rise of the modern state and the simultaneous rise of market economies — and the rise of the corporation and the rise of democracy — as if they were all one story. The *Citizens United* case, however, demands that we consider the possibility that they are not all one story. The rise of corporate power is not the same as the rise of democracy, and in fact can threaten democracy. As Charles Lindblom argued in his landmark book *Politics and Markets,* there is no essential relationship between democracy and markets. The reason that polyarchies — systems in which no monolithic elite controls the political process — are always associated with market systems has to do with the constitutional liberalism in which both polyarchies and market systems were born. Liberalism, however, is not necessarily democracy. Liberalism was not democratic in origin, but an attempt to protect and enlarge the liberties first of nobles and then of a merchant middle class. The job of liberal states was and is to protect property and

29. Anthony Giddens, *The Nation-State and Violence* (Berkeley: University of California Press, 1987), pp. 148-60. Also see Michael Perelman, *The Invention of Capitalism: Classical Political Economy and the Secret History of Primitive Accumulation* (Durham, N.C.: Duke University Press, 2000).

provide the necessary conditions for market competition. Popular rule, or democracy, was sometimes seen as an end toward the attainment of liberty, but liberty and equality were often at odds, and when they were at odds, liberty has usually trumped equality,[30] as is the case in *Citizens United*. In *Citizens United*, both the majority and the dissenting opinion agree that the First Amendment is designed to protect liberty — the freedom to speak — but it is not meant to equalize the power of those who speak. In his dissenting opinion, Justice Stevens emphasizes that equalizing the relative influence of speakers on elections is not the basis on which the McCain-Feingold Act had sought to restrain corporate electioneering.[31]

C. B. MacPherson writes that "Liberalism had always meant freeing the individual from the outdated restraints of old established institutions. By the time liberalism emerged as liberal democracy this became a claim to free all individuals equally, and to free them to use and develop their human capacities fully."[32] Despite the claim to equality, however, liberal democratic theorists accepted class division. The equality envisioned was a formal equality before the law. "The first formulators of liberal democracy came to its advocacy through a chain of reasoning which started from the assumptions of a capitalist market society and the laws of classical political economy. These gave them a model of man (as maximizer of utilities) and a model of society (as a collection of individuals with conflicting interests)."[33] Early theorists of liberal democracy did not give up on the goal of full democracy through equality, but did their best to reconcile a competitive market economy with equality. John Stuart Mill, for example, saw liberal democracy as a moral project for the improvement of humanity that would progressively overcome class divisions. Mill saw that the current system was grossly unfair, in that rewards were inversely proportional to the amount of labor a person did, but Mill thought this inequality was only accidentally related to the market system. He thought that participation in the competitive market would allow the working class to develop its own human potential, but in the meantime, the elite should be given a disproportionate share of votes, since in their present debased condi-

---

30. Charles E. Lindblom, *Politics and Markets: The World's Political-Economic Systems* (New York: Basic Books, 1977), pp. 161-69.

31. *Citizens United*, Opinion of Stevens, p. 51.

32. MacPherson, *Life and Times*, p. 21.

33. MacPherson, *Life and Times*, p. 24.

tion the lower classes could not be trusted to vote in the interest of the common good.[34]

Mill had the virtue of recognizing that class division and inequality were a problem for democracy, and he attempted to institute a political solution, however elitist, to market inequities. As MacPherson shows, however, theorists of democracy in the latter half of the twentieth century, beginning with Joseph Schumpeter, have tended to conflate the political and economic processes, so that liberal democracy is envisioned on the model of a market. Any concern about class division and the improvement of humankind has tended to give way to a more ostensibly empirical model of all people as individual rational maximizers who choose political candidates as they choose salad dressing at the supermarket. Democracy is a marketplace in which elections register people's desires as they are, just as purchases do in the economic marketplace.[35] There is no overriding *telos* or common good; each person chooses his or her own good based on his or her own preferences, and individual preferences will inevitably conflict. The market is the mechanism in both the economic and political realms that determines whose preferences prevail, with one important difference. In the economic market, minority preferences may still be met by some suppliers; in the political market — in a two-party system especially — it is winner take all. The preferences of the majority always trump those of the minority.

The model of democracy as a marketplace is certainly not the only theoretical model of democracy available,[36] but the Supreme Court seems to take it for granted. Both the majority and the dissenting minority in *Citizens United* repeatedly use the model of marketplace to describe the political arena. The majority argues that restricting cor-

---

34. MacPherson, *Life and Times*, pp. 44-64.

35. MacPherson, *Life and Times*, pp. 78-80.

36. The widely-influential account of John Rawls is less competitive and more cooperative, though it still depends on envisioning the individual as a rational maximizer of his or her own interests who, under conditions of moderate scarcity, will choose principles of justice behind the "veil of ignorance"; John Rawls, *A Theory of Justice*, rev. ed. (Cambridge: Harvard University Press, 1999). Jeffrey Stout's theory of democracy as a moral tradition based on a background of agreement rather than competition is an interesting alternative, though I find it hard to square with the actual empirical condition of democracy in the United States; Jeffrey Stout, *Democracy and Tradition* (Princeton: Princeton University Press, 2004).

porate speech will impede the "uninhibited marketplace of ideas,"[37] by restricting the ability of corporations to "compete" in the "'open marketplace' of ideas protected by the First Amendment."[38] One of the precedents that *Citizens United* overturned — *Austin v. Michigan Chamber of Commerce* — had sought to prevent "an unfair advantage in the political marketplace" by using "resources amassed in the economic marketplace,"[39] but the majority knocked down this attempted barrier between the two marketplaces by arguing that the Court had already rejected as unconstitutional the goal of "equalizing the relative ability of individuals and groups to influence the outcome of elections."[40] Speech is held to be "the means to hold officials accountable to the people," and so "the First Amendment stands against attempts to disfavor certain subjects or viewpoints or to distinguish among different speakers, which may be a means to control content."[41] The logic of the economic marketplace — that more choices are better and no one can prejudge which choices are good — is applied also to the political marketplace: "There is no such thing as too much speech,"[42] as Justice Scalia has written. Justice Stevens in dissent also recognizes the legitimacy of the "market for legislation,"[43] but wants to create "breathing room around the electoral 'marketplace of ideas'" to allow competition in that market to be fairer.[44]

The marketplace in Adam Smith's vision assumes that supply responds to demand because many sellers respond to many buyers. What happens when many individuals band together to form a corporation? The majority in *Citizens United* assumes that corporate persons have the same speech rights as individuals; democracy is the

37. *Citizens United,* Opinion of the Court, p. 19, citing a previous case, *Virginia v Hicks* (2003).

38. *Citizens United,* Opinion of the Court, p. 38; the internal quotation is from a previous case, *New York State Board of Elections v Lopez Torres* (2008).

39. *Citizens United,* Opinion of the Court, p. 34. Here the majority is quoting the *Austin* decision.

40. *Citizens United,* Opinion of the Court, p. 34. Here the majority is quoting *Buckley v Valeo* (1976).

41. *Citizens United,* Syllabus, p. 3.

42. This quote from Justice Scalia is from his dissenting opinion in the *Austin* decision; Stevens quotes Scalia in his dissenting opinion in *Citizens United,* Opinion of Stevens, p. 83.

43. *Citizens United,* Opinion of Stevens, p. 82.

44. *Citizens United,* Opinion of Stevens, p. 83.

process by which all speakers, including groups of individuals, have their say, and then the citizens or consumers choose which speech is true; the electoral system responds to consumer demand — one person, one vote. The problem is that the political market, in fact, is an oligopoly. The buyer confronts not multiple sellers, but two, in a two-party system such as that of the United States. The sellers need not respond to the buyers'/voters' demands as they would in a fully competitive system; demand is dictated by the sellers. It is true that the system gives one vote to each individual natural person. But the candidates and issues that are voted on, and the information provided to the individual voter, are largely determined not simply by demand but by *effective* demand. In an economic market, the only demand that counts is demand backed by purchasing power. In an economic market, the person with a million dollars has a million more "votes" than the person with one dollar. And so it is in the political market. The Supreme Court recognizes that money is the equivalent of speech. Those with a lot of money are much more effective at creating demand than those without. Where there is substantial inequality of wealth, there is no true democracy, unless democracy is defined in a minimal way as a lack of tyrannical dictatorship. What we have are competing elites with low citizen participation.[45] The majority in *Citizens United* astonishingly uses heavy corporate spending on elections as evidence that the people are in charge: "The fact that a corporation, or any other speaker, is willing to spend money to try to persuade voters presupposes that the people have the ultimate influence over elected officials."[46] The Court therefore dismisses the idea that people will cease to participate, even though nearly half of the electorate already sits out national elections. Wolin's view of American democracy is probably closer to the mark: "The citizen is shrunk to the voter: periodically courted, warned, and confused but otherwise kept at a distance from actual decision-making and allowed to emerge only ephemerally in a cameo appearance according to a script composed by the opinion takers/makers."[47]

Early theorists of liberal democracy feared that giving the lower classes the right to vote would overturn the class system and result in

---

45. MacPherson, *Life and Times,* pp. 87-92.
46. *Citizens United,* Opinion of the Court, p. 44.
47. Wolin, *Politics and Vision,* p. 565.

chaos. It never happened. As Wolin points out, Americans are apolitical but not alienated, patriotic and resigned or relieved to turn over their civic obligations to the experts. Why? I think it has to do with the kinds of social bodies that have largely replaced the church in the modern era. The first is the nation-state. The mysticism of nationalism has tended to occlude any discussion of class divisions. We are convinced that we are *e pluribus unum,* one united from many. Policy debate shies away from any discussion of class; those who raise the issue of class are accused of making class warfare, which strikes me as the equivalent of accusing the fire department of arson because they keep showing up at house fires. We rally around the flag and support our troops, so that we can ignore the brute fact that those who kill and die on our behalf come overwhelmingly from the lower classes. The second type of social body, whose interests have largely merged with those of nation-state elites, is the business corporation. Here too corporations have succeeded in convincing us that their interests are not private but fully public. The welfare of the whole society depends on the success of business — "It's the economy, stupid," as President Clinton's personal reminder ran — and so public officials are remarkably solicitous of business demands for favors, which include everything from direct subsidies to fighting wars for economic interests. Lindblom quotes a DuPont executive as saying "the strength of the position of business and the weakness of the position of government is that government needs a strong economy just as much as business does, and the people need it and demand it even more."[48] Lindblom comments, "The duality of leadership is reminiscent of the medieval dualism between church and state, and the relations between business and government are no less intricate than in the medieval duality."[49]

Michael Novak has notoriously applied the Suffering Servant passages in Isaiah to "the modern business corporation, a much despised incarnation of God's presence in the world."[50] Naomi Klein, on the other hand, has documented a corporate chic in which branding creates a kind of salvific mysticism around corporate identities.[51] Either way,

48. Quoted in Lindblom, *Politics and Markets,* p. 175.

49. Lindblom, *Politics and Markets,* p. 175.

50. Michael Novak, "A Theology of the Corporation," in *The Corporation: A Theological Inquiry,* ed. Michael Novak and John W. Cooper (Washington, D.C.: American Enterprise Institute, 1981), p. 203.

51. Naomi Klein, *No Logo: Taking Aim at the Brand Bullies* (New York: Picador, 1999).

corporations embody powerful social processes and, in some cases, effect a kind of mystical union among managers and consumers, a charmed circle from which workers are largely excluded. Novak is right to emphasize the inherently corporate nature of the corporation; market economics is primarily about social bodies, not lone individuals. Business corporations can and do serve social purposes in the pursuit of private profit, and Novak argues that business corporations are not just economic actors but also moral, social, and political actors.[52] The problem is that, when political discernment has been subsumed into a competitive market model based on preferences rather than any substantive *telos* or conception of the common good, there is no standard on which to judge which social purposes are to be pursued. Markets are designed for the maximization of preferences; in the absence of any equalizing considerations, those preferences with the most power win out. And power in a corporate-dominated society is based on class division, the fundamental divide between the owners of capital and those who have nothing to sell but their own labor. The business corporation embodies class antagonism, not a true social solidarity, not simply because the corporation is divided between capital and labor, but because the managers of the corporation understand their task as the maximization of shareholder value, which often comes at the expense of labor: one significant way to increase profits is to cut labor costs, that is, to decrease wages paid to workers. In the political sphere, corporations commonly use the profits generated by labor to support the interests of shareholders, often opposing the interests of labor. What we have then is our current situation: patriotic assurances that the nation and the corporation enact truly social processes that bind us all together as one, combined with a reality of ever-greater class division and political participation that is driven by and serves those with access to large amounts of money.

Justice Stevens makes a number of powerful arguments demonstrating the corrupting influence of corporate speech, but his main move is to claim that free speech rights are meant to protect individuals, not corporations. He stops well short of questioning the legal personhood of corporations, but he writes of the framers of the U.S. Constitution, "Unlike our colleagues, they had little trouble distinguishing corporations from human beings, and when they constitutionalized the right to

52. Novak, "Theology of the Corporation," pp. 220-24.

free speech in the First Amendment, it was the free speech of individual Americans that they had in mind."[53]

The problem with Justice Stevens's dissent, as I see it, is that it does not fundamentally call into question the marketization of the political process. He hopes that envisioning society as a collection of individuals will make for a fairer competition, but fairer competition is not the same as full participation, much less the pursuit of any real common good. To see society as a collection of individuals both occludes the reality of class division and prevents any true attempts to overcome those divisions through a deeper kind of solidarity. If we do not see each other as members or potential members of the same body, we cannot begin to see the political process as a healing process for the weakest of our members. From a Christian point of view, we have a strong stake in corporate personhood. The church as the body of Christ is called to see the joys and sufferings of all God's children as intimately bound together. The scandal of the rich feasting while the poor go hungry cannot be reconciled with the enactment of the body of Christ, as Paul makes clear in I Corinthians 11. The option for the poor is the church's response to class division. The church must furthermore be able to speak as a body, not a mere collection of individuals. In the recent debate over contraception and the Department of Health and Human Services' health-care mandate, the government privileged the rights of individuals over the rights of corporate bodies like the church. For this reason, some within the church welcomed *Citizens United* as a vindication of the rights of corporate persons like the church to speak. I think this is a mistake. The majority in *Citizens United* disavows any sort of distinction among types of corporate bodies, or indeed among speakers of any kind; according to the Court, "the First Amendment generally prohibits the suppression of political speech based on the speaker's identity."[54] The Court thus claims to be blind to the exercise of power while eliminating the ability to make political decisions on the basis of anything but raw power. But Christians need not feign such blindness; there are important distinctions between class-divided business corporations whose goal is the pursuit of profit, and churches, unions, farmer cooperatives, nonprofit corporations, charitable organizations, credit unions, and other bodies who can make greater claims to promote solidarity and common goods.

53. *Citizens United,* Opinion of Stevens, p. 37.
54. *Citizens United,* Opinion of the Court, p. 34.

The church's goal is to speak as a corporate person on behalf of the poor, to promote organizations of true social solidarity, and also to encourage businesses to pursue legitimate profit within the wider *telos* of an economy of love. As Pope Benedict XVI writes in his encyclical *Caritas in Veritate* — which I will discuss in more detail in chapter 6 — love must be "the principle not only of micro-relationships (with friends, with family members or within small groups) but also of macro-relationships (social, economic, and political ones)."[55] The pope continues:

> When both the logic of the market and the logic of the State come to an agreement that each will continue to exercise a monopoly over its respective area of influence, in the long term much is lost: solidarity in relations between citizens, participation and adherence, actions of gratuitousness, all of which stand in contrast with *giving in order to acquire* (the logic of exchange) and *giving through duty* (the logic of public obligation, imposed by State law). In order to defeat underdevelopment, action is required not only on improving exchange-based transactions and implanting public welfare structures, but above all on gradually *increasing openness, in a world context, to forms of economic activity marked by quotas of gratuitousness and communion.* The exclusively binary model of market-plus-State is corrosive of society, while economic forms based on solidarity, which find their natural home in civil society without being restricted to it, build up society.[56]

What it means to enact the body of Christ in this context is not to despair of the state of corporate-state power, but to build businesses and communities of true participation and solidarity. I will discuss one experiment in this kind of solidarity in the next chapter.

---

55. Benedict XVI, *Caritas in Veritate,* §2; http://www.vatican.va/holy_father/benedict_xvi/encyclicals/documents/hf_ben-xvi_enc_20090629_caritas-in-veritate_en.html.
56. Benedict XVI, *Caritas in Veritate,* §39.

CHAPTER TWO

WESTPHALIA AND BACK:

COMPLEXIFYING THE

CHURCH-WORLD DUALITY

S OME YEARS AGO, I was staying with an aunt and uncle in Winona, Minnesota, when I came upon an old Catholic primary school geography textbook in a spare bedroom that had previously been occupied by a now grown-up cousin. The book was entitled *World Neighbors;* it was published in 1952 by William H. Sadlier, Inc., still today a major publisher of educational materials for public and nonpublic schools, as well as catechetical materials for Catholic schools. The book's foreword announced "the beginning of an era in Catholic education," but to contemporary eyes it looks more like a relic from the far distant past. Particularly fascinating is the depiction of a small town in Iowa called Westphalia, presented in a section entitled "A Study of a Community." It is an entirely Catholic town, settled by German immigrants, where the social and economic life of the community is organized through the parish, whose pastor reigns like a benevolent despot. It seems to belong to a much earlier era: the Middle Ages. The fact that it is mid-twentieth-century America seems to mark it as an anachronism, a last-ditch effort to keep the modern world at bay. As we know with the benefit of hindsight, the life represented by Westphalia, Iowa, was not the beginning of an era, but the end of one. The insular Catholic universe it represented was about to be swept away by the changes of Vatican II and, more generally, the 1960s. Rather than huddling together and trying to protect the church from the world, the church would throw its arms open to the world and embrace modernity. Instead of seeing the world as one big opportunity for sin from which the church must stand apart, we would recognize the essential goodness of the world and seek to locate the church in the world, always trying to transform the world from within.

So goes the familiar story. As a broad characterization of changes in the Catholic orbit in the late twentieth century, it is not entirely inaccurate. And as a cautionary tale against nostalgia for a lost world, it is salutary. Those who want to return to a lost world usually end up making a mess of this one. Nevertheless, as a neatly progressive tale, the familiar story is incomplete and oversimplified. It fails to appreciate the efforts, sometimes successful, to bring the gospel to bear on material life in quite sophisticated ways. In dismissing these efforts, it fails to recognize what the past has to teach us today as we negotiate our way through the postmodern world.

I will begin with the story of Westphalia, circa 1952, then turn to the way that social milieu is narrated by the standard understanding of the church-world duality after Vatican II. I will argue that "world" has multiple meanings, and that the standard narrative does not do justice to the way that Westphalia engaged with the world. I will, finally, suggest some things that can be learned from complexifying the church-world dualism. I intend this chapter as a bridge-building exercise; rather than siding with factions who would either dismiss or romanticize the pre-Vatican II church in America, I will argue that we can attain a more nuanced view of that church by attending to a more nuanced view of the church-world relationship.

I. Journey to Westphalia

World Neighbors makes clear on page 1 that Catholics do not study geography out of idle curiosity. We need to know the land where God has put us and know about our fellow children of God in order that we may love them, and thus "do our part in helping God's Kingdom come."[1] The first section of the book deals with the land of the United States — rivers, lakes, climate, etc. — and the second deals with the people of the United States, "a Nation of Many Peoples." Within this second section is a subsection on community life in the United States, in which Westphalia is featured as a kind of ideal. "In this community there are

1. Sister M. Juliana Bedier, *World Neighbors* (New York and Chicago: W. H. Sadlier, 1952), p. 1.

33

no poor people, no very rich, but all are comfortable, prosperous, hard-working, most of them farmers. There is no crime, no jail, no police force. The Ten Commandments are the Law here, says the Pastor, Father Hubert Duren. The Community and the Parish are here one and the same."[2] Although there are only a hundred families, Westphalia boasts "15 of its sons in the priesthood, 96 girls are nuns, 17 boys monks or Brothers, and 18 boys are in the armed forces."[3] The town's year is organized around the liturgical calendar and special occasions such as the blessing of fields by the pastor each spring.

Westphalia was not always such a happy place, the textbook reports. "When Father Duren came to Westphalia years ago, he found the people poor, all their earnings draining out to the big towns where they bought supplies. There was no good school, no way of marketing produce for fair returns, no amusement for young people. Families were breaking up, drifting away. He taught the people the principles of co-operation; organized a Credit Union, thus keeping money in the community and providing a fund to improve farms and livestock. He set up a co-op store where farmers buy supplies."[4] The cooperative store gave the farmers control over processing and marketing their own meat and dairy products, and returned the profits to them, since they were its owners. In turn, the community built a cooperative beauty parlor and a cooperative garage. They used the profits from these ventures to build a school "where children are taught to co-operate, to esteem rural life, to live as happy, productive members of the Community, following the Church's social teaching and the liturgy through the year."[5] The community also built a recreation hall for dances, shows, and parties, a clubhouse with a soda fountain and billiard tables, and a baseball field. The people of Westphalia are shown enjoying these amenities in a gallery of pictures that accompanies the text. The pictures concentrate on the Zimmerman family, various of whose fourteen children are shown shoveling alfalfa, repairing a hog feeder, receiving communion at daily Mass, visiting the soda fountain and the credit union, and relaxing at home, where Don and Jerry pop corn, Joey and Celia wash dishes, and Michael makes rosaries.

2. Bedier, *World Neighbors,* p. 64.
3. Bedier, *World Neighbors,* p. 64.
4. Bedier, *World Neighbors,* p. 65.
5. Bedier, *World Neighbors,* p. 66.

Residents of Westphalia who remember it from that time speak of constant social activity surrounding the parish. Movies followed Sunday night devotions. There were plays, band concerts, baseball games, monthly meetings of the Rosary Society for women and the Holy Name Society for men, parish picnics, bingo nights, and special processions on feast days with townspeople carrying a large rosary, each bead as large as a softball. As one longtime resident says, "Religion was woven into our everyday life at that time."[6] There were no sharp distinctions between religious, social, and economic life. Support for the local businesses — "People knew that if the community was to prosper one had to support the businesses" — was a religious duty as much as it was a social pleasure. "Saturday nights people would come to the Co-op Grocery store to buy groceries for the week. This gave everyone a chance to visit with friends."

The center of the community was, without question, Father Duren, shown in the textbook chomping a cigar and playing billiards at the clubhouse. Longtime residents remember Father Duren as a tall man, "demanding, but gentle," who composed music, painted, hand carved furniture, and built his own home with an energy-saving cooling system of his own design. In addition to the feats mentioned in the textbook, Father Duren also built and stocked an artificial lake for the community to fish and built two shrines, one to Our Lady and the other to Saint Isidore, patron saint of farmers. The success of the community did not happen by accident, the textbook reports. Father Duren "follows a 5-point program in which religion, education, recreation, commerce, and credit are organized with the Church as the center of life in community and family. He calls it the Complete Life, Christian, American, and democratic. He believes Americans should rebuild their small communities. We should all unite under God and move in the direction of security on earth and in eternity. Westphalia shows it can be done."[7] The textbook reports that young people no longer wish to leave the small town, but it does not mention what some old-timers in the

---

6. A dozen residents of Westphalia who remember the time to which the textbook refers were kind enough to complete questionnaires that I sent them. I am extremely grateful to Lorene Kaufmann, parish secretary of St. Boniface Church in Westphalia, for all her kindnesses and help in soliciting responses from people in Westphalia. All subsequent quotes from residents of Westphalia are taken from these completed questionnaires.

7. Bedier, *World Neighbors*, p. 67.

community have told me: the young people had to ask Father Duren's permission to go to a dance in another town. As one resident reports, "Mostly everything that went on went through him." Not everyone was pleased. Though most reminisce fondly about Father Duren, one says, "He had his favorites, people who were brainwashed to his program. If not, he didn't care much for you."

II. Narrating Westphalia

It is easy for a contemporary reader to laugh and shake one's head at such a neat and tidy Catholic enclave. The account in the textbook is doubtless somewhat romanticized; people surely chafed at Father Duren's authority. Recent revelations of priestly abuse of authority cannot help but make contemporary readers wary of such forty-year reigns in which the pastor's leadership is unquestioned. Even if the textbook's account of life in Westphalia circa 1952 is essentially accurate, however, few Catholics today would wish to return to such a time and place. Attempts like that of Ave Maria, Florida, to re-create a kind of cohesive Catholic culture in Catholic enclaves have been marginal efforts and marred with controversy.

The standard way to narrate communities like Westphalia centers on the church-world dualism and pivots around the Second Vatican Council.[8] In brief, the story goes like this: once Catholics huddled in all-Catholic ghettos, at odds with the world. After Vatican II, Catholics came confidently to embrace the world, and became leaven in a pluralistic society. A typical account is that of Charles Curran's 2011 book *The Social Mission of the U.S. Catholic Church: A Theological Perspective*. Curran makes clear that his book is not simply a history of the social mission of the Catholic Church in America, but is a theological interpretation of that history.[9] Chapter 1, entitled "Early Historical Context

8. For example, see Jay P. Dolan, *The American Catholic Experience: A History from Colonial Times to the Present* (Notre Dame: University of Notre Dame Press, 1992); Richard Gula, *Reason Informed by Faith: Foundations of Catholic Morality* (Mahwah, N.J.: Paulist, 1989); and James McEvoy, "Church and World at the Second Vatican Council: The Significance of *Gaudium et Spes*," *Pacifica* 19 (February 2006): 37-57.

9. Charles E. Curran, *The Social Mission of the U.S. Catholic Church: A Theological Perspective* (Washington, D.C.: Georgetown University Press, 2011), pp. x-xi. Page references to this work have been placed in the text.

and Taking Care of Our Own," is a brief overview of the history of the immigrant Catholic Church in the nineteenth century. The title of the chapter tells the story. Poor and unwashed immigrants from Catholic homelands in Europe flooded the United States over the course of the nineteenth century, often incurring the hostility of the native Protestants, both for social reasons — the poor and foreigners are often disdained — and for theological reasons: "The greatest problem many Americans had with the Catholic Church was its failure to accept religious freedom and the basic principles of the U.S. Constitution" (p. 5). Catholics tended to think that religious freedom was acceptable only if it was impracticable to offer official recognition to the Catholic Church as the bearer of truth. Error, after all, had no rights. The erroneous tended to disapprove of this view of the world, and nativist reactions against Catholicism sometimes turned violent. The Catholic response was to form their own parochial schools, since public schools were essentially Protestant schools. Extensive efforts at poor relief undertaken by Catholic religious orders were in part motivated by the desire to keep Catholic children out of the care of publicly funded efforts, run by Protestant groups, to reform and improve the poor. Catholic laborers banded together into Catholic labor unions, beginning in 1869, and Catholic religious orders founded an extensive system of Catholic hospitals, which did minister to non-Catholics in times of crisis (pp. 5-11). Catholic efforts before World War I, according to Curran, were largely directed to "taking care of our own" and not to addressing "the reform of U.S. social institutions" (p. 6). In addition to dealing with the hordes of poor Catholic immigrants, however, Catholics tried to present themselves as good, patriotic Americans, to lessen the stigma of foreigner with which they were often marked.

Curran's second chapter tells the story of the social mission of the church from World War I to the Second Vatican Council, the period in which the *World Neighbors* textbook was produced. After the bishops formed the National Catholic War Council to show Catholic support for the American cause in World War I, the bishops — through the later-renamed National Catholic Welfare Conference (NCWC) — began to address public policy issues under the leadership of John A. Ryan, who directed the NCWC Social Action Department from 1920 to 1945. Curran calls Ryan's efforts "the first attempts by the U.S. Catholic Church to develop its social mission" (p. 15). All the previous efforts do not count as "social mission" for Curran because they do not address American society as a whole. Ryan saw the church as a hierarchical institution whose primary business was the saving of souls. In this sense, as Curran points out, his thought obeyed the neoscholastic distinction between natural and supernatural orders. But Ryan thought that the moral law necessary to the salvation of souls also included social and economic issues such as a living wage. The other key figure in Curran's pre-Vatican II narrative is John Courtney Murray, though in many ways Murray was ahead of his time, laying the groundwork for Vatican II. Murray was in the vanguard of emphasizing the independence of the laity from direct obedience to the hierarchy in social matters. Rather than the Catholic Action model, in which laypeople addressed social issues from within an organization juridically subject to the bishops, Murray called for Catholic action, with a small *a,* in which laity played a direct role in the secular institutions of civil society to bring about a more just society. Murray also defended intercreedal cooperation with non-Catholics for a better world (pp. 17-18).

Curran provides an overview of the different kinds of Catholic groups working in the pre-Vatican II period: organizations of Catholic labor unionists, sociologists, and economists; the Legion of Decency; the Catholic Association for International Peace; the Catholic Worker Movement; efforts to promote anticommunism and to fight racism; community-organizing efforts in collaboration with Saul Alinsky; the Catholic Family Movement; and others. The 1930s through the 1950s were, Curran says, "a golden period of Catholic action" (p. 36). As immigration slowed and Catholics moved toward the American mainstream, Catholic attention moved from taking care of Catholic immigrants to the concerns of the broader society. There was an impressive range of Catholic organizations hard at work to bring Catholic social teaching to fruition in America, from organizations like the Legion of Decency that looked to the hierarchy for guidance to the majority of efforts, which were led by laypeople. There were large Catholic organizations dedicated to bringing Catholic teaching directly to bear on labor, war, economy, racism, poverty, and family — all the great issues of the day.

Most of these organizations collapsed in the 1960s. Curran explains the collapse in part sociologically: Catholics went to college on the G.I. Bill after World War II, became affluent, and moved to the suburbs, away from tight-knit parish units. The newly prosperous and more Americanized Catholics were less likely to look to the church for guidance. But beyond sociology, Curran is more interested in giving a theological account of the changes in Catholic social action. In chapters 3 and 4 of his book, he narrates the changes as an effect of the changes in the way the Catholic Church viewed itself and its own relationship to the world in the wake of Vatican II. According to Curran, pre–Vatican II treatises on the church were defensive, concerned to protect the church from Protestantism and secularism. The institutional and hierarchical aspects of the church were emphasized, and the church itself tended to be identified with the kingdom of God. There was a two-tiered division of labor between those called to leave the world for the perfection of the religious life, and those laity called to live in the world. Vatican II, on the other hand, tended to present the church as a mystery, a sacrament in and to the world, rather than a bulwark against the world. The call of the laity to perfection was emphasized, and the church was seen not as the kingdom, but as a pilgrim community called to witness to the kingdom as it journeys through the world (pp. 41-42).

Curran writes that the church's ecclesiology changed in Vatican II, but he also wants to claim a "significant continuity in the understanding of the Catholic Church throughout the centuries" (p. 42). Rather than turn to some classical Catholic theological sources, however, he turns instead to Protestant sociology of the twentieth century, that of Ernst Troeltsch and Max Weber. Weber's distinction between church and sect was developed by Troeltsch into a three-part typology of church, sect, and mysticism. The last term goes unused by Curran, who adopts the basic contrast between church and sect as the framework for analyzing Catholic social action in the United States. Those Christians who follow the sect type, as exemplified by the Amish and other Anabaptist groups, see themselves as a small minority who follow the Sermon on the Mount strictly; they see "themselves in opposition to the world around them. . . . [I]f one does not detach from the rest of the world one ultimately has to compromise these Christian tenets. Sectarians believe themselves to be called as faithful witnesses to the Gospel message, not called to transform society" (p. 42). The church type, exemplified by the Catholic Church, is a large group "that exists within the world and works to influence existing cultural, political, and economic structures. The church type moderates the radical ethic of Jesus" (p. 43).[10] The basic contrast between sect and church is

10. I consider more such critiques of "sectarianism" in chapter 13.

between those who detach themselves from the world and those who work within the world.

Curran comments that Troeltsch used the term "sect" as descriptive, not evaluative. But he adds, "Troeltsch's approach is sociological and descriptive but it points to aspects that are normative for the Catholic Church" (p. 43).[11] The Catholic Church in Curran's view clearly conforms to Troeltsch's church type, not only descriptively but also normatively. Curran then parses this normative judgment about the Catholic Church into four related types of inclusivity: in relation to Catholic Church membership, in its concern for all of reality, in its basic approach to theology ("both-and," not "either-or"), and in recognizing different levels of morality with different degrees of certitude. The second mark of inclusivity is especially relevant to the relationship of church to world, and according to Curran clearly distinguishes the church type from the sect type. The church does not withdraw from the world, but is concerned about the world as a whole. At the same time, the church recognizes that the world has its own autonomy that must be respected; but this cannot mean that God's wishes for the creation can be ignored. With regard to the relationship of church and state, after Vatican II the Catholic Church no longer seeks to subordinate the state to itself, but rather seeks to work for justice within the structures of the state. The theological justification for this embrace of all of reality is the fact that creation is the good gift of a good God. "The created, the natural, and the human are not evil" (p. 47) but rather mediate the presence of God to us. The sacraments of the church display this embrace of mediation:

> The Eucharist is basically a celebratory meal recalling the many meals Jesus celebrated with his disciples, including what we call the Last Supper. The celebratory meal is the primary way in which human families

11. After discussing the various types of inclusivity that come with being a church, not a sect, Curran returns to sociology and cites various surveys indicating that the number of committed Catholics has dropped in the United States over the past several decades, and that many American Catholics are looking to individual conscience rather than to the church for guidance on moral issues. Curran concludes: "Sociological surveys by their very nature can never be normative or prescriptive, but they indicate in their own way that the Catholic Church is a big church, inclusive of saints and sinners and of the more or less committed, in which there is both unity on core issues and diversity on more peripheral issues" (*Social Mission*, p. 53).

and friends gather together to celebrate their love and friendship for one another. . . . So the liturgy takes over the fundamental sharing inherent in a meal and makes the meal the primary way in which Christians celebrate God's love and their commitment to love God and neighbor. (p. 47)

In the following chapter, Curran takes this post–Vatican II understanding of the Catholic Church and shows its effects on the social mission of the church. According to Curran, in the pre–Vatican II church, the mission of the church was seen as twofold. Divinization, the work of sanctifying the people, was the job of the clergy and religious. Humanization, working for the betterment of the world, was the role of the laity. The main development in the wake of Vatican II, according to Curran, has been the integration of the two missions into one (pp. 57-58). Now the transformation of the world is seen as an integral aspect of the preaching of the gospel. This is a direct result of the Vatican II emphasis on the dialogue between the church and the world (pp. 58-59). As a result of this breaking down of the supernatural/natural dichotomy, the roles of clergy, religious, and the laity have changed as well. The full gospel dignity of the laity's work in the world has been recognized, while the clergy and religious have come out of their confinement in the supernatural sphere to become actively involved in working for the transformation of the world. The Leadership Conference of Women Religious, for example, has claimed working for a more just and peaceful world as integral to its calling (p. 66). An important manifestation of this active embrace of the world has been the breaking down of the triumphalism and separatism of the Catholic Church. We have moved out of the "Catholic Ghetto" (p. 76). The church no longer seeks to foster specifically Catholic social organizations, but rather encourages Catholics to work together with all people of good will, of another religion or none at all, to foster justice in a pluralistic society. At the same time, Catholics now work with others through the mechanism of the state. Structural change through public policy is the most important way the Catholic Church works to transform the world. "From a theoretical perspective, there is no doubt that structural change is a very effective way to correct injustice, which explains the Church's present-day emphasis on change in public policy on a number of issues" (p. 71). At the same time, Curran gives a nod to the principle of subsidiarity, which shows the coherence of Catholic social teaching with the limited constitutional government of American democracy. Government should only intervene to do what voluntary associations cannot do on their own (pp. 72-73).

Overall, Curran's narration of changes in Catholic social mission in America is a progressive tale. We have moved from huddling together in Catholic ghettos like Westphalia to embracing the world in all its plurality. Catholic Charities and Catholic health-care institutions now receive significant government funding and mostly resemble secular institutions, but this is simply a flowering of the Catholic emphasis on mediation and the desire to avoid being a "sect" (pp. 81-85). The death of most Catholic social action movements in the United States is attributed to Vatican II, and celebrated. "The very concept of Catholic Action no longer made sense after Vatican II, when action on behalf of justice and the transformation of the world were seen as the constitutive dimension of the preaching of the Gospel and the mission of the Church" (p. 92). Why Catholic Action does not qualify for this conception of "action on behalf of justice and the transformation of the world" is not clear, except that, in Curran's view, the more justice and transformation of the world are seen as constitutive of the church, the more the church should come to be constituted by the world. Curran explains that we have moved beyond hierarchical church documents that

> see the Church and the world as two previously constituted entities that then enter into dialogue and relationship with one another. But political and liberation theologians do not understand faith as an independently constituted reality illuminating the political or economic sphere. The prior question is how the commitment to struggle for the poor and against injustice affects faith itself. Commitment to this struggle is the horizon that shapes our understanding of faith itself and of the Church. (p. 59)

Curran mentions no reciprocal relationship whereby the world is constituted by the church. The world is simply out there, a reality with which the church must reckon.

III. Church and World

Curran's tale is attractive because, like all progressive narratives, it allows us to see our current situation as superior to what came before.

Once we were huddled against the world, and now we have turned toward the world and embraced it in order to transform it. Who besides sociopaths want to go back to such a negative and defensive attitude toward the world? I think Curran's narrative is problematic — not because I wish to return to the pre-Vatican II church, but because it oversimplifies the relationship of the church to the world by reading it through the church/sect dualism, and in doing so too easily dismisses the relevance of pre-Vatican II efforts to conform the world to the gospel.

The problem begins with the fact that Curran — without recognizing the difference among them — uses the church/world duality in at least three different ways:

A. It follows the Catholic/non-Catholic binary, such that embrace of the world means the embrace of non-Catholics.

B. It follows the God/creation or supernatural/natural binary, such that embrace of the world means recognizing the goodness of the created order and the way it mediates God's presence to us.

C. It follows the Christ/culture or faith/daily life or religious/social binary, such that embrace of the world means integrating the gospel with economic and political and social realities.

Conflating these three meanings of church/world leaves Curran without sufficient nuance to recognize more than two different approaches to the church/world question. We are left with a choice between church type and sect type — or, as I would suggest, to question the very categories with which he is operating.

The breaking down of barriers between non-Catholics and Catholics in the post-Vatican II era should be recognized as an unqualified gain. To describe this movement as an embrace of the world by the church, however, is misleading. The ecumenical movement, from the Catholic point of view, is rather a recognition that those who were previously anathematized as belonging to the realm of perdition and not to the church are now recognized as belonging to the one church of Christ, even though not yet in full communion with the Catholic Church. The "realm of perdition" — those whose salvation is in serious jeopardy by reason of their obstinate refusal to recognize Christ — corresponds to the Johannine use of "world" *(kosmos)* to mean that part of creation that is still in rebellion against Christ's definitive rule (see, e.g., John 12:31; 16:11; 18:36). This use of the church/world duality as corresponding to those who follow Christ/those who are in rebellion against Christ — let's call this sense D — is not employed by Curran at all, despite its biblical pedigree.

Sense D is the primary way the Gospel of John uses the term "world," but John also uses it secondarily as in B to denote the created order.[12] In this case, however, the world is not located in a duality with the church; the church is part of the created order. Curran, of course, would agree. But he thinks there is a type of Christian — the sect type — that overlooks the goodness of the created order that came into being through Christ (John 1:10), and thus turns its back on the world, trying to maintain its own purity against the evils of the created order. For Curran, then, the two different uses of the term "world" in the Gospel of John reflect not two quite different meanings of the word *kosmos* — used by the author of the Fourth Gospel in two quite distinct contexts — but rather two different types of being church, one that has a positive view of creation and one that has a negative view. The church/world relation then becomes a matter of the church's attitude toward the world, whether one shuns it or embraces it. But the choice that is being presented to the readers of the Gospel of John is not yes or no to creation, as the Gnostics thought, but yes or no to Christ's reign. The corresponding light/ dark and ascending/descending dualities in John do not correspond to spirit/matter — which would be a Gnostic reading — but rather to those who accept Christ's kingdom/those who reject it. The Gospel of John is not trying to get the reader to say yes to creation (the secondary use of *kosmos*) but to say no to sin (the primary use of *kosmos*), although, of course, creation is assumed to be good, as the echoes of Genesis 1:1-5 in John 1:1-5 make obvious.

Troeltsch's church/sect distinction is equally distorting if it is the lens through which one approaches the relationship between the gospel and economic, political, and social life (option C). For Curran, the church/world duality corresponds to the religious/social or Christ/culture duality. The sect type of Christians consists of those who detach

---

12. The marginal comment on John 1:10 in *The New Oxford Annotated Bible* notes that "The primary meaning of *world* in the Fourth Gospel is the fallible social systems and social relations created by humanity . . . but it also denotes physical creation, including humanity."

themselves from the world, by which is meant the larger surrounding culture and its economic, political, and social life. The church type embraces the world by participating in that life, thus breaking down all these dichotomies and helping to spread the kingdom of God by transforming the world from within. If presented in these terms, who would not want to be church type rather than sectarian? When B and C are conflated, it seems especially obvious that the church does not want to turn its back on God's good creation, but rather to embrace the grace found in all natural things, and thus participate fully in the world in all its dimensions, economic, political, and social.

But there are good reasons to reject the choice between church and sect, because of its distorting effect on church/world discourse. To begin, Troeltsch's typology fits awkwardly in Curran's own narrative. If the Catholic Church is normatively church type and not sect type, why did the pre–Vatican II Catholic Church refuse to embrace the world in the way that Curran narrates? Curran fails to explain why, if the church type is in the Catholic Church's DNA, it took until after Vatican II to realize it. It may be that the immigrant experience in America produced a particularly long-lasting collective amnesia in the American Catholic community, one that was righted only when Catholics entered the mainstream of American society in the 1960s. It may be, on the other hand, that the very terms of Troeltsch's typology are insufficient to understand the experience of the Catholic Church in America.

In traditional Catholic usage, the distinction between church and sect was determined not by a particular group's attitude toward the world, but by that group's attitude toward the church. A sect was a group that rejected church authority. From the Catholic point of view, what made the Waldensians a sect and their contemporaries the Franciscans a religious order within the church had nothing to do with differences in their attitudes toward the "world." Both were equally "unworldly" in the sense of D above — rejecting, through evangelical poverty and the renunciation of violence, the powers and principalities of the *kosmos* — and both were equally "worldly" in the sense of B above, embracing the natural world as God's good creation.[13] With regard to C, both were

---

13. The followers of Francis are well-known for their positive regard for the natural world, as in Francis's *Canticle of the Sun,* and I can find no evidence of any dualism among the Waldensians, despite their proximity to the Cathars. Reinarius Saccho's 1254 list of accusations against the Waldensians contains no hint of ontological dualism or

either shunning the world or seeking to transform the world's attitudes toward power and material goods, depending on how one narrates it. But the key difference, what made the Waldensians a sect in Catholic eyes, was not their attitude toward the world, but their rejection of church authority, in sharp contrast with the Franciscans.

For Troeltsch, on the other hand, "The Franciscan movement belonged originally to the sect-type of lay religion."[14] Eventually, Troeltsch says, the Franciscans split into two factions, those that remained true to the sect type (the various kinds of Franciscan "Spirituals") and those who were domesticated into the church-type system. What marks the original Franciscan (and Waldensian) spirit as sectarian was its rigid adherence to what Troeltsch calls the "Law of Jesus."[15] According to Troeltsch, Jesus' message was purely religious, and did not, at first, produce a social ethic; "in the whole range of the Early Christian literature — missionary and devotional — both within and without the New Testament, there is no hint of any formulation of the 'Social' question; the central problem is always purely religious."[16] Because it shuns the social, Troeltsch writes of the gospel ethic: "Its first outstanding characteristic is an unlimited, unqualified individualism."[17] The Sermon on the Mount was not intended to provide an ethics or a politics by which the social order could be maintained; it was instead a manifesto for the pure, who would await the parousia in isolation from the mainstream of society. When the Roman emperor converted to Christianity in the fourth century, the church type came to the fore, in which the teachings of Jesus were moderated to accommodate the realities of the social world, which simultaneously created the opportunity for clearly defined sects within the Christian movement to separate themselves out from the world. Just as Curran does not consider the Catholic Church to have had a "social mission" until it was ready to address the whole of society, so Troeltsch uses the term "social" to refer only to an ethic that is directed at governing society as a whole. In other words, the very terms in which Troeltsch casts his supposedly descriptive analysis are dictated

a negative attitude toward material creation. Saccho's list can be found at http://www.fordham.edu/halsall/source/waldo2.html.

14. Ernst Troeltsch, *The Social Teaching of the Christian Churches,* trans. Olive Wyon (New York: Harper and Row, 1960), p. 355.

15. Troeltsch, *Social Teaching,* pp. 355-58.

16. Troeltsch, *Social Teaching,* p. 39.

17. Troeltsch, *Social Teaching,* p. 55.

from the point of view of the church type. Troeltsch assumes that, even in the ancient and medieval worlds, there was such a thing as "society" as a whole. He assumes, furthermore, that religious/social, religious/ political, and religious/economic are binaries that are not simply modern but apply to the premodern world as well.

All these assumptions are dubious. As the ferment of political theologies of the last few decades has made abundantly clear, Jesus' message was not inherently apolitical or asocial; the kingdom of God was directly relevant to the kingdoms of the world. The kingdom of God did not have to come to resemble the kingdoms of this world in order to become social or political. There is no good reason to assume that Jesus' teachings must be adjusted to address society as a whole in order to move from the purely religious to the social. First, "society as a whole" is a modern Western concept; secondly, religion as something separate from political and social life is also modern. Indeed, as historian John Bossy notes, the modern concepts of religion and society are like twins, both created when the early modern state was creating a unitary society governed by a sovereign out of the medieval patchwork of *societates,* semi-autonomous guilds, clans, cities, and other organic associations with overlapping jurisdictions and loyalties. Bossy writes that the development of the modern idea of society was "a successor effect of the transition in 'religion,' whose history it reproduced. One cannot therefore exactly call Religion and Society twins; but in other respects they are like the sexes according to Aristophanes, effects of the fission of a primitive whole, yearning towards one another across a great divide."[18] The "primitive whole" of which Bossy writes is the premodern inseparability of "religion" from life as a whole. *Religio* in the premodern West was a subvirtue of the cardinal — not theological — virtue of justice, which did not belong to a separate, "supernatural" realm of activity; not until the dawn of the seventeenth century was *religio* identified as *supernaturalis.*[19] There was a division of labor between

18. John Bossy, *Christianity in the West, 1400-1700* (Oxford: Oxford University Press, 1985), p. 171. The fact that such fission is commonly associated with the Treaty of Westphalia (1648) is an irony not lost on me. "Westphalia" is often used as shorthand for the system of nation-states that superseded Christendom.

19. Ernst Feil, "From the Classical *Religio* to the Modern *Religion:* Elements of a Transformation between 1550 and 1650," in *Religion in History: The Word, the Idea, the Reality,* ed. Michel Despland and Gérard Vallée (Waterloo, Ontario: Wilfred Laurier University Press, 1992), p. 35.

kings and priests, but not between "religion" and "politics." As Aquinas makes plain, both *religio* and acts of governance were directed toward the same end, the enjoyment of God, and right *religio* was necessary for good governance.[20]

Troeltsch, following Weber, attempted to resist the Marxist or Durkheimian reduction of religion to the social, and so defined religion as essentially asocial and belonging to the realm of value. Politics, on the other hand, is defined in terms of influencing the leadership of a state, that is, the one and only public realm, where instrumental rationality holds sway.[21] Religion, then, is an essentially interior impulse that can have an effect on society and the political, but if religion seeks to be influential, it must come to terms with, and accommodate itself to, the sphere of social life, which is a given and runs according to its own logic. Those who accept this process of accommodation are church types; those who reject it to maintain the purity of religion are sect types.

To accept Troeltsch's terms and to fit them into a church/world duality is to straitjacket the different possibilities of church engagement with the world. Contrary to Curran's contention that being church type is normative for Catholicism, Troeltsch's is a distinctly liberal Protestant project that locates the essence of religion in an asocial interiority, rather than in the daily engagement of the Christian with the material world that is penetrated by the grace of God. In Troeltsch's scheme, the social is equated with the one society bounded by the state, thus eliminating from view any other kind of social and political action that tries to imagine a plurality of social spaces. Thus Troeltsch ignores everything from the complex medieval space of overlapping *societates;* to Catholic experiments in corporatism and distributism in the late

---

20. Thomas Aquinas, *On Kingship to the King of Cyprus,* trans. Gerald B. Phelan (Toronto: Pontifical Institute of Mediaeval Studies, 1949), 60 (bk. II, chap. 3); also Thomas Aquinas, *Summa Theologiae* II-II.10.10. I treat the genealogy of the concept of religion at much greater length in my book *The Myth of Religious Violence: Secular Ideology and the Roots of Modern Conflict* (New York: Oxford University Press, 2009), chap. 2.

21. Weber's famous essay "Politics as a Vocation" defines politics this way: "We wish to understand by politics only the leadership, or the influencing of the leadership, of a *political* association, hence today, of a *state.*" The state, in turn, is defined thus: "a state is a human community that (successfully) claims the *monopoly of the legitimate use of physical force* within a given territory." Max Weber, "Politics as a Vocation"; http://anthropos-lab.net/wp/wp-content/uploads/2011/12/Weber-Politics-as-a-Vocation.pdf.

nineteenth and early twentieth centuries; to the English pluralism of John Neville Figgis and G. D. H. Cole in the 1920s and 1930s; to Rowan Williams's call for recognition of different spaces of law in Britain; to contemporary calls for "radical democracy," a recognition of a pluralism of grassroots experiments in self-governance that go beyond the dreary exercise of voting for one of two corporation-sponsored candidates once every four years. Rather than assuming that there is one "world" out there, one dominant culture that we must either embrace or reject, it is both more empirically correct and more theologically faithful to see and imagine multiple ways of engaging with God's good creation while attempting to transform sin into the kingdom of God.

Vatican II does not represent the embrace of the church type over the sect type, the turn from detachment from the world to living in the world. The treatment of the church/world relationship in the documents of Vatican II is carefully nuanced. All four of the above valences of the church/world duality can be found in *Gaudium et Spes,* with different approaches to each. In the preface, the "world of men" is defined as "the whole human family along with the sum of those realities in the midst of which it lives; that world which is the theater of man's history, and the heir of his energies, his tragedies and his triumphs; that world which the Christian sees as created and sustained by its Maker's love, fallen indeed into the bondage of sin, yet emancipated now by Christ."[22] As in option B, the world is here the whole of creation, essentially good but fallen and redeemed. But *Gaudium et Spes* also uses "world" to mean that part of creation that stands outside the church (A): the council "sets forth certain general principles for the proper fostering of this mutual exchange and assistance in concerns which are in some way common to the world and the Church" (§40). In the same paragraph, the council also expresses "high esteem" for the way that "other Christian Churches and ecclesial communities" are working toward the same goal, and expresses confidence that the Catholic Church can be "helped by the world" in preparing the ground for the gospel (§40). The "world" in *Gaudium et Spes* is also used in sense C, as referring to the temporal activities of economics, politics, and social life; this is what is

22. Vatican II, *Pastoral Constitution on the Church in the Modern World (Gaudium et Spes), §2;* http://www.vatican.va/archive/hist_councils/ii_vatican_council/documents/vat-ii_cons_19651207_gaudium-et-spes_en.html. References to *Gaudium et Spes* are placed in the text.

meant when the church appeals to those who live "in the world," as in "the Church requires the special help of those who live in the world, are versed in different institutions and specialties, and grasp their inner-most significance in the eyes of both believers and unbelievers" (§44). These temporal activities or "earthly affairs" possess a certain sort of autonomy. "If by the autonomy of earthly affairs we mean that created things and societies themselves enjoy their own laws and values which must be gradually deciphered, put to use, and regulated by men, then it is entirely right to demand that autonomy" (§36). The document goes on to claim the "rightful independence of science" and deplores those who consider faith and science to be mutually opposed. The document is then careful to distinguish true autonomy from false autonomy, re-jecting the idea that "created things do not depend on God, and that man can use them without any reference to their Creator" (§36). This paragraph is then followed by an admonition to reject the world, in the sense of D. "That is why Christ's Church, trusting in the design of the Creator, acknowledges that human progress can serve man's true happiness, yet she cannot help echoing the Apostle's warning: 'Be not conformed to this world' (Rom 12:2). Here by the world is meant that spirit of vanity and malice which transforms into an instrument of sin those human energies intended for the service of God and man" (§37).[23] *Gaudium et Spes* thus presents a nuanced approach to church and world. It calls us to recognize the goodness of creation, fallen and then re-deemed by Christ, and cooperate with non-Catholics to transform earthly affairs while resisting being conformed to the evils of the world.

The devil, of course, is in the details. What does it mean to say "The council brings to mankind light kindled from the Gospel, and puts at its disposal those saving resources which the Church herself, under the guidance of the Holy Spirit, receives from her Founder" (§3)? Are there Christian approaches to economics, for example, or do Christians learn economics from the "science" of economics the way everyone else does? Do Christians try to create different economies, or is there one "economy" — one "world" — in which we all participate, for better or for worse?

23. The Latin text of *Gaudium et Spes* has *saeculo* for "world" here, whereas the texts cited for senses A, B, and C all use a declension of *mundus*. Paul, in the cited text from Rom. 12, uses a derivation of *aeon* instead of *kosmos;* the Gospel of John, on the other hand, uses *kosmos* for both the positive and negative senses of "world."

IV. Westphalia Today

Answering such questions in the abstract leads to distorting oversimplifications about the embrace or rejection of "the world." What interests me about Westphalia is that it provides an occasion for reflection on church and world in the concrete. The picture we see is complex. In 1952, there was not much contact with the non-Catholic world (A). There were no non-Catholics in Westphalia, and as in many other Catholic environments pre–Vatican II, Catholic identity was a source of pride, in both the positive and negative senses of the word. Clericalism and a stifling uniformity were often symptoms of this detachment from the non-Catholic world. Ecumenism and interreligious dialogue in the post–Vatican II Catholic Church are unqualified gains.

At the same time, Westphalia in 1952 was not at all disengaged from the natural world (B) or the temporal affairs of economic and social life (C). Indeed, in significant ways Westphalia was more engaged with the world than are many Catholics post–Vatican II, when the collapse of Catholic social action organizations and the move to the suburbs limited the temporal engagement of many American Catholics to voting. Neither politics nor economics for the people of Westphalia in 1952 was an abstruse discipline dominated by experts to whom one must defer; it was a community project of cooperative ventures that required the active participation of all the members of the body of Christ in Westphalia, their active involvement in each other's lives. "The economy" was not an abstract and incomprehensible unity of which Westphalia was a tiny and insignificant part, buffeted daily by decisions made far away by people of which one had no understanding and over which one had no control; economy was simply the sum of face-to-face transactions that one had with neighbors and fellow communicants. The people of Westphalia were profoundly engaged with the world. They grew food or knew where it came from. Commodities were not abstractions that appeared on shelves out of nowhere, and profits on services like the garage and the beauty parlor did not disappear into the ether of "the financial system" but circulated as credit among the members of the community, who had to earn each other's trust. For better and for worse, people were in each other's business, in all senses of that word. By no means were they "detached from the world."

Westphalia has changed, along with both the church and rural America. The school is closed, the credit union moved to Harlan, the co-op is gone. People shop at the Walmart in Denison, and shopping is not an occasion for socializing. "We still have our church, but young people grow up, graduate and move on because there are no jobs here. Large farms are becoming more prevalent. Not good for keeping a small town prosperous." According to another longtime resident, Father Duren predicted this. "He said back in the '50s how the family farms would be bought up by corporations and here it is today — it's a different world in all respects." St. Boniface Parish in Westphalia shares a priest with two other towns. In some ways, this is a gain. People appreciate the new role of the parish council, and one parishioner reports that now "the people of the parish have a say in what goes on — not only in parish life but in family life also." But all who responded to my questionnaire report some version of the following: "The feeling of community life is now very different with less cooperation from the members." "Religion is sort of on the back burner for a lot of the people." And this summary: "Most of what was gained by hard work and vision has been lost in this community. We have our church and clubhouse and ball park. I think as time progressed people didn't hold on to their vision of a prospering community and we lost it."

The causes of the challenges that Westphalia faces along with much of rural America are many. They include the enormous concentration of the power of agribusinesses and government policies that have, especially since the 1970s, favored corporate interests in agriculture.[24] Beyond rural America, consumerism has detached people from production and producers. We talk of "the global economy" increasing interaction among people, but the reality is of increasing detachment from the material world and from each other.[25] As Wendell Berry has written, we have given proxies to corporations to produce all our food, clothing, and shelter, and are rapidly giving proxies to corporations and the state to provide education, health care, child care, and all sorts of services that local communities used to provide. As Berry says, "Our major economic practice, in short, is to delegate the practice to others."[26] The post-Vatican II era is, in this sense, characterized not by engagement but by a profound disengagement with the world.

24. See, for example, Michael Pollan, *The Omnivore's Dilemma: A Natural History of Four Meals* (New York: Penguin, 2006).

25. I discuss this in more detail in my book *Being Consumed: Economics and Christian Desire* (Grand Rapids: Eerdmans, 2008).

26. Wendell Berry, *Citizenship Papers* (Washington, D.C.: Shoemaker and Hoard, 2003), p. 64.

The recent movement to promote locally-grown food and community-supported agriculture (CSA) shows that, in some ways, Westphalia was ahead of, not behind, the times. Nostalgia is not the point. The solution today is not to try to re-create Westphalia in 1952. Westphalia can, nevertheless, contribute to the "vision" of a prospering community to which the resident last cited above referred. Ideas about how to engage the world will vary with each different context. But the church should not abandon the hope that the followers of Christ can contribute distinctive visions of how to engage the temporal order, how to create new spaces of engagement with earthly life that do not simply bow to the inevitability of "the world."

What matters about Westphalia, in other words, is not simply the town itself, but the fact that *World Neighbors* told the story. Today, the geography textbooks my children use in our Catholic school are the same as those used in public schools. They learn about "the economy" as if it were simply out there, a given fact obeying its own laws. *World Neighbors,* on the other hand, covers economics in a chapter entitled "Sharing Goods through Trade." There, Catholic school students learned that God has distributed treasures and skills in different ways so that we must interact with each other to get what we need. Those engaged in trade should seek first to supply others' needs, and only take a reasonable profit. Advertisers should not lie. Prices should be set according to the principle of the just price, not supply and demand. The "Christian merchant" will pay good wages, allow fair working hours, let his workers have some say in the management of the business, and let them own shares in the business, for "Christ says that the hireling shepherd runs away when the sheep are in danger."[27] The text acknowledges that the battle is uphill: "in American business life, religion is not a great power. Even Catholics have largely lost the sense of obeying Christ in everyday life. Church is too often thought to be for Sunday, and religion is limited to saying one's prayers."[28] But the text hopes to provide a vision of a different world, to spur the imaginations of young people to create economic spaces where the eternal breaks into the temporal, to resist simply passively accepting "the economy" as if it were fated and impervious to the impact of the gospel. The book's foreword announces that it was "designed to show the Church at work in the world, and to

27. Bedier, *World Neighbors,* pp. 189-92.
28. Bedier, *World Neighbors,* p. 190.

study human beings in their spiritual and religious aspects as well as in their ability to produce economic and material wealth."[29]

What it would mean to be "the Church at work in the world" today must surely include working alongside other people of good will from other faiths and none. But it also must mean overcoming the temptation to separate "religion" from everyday life, and accept dominant systems as given. Today's Christians can take inspiration from previous attempts, like that of Westphalia, to knit together our spiritual lives with our material lives, and thus become more "worldly."

In the next chapter, I consider more reasons why the theory and practice of economics are not best left entirely to experts.

29. Bedier, *World Neighbors*, p. ii.

CHAPTER THREE

ORTHODOXY AND HERESY

IN DEPARTMENTS OF ECONOMICS

I N 2003, THE economics department at the University of Notre
Dame was split into two departments. Economics and Econometrics — to which seven professors were assigned — was to pursue
mainstream economics focused on quantitative analysis. Economics
and Policy Studies — to which eighteen professors were assigned —
was to carry forward the more heterodox type of economics for which
Notre Dame had become known. In this department would huddle the
historians of economics, the Marxists, and those who questioned the
reigning paradigms of academic economics. At least since the 1970s,
Notre Dame's economics department had been known for taking cur-
rents in Catholic social thought seriously, and bringing in a distinctive
emphasis on social justice, labor, and development not found in most
economics programs granting doctoral degrees, where the emphasis
was on supposedly value-neutral analysis of economic facts and behaviors. Alas, that department also tended to be ranked in the lowest
quartile of doctorate-granting economics departments, in part because
leading journals would not publish its work. "There are some journals
that focus on heterodox economics," as the neoclassicist chair of the
economics department noted. "Most of them don't even rank in the top
50, which means that they don't have a great deal of impact."[1] And so

1. Richard Jensen, quoted in Gill Donovan, "Economics Split Divides Notre
Dame," *National Catholic Reporter,* April 4, 2004; http://natcath.org/NCR_Online/
archives2/2004b/040904/040904c.php.

a separate department of econometrics was created with a mandate to publish in more acceptable journals.

Not everyone was pleased. In an open letter, members of the Notre Dame community criticized mainstream economics for giving the false impression that economics is a value-free "natural science" and for avoiding any questioning of such assumptions: "this perspective ignores the reality that neoclassical theory's starting assumptions and supporting logic carry an embedded ethics and have serious social implications."[2] Even neoclassical economist Robert Solow of MIT wrote to Notre Dame's president, calling the split a "cruelly bad idea" and arguing that "Economics, like any discipline, ought to welcome unorthodox ideas, and deal with them intellectually as best it can. To conduct a purge, as you are doing, sounds like a confession of incapacity."[3]

The split, it turned out, was temporary. In 2009, Notre Dame announced it was dissolving its Economics and Policy Studies Department. Faculty in that department would be dispersed to other departments in the university, most being unwelcome in the triumphant mainstream department. "In light of the crash of the economy, you would think there would be some humility among economists, some openness to new approaches," commented economics professor emeritus Charles Wilber. "There's not a lot."[4]

The borrowing of theological language — "orthodox" versus "heterodox" — to characterize this debate ought to tell us something interesting about economics as a discipline. On the one hand, defenders of neoclassical approaches tend to speak of economics as a science because of its reliance on quantitative analysis and its supposed descriptive and predictive power. On the other hand, they dismiss other approaches as "heterodox," which indicates that *belief*, or *doxa*, is in fact what is at issue, despite the claim of science to have superseded mere belief. Indeed, defenders of a secularist model of the university claim that it is precisely the overcoming of the cramped limitations of orthodoxy that most marks the success of the secular university over the previous faith-based model. Perhaps some would claim that orthodoxy and heterodoxy are just metaphors when used to describe the science

2. The letter can be found at http://paecon.net/petitions/petitionNotreDame.htm.
3. Quoted in Donovan, "Economics Split."
4. Charles K. Wilber, quoted in David Glenn, "Notre Dame to Dissolve the 'Heterodox' Side of Its Split Economics Department," *Chronicle of Higher Education,* September 16, 2009; http://chronicle.com/article/Notre-Dame-to-Dissolve/48460/.

of economics. Those on the losing side of the battles for institutional recognition at Notre Dame and other places are unlikely, however, to experience these terms as "mere" metaphors. They are terms that do real work to mark out what kinds of inquiry are acceptable and what kinds can be safely ignored.

In this chapter I explore the ways that economics as a discipline is described and the work those descriptions do in situating economics within a faith-based university. I examine three different images Christian economists use to describe economics: economics as science, economics as ethics, and economics as theology. I argue that only by examining the theology implicit in economies and economics can a fully satisfying science of economics emerge.

I. Economics as Science

"To have influence in the academic discussion, it is important to excel in one's discipline. It takes quality scholarship, as defined by the mainstream, to get a seat at the discussion table."[5] Thus begins an essay by economist Judith Dean on being a Christian economist. Her approach is probably quite similar to what the administration at Notre Dame had in mind when moving in a more mainstream direction: the goal of a Christian institution is to have influence, to influence society for the good, and one cannot have influence unless one is respected by one's academic peers. When asked by a student, "If I were to take your course in econometrics, would I be able to tell you are a Christian?" Dean answered no. But she emphatically denies that she has thereby compromised her Christian faith, any more than C. Everett Koop has compromised his just because the way he does surgery varies not at all from techniques used by non-Christian colleagues.[6] While acknowledging that Christian economists should sometimes play the role of "philosopher," challenging the philosophical presuppositions of their field, Dean's preferred image for what Christian economists do is that of "research physician." She sees her role as improving the health of the

5. Judith M. Dean, "The Christian Economist as a Mainstream Scholar," in *Faithful Economics: The Moral Worlds of a Neutral Science*, ed. James W. Henderson and John Pisciotta (Waco: Baylor University Press, 2005), p. 25.

6. Dean, "The Christian Economist," pp. 25-26.

economy. Just as a research physician must have a solid understanding of the human body, carrying out empirically-verifiable experiments on the effectiveness of various treatments, so must an economist apply technical expertise to diagnosing and curing a sick economy.[7]

There will be no difference, according to Dean, between a Christian and a secular economist on the question of "technical methodology." The Christian's faith will make a difference, however, in three areas: (1) in the choice of research topics, a "Christian's choices will reflect God's priorities"; (2) in the formulation of research questions, "the choice of definitions of terms should be affected by [his or her] faith"; and (3) in the way she or he evaluates potential solutions to problems, "evaluation of potential solutions should use both transcendent and immanent criteria." What this last indicates is that both criteria from economics, such as efficiency, and criteria from Christianity, such as "ethical treatment of human beings," should have an influence on formulating solutions.[8] As an example, Dean discusses her research on removing nontariff restrictions on textile exports from developing countries to developed countries. Her faith motivated the choice of research topic because of the issue's effect on the poor, one of God's priorities. Her faith, she says, affected her choice of methods in that she chose criteria that would not underestimate the number of trade barriers that really inhibit trade.[9] Finally, in terms of potential solutions, she was able to give an accurate assessment of whether or not removal of the barriers would be detrimental to poor countries.

It seems clear that her training as an economist has prepared Dean to make a potentially useful contribution to a debate important to poor countries. Her Christian faith has motivated her to do honest analysis and come up with a solution based on what she believes would benefit the poor. What is unclear is whether and how Christianity actually provides content, not just motivation, for her economic analysis. Dean is trying admirably to explain the influence that Christian economists can and should have, but the language of Christian belief — that is, what Christians think is true about the world — quickly turns into the language of motivation to do the right thing. What counts as the right thing is generic: being honest and helping disadvantaged people.

7. Dean, "The Christian Economist," p. 28.
8. Dean, "The Christian Economist," p. 30.
9. Dean, "The Christian Economist," p. 32.

The problem with articulating a genuine impact of Christianity on economics comes with the power of the scientific metaphor Dean uses, and the sharp distinction between descriptive and normative activities that it reinforces. If an economist is to be likened to a research physician, then economics takes on the aura of a "hard" science, itself a metaphor that indicates the unyielding and given nature of facts. In such a view, economic facts are simply out there, a reality that one bumps into as one bumps into a chair. The economist then must seek to understand those facts, just as a research physician seeks to understand the human body, using the best instruments and techniques at his or her disposal. The task at this stage is purely descriptive. Subsequently, one may or may not apply various values in determining what to do with those facts. But that is another enterprise in which the economist might or might not wish to engage.

The story that mainstream economics likes to tell about itself is one of the progressive separation of the analysis of fact from that of value, and the eventual congealing of the former analysis into a proper science. Roger Backhouse's history of economics, for example, describes the inklings of economics in the medieval scholastic debates over the morality of usury. Though primarily concerned with ethics, ethical questions inevitably required people to think about the way in which economic activities "actually worked."[10] This distinction — a basic duality between "moral questions" and "what is actually going on in the world and what can be done"[11] — gradually opened up into a full-blown separation of economics from theology first, then from philosophy and politics. Eventually, in the twentieth century, economics emerged emulating science, with its own distinct, and thoroughly mathematized, methodology.

Given the prestige of the natural sciences, there are obvious advantages for economists in presenting what they do as scientific. There are reasons to think, nevertheless, that economics is *not* best understood

10. Roger Backhouse, *The Ordinary Business of Life: A History of Economics from the Ancient World to the Twenty-First Century* (Princeton: Princeton University Press, 2004), p. 41.

11. Backhouse, *Ordinary Business of Life*, p. 65. For example, Backhouse describes the emergence of proper economics in the early modern period this way: "Instead of disputing the morality of profit, such writers were beginning to take profit-seeking behaviors for granted and attempted to work out its implications" (p. 65). It is not clear why taking profit-seeking behaviors for granted is not a type of moral judgment.

on the model of the natural sciences. There is an extensive literature calling this model into question and arguing that economics has made only negligible progress in describing the world and predicting human behavior. Those calling it into question, however, are those labeled "heterodox," who find themselves largely excluded from the privileged circle of influential economists. Economics as science is something of an echo chamber in which the very application of the metaphor of "hard" science to economics prevents some forms of inquiry that might truly be called scientific from questioning the assumptions on which the discipline often operates.

Sheila Dow's book *Economic Methodology: An Inquiry* finds that "it is extraordinarily rare for empirical evidence [in economics] to settle a theoretical dispute."[12] An example of the malleability of empirical data is a 1991 article by David Hendry and Neil Ericsson on econometric analysis of U.K. money demand, in which the authors used data provided by Milton Friedman and Anna Schwartz and came up with opposite conclusions to those reached by Friedman and Schwartz.[13] Hendry's earlier article "Econometrics: Alchemy or Science?" explores some of the same problems.[14] The scientific status of econometrics has been questioned both inside and outside the field, leading to conclusions like that of Wassily Leontief that "in no other field of empirical inquiry has so massive and sophisticated a statistical machinery been used with such indifferent results."[15] Edward Leamer, in an article entitled "Let's Take the Con out of Econometrics," has written that "economists have inherited from the physical sciences the myth that scientific inference is objective, and free of personal prejudice. This is utter nonsense . . . the false idol of objectivity has done great damage to economic science."[16] The main problem, according to Leamer, is that

12. Sheila Dow, *Economic Methodology: An Inquiry* (Oxford: Oxford University Press, 2002), p. 36, quoted in Clive Beed and Cara Beed, *Alternatives to Economics: Christian Socio-Economic Perspectives* (Lanham, Md.: University Press of America, 2006), p. 160.

13. David Hendry and Neil Ericsson, "An Econometric Analysis of UK Money Demand in Friedman, M. and Schwartz, A., 'Monetary Trends in the United States and the United Kingdom,'" *American Economic Review* 81, no. 1 (1991): 8-38.

14. David Hendry, "Econometrics: Alchemy or Science?" *Economica* 47, no. 188 (1980): 387-406.

15. Wassily Leontief, "Theoretical Assumptions and Nonobserved Facts," *American Economic Review* 61, no. 1 (1971): 1-7, quoted in Beed and Beed, *Alternatives to Economics*, p. 205.

16. Edward Leamer, "Let's Take the Con out of Econometrics," *American Eco-*

economists tend to select the set of estimated models that yield "the most congenial results."[17]

The search for laws is generally understood as marking a science, but the presence of laws in economics that are equivalent to the law of gravity in physics is much disputed. *The New Palgrave Dictionary of Economics* claims that "no scientific law, in the natural scientific sense," has been found in economics, and "the list of generally accepted economic laws seems to be shrinking."[18] Laws in economics — for example, "agents always perform those actions with greatest expected desirability,"[19] or "in all capitalist societies, the likelihood of getting out of unemployment falls as the unemployment rate increases"[20] — have been criticized for being vague and self-evidential, or simply the codification of commonsense observation. That bond prices have an inverse relationship to interest rates is an observation that can be made by experience in markets. When the language of "law" is pressed to conform to the model of law in the natural sciences, the results are inevitably distorting. As Backhouse writes, "we cannot 'see' many economic concepts in the same sense as we can see a polyhedron," and furthermore, there is a "lack of agreement on the basic concepts that economics should be seeking to explain."[21] Preferences, utility, desires, intentions, motives, class, and a host of other terms are not fixed in the same way that independent variables necessary to natural sciences are. Often human economic behavior is described in terms of preferences, but the preferences are in turn explained by the behaviors. As Alexander Rosenberg comments, "the crucial explanatory variables are characterized and individuated by the very events whose occurrence they are cited to explain."[22] Similar observations have led Rosenberg

nomic Review 73, no. 3 (1983): 36, quoted in Beed and Beed, *Alternatives to Economics,* p. 206.

17. Leamer, "Let's Take the Con," p. 206.

18. Stefano Zamagni, "Economic Laws," in John Eatwell, Murray Milgate, and Peter Newman, *The New Palgrave Dictionary of Economics* (London: Macmillan, 1987), p. 54, quoted in Beed and Beed, *Alternatives to Economics,* p. 231.

19. David Papineau, *For Science in the Social Sciences* (London: Macmillan, 1978), p. 81, quoted in Beed and Beed, *Alternatives to Economics* , p. 257.

20. Mario Bunge, *Finding Philosophy in Social Science* (New Haven: Yale University Press, 1996), p. 28, quoted in Beed and Beed, *Alternatives to Economics,* p. 257.

21. Roger Backhouse, *Truth and Progress in Economic Knowledge* (Cheltenham: Edward Elgar, 1997), pp. 206-7, quoted in Beed and Beed, *Alternatives to Economics,* p. 240.

22. Alexander Rosenberg, *Sociobiology and the Preemption of Social Science* (Baltimore:

to conclude that rational choice theory has the "predictive accuracy of common sense."[23] A slightly more jaundiced view is that of Clive and Cara Beed, who write that in economics " 'Theory' is no longer seen as propositions purporting to describe, explain, or predict the real world. It is becoming schemata describing how the real world might look if people behaved in the way the theory suggested."[24]

This brief compendium of doubt is not meant to constitute a complete argument that economics is not a science; it is meant only to indicate that there are serious reasons for having this argument.[25] The problem is that universities — even Christian universities like Notre Dame — tend to be structured to preclude such arguments. The metaphor of economics as science ensures that "philosophical" arguments about the status of economics as a science cannot take place in economics departments, precisely because they see what they do as an analysis of fact, leaving arguments about deeper "values" to others.

II. Embedded Ethics

There are Christian scholars who more directly challenge the idea of a value-neutral economics. According to Lorna Gold, the dominant idea that economics is the dispassionate study of self-interested rational individual actors has helped to create the reality it purportedly describes. What this indicates is that the difference between descriptive and normative is not always as neat as the advocates of economics as science would have it. Gold advocates a Christian business model in which "[a]n instrumental economic rationale, in a sense, is subdued or 'framed' by the communitarian ethic in practice."[26] According to

Johns Hopkins University Press, 1980), p. 74, quoted in Beed and Beed, *Alternatives to Economics*, p. 226.

23. Alexander Rosenberg, *Economics: Mathematical Politics or Science of Diminishing Returns?* (Chicago: University of Chicago Press, 1992), p. 134, quoted in Beed and Beed, *Alternatives to Economics*, p. 271.

24. Beed and Beed, *Alternatives to Economics*, p. 299.

25. A summary of heterodox critiques of the "scientific" status of economics is found in Beed and Beed, *Alternatives to Economics*, chaps. 7-12, from which the above two paragraphs of this chapter are mostly taken.

26. Lorna Gold, *New Financial Horizons: The Emergence of an Economy of Communion* (New York: New City Press, 2010), p. 77.

Gold, the goodness of a business depends on the culture in which it is embedded.[27] The metaphor of embedding comes from Karl Polanyi, who famously described how markets are embedded in culture but have gradually come to be seen as separate and independent of culture, to the point where culture can be described as an epiphenomenon of markets. But, as Gold points out, Polanyi saw the independence of markets as an illusion; they are in fact embedded in and require a certain kind of culture, for better and for worse. The same point is typical of Catholic social teaching, especially as articulated by Pope John Paul II. As he writes in *Centesimus Annus*, "If economic life is absolutized, if the production and consumption of goods become the centre of social life and society's only value, not subject to any other value, the reason is to be found not so much in the economic system itself as in the fact that the entire socio-cultural system, by ignoring the ethical and religious dimension, has been weakened, and ends by limiting itself to the production of goods and services alone."[28]

The metaphor of "framing," or "embedding," circumscribes the autonomy of economics. If economics is somehow located "within" culture, which includes religion and ethics, then Christianity will certainly have an effect on how economics is practiced. If we picture economics and culture in this metaphor as concentric circles, with culture as the larger of the two circles, it remains unclear to what extent the circles interpenetrate; to what extent does Christianity, for example, actually alter what is going on inside of the inner circle of economics? There are different ways that this question gets answered, but most commonly the effect on economics is an "ethical" effect.

I will illustrate this effect with an essay by Rebecca Blank,[29] dean of the public policy school at the University of Michigan. Blank more directly than Dean challenges the value-neutrality of economics, refusing to carve out a "technical methodology" where Christianity does

27. Gold, *New Financial Horizons*, pp. 9-10.

28. Pope John Paul II, *Centesimus Annus* (1991), §39; http://www.vatican.va/holy_father/john_paul_ii/encyclicals/documents/hf_jp-ii_enc_01051991_centesimus-annus_en.html. Avery Dulles thinks the most significant contribution of Catholic social thought to economics is the view of economics as embedded in culture; see Avery Dulles, S.J., "*Centesimus Annus* and the Renewal of Culture," *Journal of Markets and Morality* 2, no. 1 (Spring 1999): 4.

29. Rebecca M. Blank, "Market Behavior and Christian Behavior," in *Faithful Economics*, pp. 35-49. Page numbers have been placed in the following text.

not penetrate. Blank describes the benefits of the competitive model of markets for predicting behavior, rewarding creativity, fostering efficiency, and doing so without central planning. Nevertheless, Blank questions the assumptions about human behavior in markets that a typical student would encounter in an introductory economics course. Individuals are assumed to act always to maximize their self-interest. They are assumed to know their own preferences and to have the information they need. The individual is the key actor in this model; aggregate demand is simply the sum of individual decisions, explained by individual preferences. Finally, more is assumed to be better; more goods are better than fewer, more choice is better than less (pp. 37-38).

Blank says that these assumptions about human behavior are often accurate; people make decisions at the grocery store based on what they like, what the price is, and how much money they can afford to spend. Blank recognizes that economists are also not blind to situations in which this ideal account of the market does not work. Economists analyze how lack of full information can lead to noncompetitive market outcomes, as can externalizing costs and a host of other factors. Nevertheless, the simple competitive market model is the starting point for economic analysis, and it is, as Blank says, a "public icon" (p. 39). We find the behaviors it describes as obvious — of course people will buy less of something if the price rises — but, as Blank says, "this seems obvious only because the economic competitive model is deeply embedded in the culture and experience of those who grow up in market economies. Persons living in non-market economies would not necessarily find these behavioral responses self-evident" (p. 40).

Writing from a Christian point of view, Blank contrasts the behavioral assumptions of the market model with "some of the widely held Christian messages about what constitutes 'right action'" (p. 40). "First, Christian faith calls people into community with each other" (p. 40). "Second, the Christian faith calls people to be other-interested as well as self-interested" (p. 42). The model for this love is the love that people experience from God, as demonstrated in the life and death of Jesus Christ. Third, Christianity affirms the abundance of life in terms not of material goods but of spiritual blessings. Fourth, choices are not morally neutral for the Christian; some preferences are better than others, and they should be evaluated on whether or not they turn one toward God. Fifth and finally, "Christian faith demands that Christians be concerned for the poor and those in need" (p. 43). Given these five requirements of Christian faith for economic behavior, Blank concludes with some reflections on how Christians can practice other-interest in the global market. We have no choice whether or not to participate in the market economy, any more than we can choose whether or not to be human. We can, however, make better choices in our purchases and become active in global groups, including the church, that are advocating for better conditions for all (pp. 43-49).

Blank's approach is helpful insofar as it makes clear that economic models are not value-neutral. Written into basic presuppositions of the neoclassical economic model of market behavior are certain assumptions about human behavior that in some cases contradict the Christian ideal of human behavior. In neoclassical models there is — as the writers of the Notre Dame open letter said — an "embedded ethics," one often directly at odds with Christian ethics. One cannot withdraw from the market, but a Christian can apply Christian norms of behavior to move the market toward more equitable and loving outcomes. Economic activity enjoys only a qualified measure of autonomy from other spheres of human life. The implication is something like what one finds in Catholic social thought: markets are a qualified good, but they should be seen as under the watchful eye of a broader culture informed by Christian norms. Blank never spells out how this approach makes a difference for how she teaches economics at a secular university. She is probably constrained as to how Christian norms might be contrasted with market norms, though she could at least make the students aware that what they are getting in their economics classes is not norm-free. At a Christian university, one could presumably go further and supplement the typical economics curriculum with an examination of Christian norms in the marketplace.

As helpful as this approach could be — and as much of an improvement as it would be on the approach taken by many Christian universities, where economics courses are indistinguishable from what is on offer at secular universities — I am not convinced that it gets to the heart of the issue. The fact/value divide is qualified but remains in place, because the confrontation between neoclassical economics and Christianity remains at the level of ethical norms. The Christian contribution to economics is given in terms of what Christianity says we ought to do; it does not confront neoclassical models on the question of fact. Christians are, for example, called to live in community; we are not told that individualism is in fact a fiction, and a dangerous one at that. In the Christian view, all humans (not just Christians) are in fact created by a good God in the image of God, a fact that means we are essentially other-oriented in our very being. The comparison between Christianity and market models as worldviews should be at the level of fact, not merely values.

III. Economics as Theology

There is a third type of image for economics that reveals this confrontation more directly: the image of economics as a kind of theology. Here theology is understood not simply as a set of values that generates certain norms of behavior, but as a comprehensive set of doctrines about how God and the world God made really are. Theology makes claims about God and the world, claims that imply an ethical stance but are not exhausted by that stance. Theology does away with sharp distinctions of fact and value by indicating that how we behave in the world is a function of seeing rightly how the world really is, in light of its creation by a good God.

Robert H. Nelson, a non-Christian economist, has perhaps done more than anyone to pursue the image of economics as theology. Nelson is not always consistent with his terms: economics is sometimes "religion," sometimes "priesthood," and sometimes "theology" in his writings. It is not entirely clear if economics is theology for a market religion, or if the practice of professional economics is itself a religion. He seems to lean toward the latter; economics, and not the economy, is a type of religion. He states his basic point this way: "Modern economics offers its own worldview, one that stands in sharp contrast to the Christian worldview."[30] Nelson came to this realization while working as an economist at the U.S. Department of the Interior. There he realized that economists rarely had influence through analyzing facts; they had influence by persuading others to act in accordance with an entire way of seeing the world that amounted to a religion.[31] "To the extent that any system of economic ideas offers an alternative vision of the 'ultimate values,' or 'ultimate reality,' that actually shapes the

30. Robert H. Nelson, "The Theology of Economics," in *Faithful Economics,* p. 89.
31. Robert H. Nelson, *Economics as Religion: From Samuelson to Chicago and Beyond* (University Park: Pennsylvania State University Press, 2001), p. xvi.

workings of history, economics is offering yet another grand prophecy in the biblical tradition. The Jewish and Christian bibles foretell one outcome of history. If economics foresees another, it is in effect offering a competing religious vision."[32] Economics does not just suggest other ways of acting in the world, but presents an alternative vision of "ultimate reality," the forces that are driving history. What this means for Nelson is that Christian attempts to reconcile orthodox economics with Christian theology are doomed to fail. "There has been a long conflict in the modern era between — as I would put it — secular religion and Christian religion. It seems to me that scholars have to make a choice. It is one or the other. Otherwise it is like saying that you are a Christian and a Muslim simultaneously."[33]

It is commonly recognized that academic economics has grown from ecclesiastical roots, from the Reverend Malthus at the beginning of the nineteenth century to social gospeler Richard Ely — founder of the American Economic Association — at the end of century. The usual story told, however, is of the rapid secularization of economics thereafter as it found a home in universities that were busily shedding their denominational identities in the interest of embracing the German model of *wissenschaftlich* higher education.[34] Nelson tells the story differently, as not the secularization of economics but the conversion to a new, progressive religion. Original sin was replaced by an original competition over scarce goods. The salvation story was that economic progress would save the world. Progressive economists like John Bates Clark in the late nineteenth century made explicit reference to God guiding the economy toward the good. Eventually Clark simply replaced these references to God with references to "natural law," which was still part of God's dispensation. Once the shift was made to laws of nature that govern human behavior, however, the "scientific" quest to uncover those laws could commence, and reference to God could become purely optional, at best.[35]

Both the old and the new religions were striving for the achievement of heaven on earth. Contrary to the common view that orthodox economics treats people as crassly self-interested, Nelson sees econ-

32. Nelson, *Economics as Religion*, p. 23.
33. Nelson, "The Theology of Economics," p. 90.
34. Nelson, *Economics as Religion*, pp. 41-42.
35. Nelson, *Economics as Religion*, pp. 102-3.

omists as offering a distinct kind of social salvation. It may be that self-interested behavior can help achieve that goal, but fulfilling self-interest is not the goal itself.[36] If this is true, then the theological import of Adam Smith's idea of the "invisible hand" of the market is not that there is an ethic of self-interest embedded in neoclassical economics, but rather that such economics serves as a type of theodicy that explains how divine providence turns evil into good. Nelson does not, however, think that economics offers a uniform theological point of view. Nelson identifies a direct parallel between the Catholic/Protestant split and the divide between progressivist and Chicago-school economists. Progressivists are those who have a strong belief both in the perfectibility of human society through economic progress and the necessity of a class of scientific managers to guide that progress through the application of rational principles. Nelson uses Paul Samuelson and his influential textbook as an example of progressivism. Despite the textbook's insistence that economics is a hard science, Nelson finds a doctrinaire insistence on change, efficiency, and other contestable values that issue from an optimistic anthropology. Progressivists, says Nelson, are like Catholic theologians, who both underplay the damage done by original sin and believe in a clerical elite to guide the laity to salvation.[37] The Protestants in this story are the Chicago school, people like Frank Knight, whose account of original sin casts doubt on the ability of a technocratic elite to act in the public interest. Self-interest is endemic, which is why economic decisions are best left to the individual, not to the government, which can only represent self-interest writ large.[38]

A similar approach to Nelson's can be seen in Philip Goodchild's book *Theology of Money*. But while Nelson uses the language and vocabulary of theology and religion rather loosely to suggest that economics offers an alternative way of seeing the world — a worldview — to that of Christianity, Goodchild's work is more precisely theological, in that it attempts to show that money formally occupies the place that God once occupied in Christian society. It is theological, that is, because it is about God, not simply about anthropology or soteriology. Goodchild also extends the range of his analysis beyond the work of professional economists to the market economy as a whole.

36. Nelson, "The Theology of Economics," pp. 93-95.
37. Nelson, *Economics as Religion*, pp. 49-88.
38. Nelson, *Economics as Religion*, pp. 119-38.

Goodchild begins his theological reflections with the opposition that Jesus posited between God and wealth, or Mammon (Matt. 6:24). What is in question is not simply ethics, but metaphysics; Jesus puts the power of God and the power of money into opposition.[39] It is not so much that people actually worship money or accumulate it for its own sake. It is rather that, in modern society, time, attention, and devotion are organized by the social institution of money, in ways that are directly in opposition to God. Money is the one thing that guarantees access to all the benefits and pleasures and goods of modern life. Money is therefore the one thing that unites all the diverse people of the world. Money takes the place that God once held, as the source of the value of values (pp. 4-7).

It would be a mistake to place money and God on opposing levels of reality, as if God were transcendent and spiritual on the one hand, and money were mundane and material on the other. As Goodchild shows, money is not a tangible thing, but is essentially a system of social obligations based in debt. The modern money system originated in banks creating notes that represented loans and in turn could be used to pay off further obligations. Credit came to occupy the space that coinage alone had previously occupied, and the whole system depended on confidence and trust. Furthermore, money can be created from speculation. A bank can create money by loaning to a speculator, whose assets can rise in value because of the very activity of speculation, as with pre-2008 house prices. If the speculator can sell the assets while the value is high, he or she can repay the loan and keep the difference. Goodchild refers to this as making money "out of pure thought" (p. 16). Money, like God, transcends the merely material.

The value of money is transcendent; no one has ever seen a dollar, only a promise to pay a debt marked by a value called a dollar. Money is the supreme value, since all other social values are realized in its terms. Furthermore,

> The value of assets is determined not by their intrinsic worth but by their expected yield, their anticipated rate of return. The value of assets is determined by speculative projections. Moreover, even if these anticipations prove misguided, at every stage the value of assets is de-

39. Philip Goodchild, *Theology of Money* (Durham, N.C.: Duke University Press, 2009), pp. 3-4. Page numbers have been placed in the following text.

termined by the next wave of anticipations about the future. Thus, the future never ultimately arrives: it is purely ideal. Financial value is essentially a degree of hope, expectation, trust, or credibility. Just as paper currency is never cashed in, so the value of assets is never realized. It is future or transcendent. (p. 12; see also p. 170)

The structural parallels between the positions that God and money occupy in different types of society, however, do not mean that God and money offer the same things. Indeed, what is on offer provides the sharpest contrast.

Where God promises eternity, money promises the world. Where God offers a delayed reward, money offers a reward in advance. Where God offers himself as grace, money offers itself as a loan. Where God offers spiritual benefits, money offers tangible benefits. Where God accepts all repentant sinners who truly believe, money may be accepted by all who are willing to trust in its value. Where God requires the conversion of the soul, money empowers the existing desires and plans of the soul. (p. 11)[40]

Because money occupies the place of God, Goodchild uses the term "religion" to describe the system of social obligations that money puts in motion. "Being transcendent to material and social reality, yet also being the pivot around which material and social reality is continually reconstructed, financial value is essentially religious" (p. 12). When money is created as a debt, it holds its value only as long as there is trust in the commitment to repay the debt. The money system is not only a system of inclusion through trust and social obligation, but also a system of exclusion for those without the wealth or willingness to complete such obligations. Goodchild says that debt occupies the position of religion in society (p. xiv), but there is a crucial difference between the financial system and what he calls "traditional religion." That difference is the lack of consciousness about the transcendent status of money in the former. We regard God as shrouded in mystery and beyond human manipulation, but we continue to see money as mundane, an object of human control, and a mere means to other ends. In

---

40. The parallels extend also to the doctrine of creation; according to Goodchild, God presides over a world created good as it is, whereas money constantly seeks to change the world through creative destruction (*Theology of Money*, p. 211).

fact, money has become our end, though we refuse to acknowledge it. "It is in modern life that alienation is complete and the consciousness of humanity departs entirely from the conditions of its existence. It is in modern life, rather than religious life, where ideology is most fully instantiated" (p. xv).

The profession of economics is part of that ideological apparatus that keeps us from recognizing the transcendent nature of the money economy. The so-called science of economics is concerned with the effects of money on value, but value is only measured in terms of money. Economics carefully chooses for its object of study only that which is exchangeable, which imposes exchangeability as a value and a form of evaluation (p. 16). What is needed, according to Goodchild, is the rescue of evaluation from its subordination to the demands of those with access to money. This requires the recognition that a true science of evaluation is necessary, and this science must be consciously theological. Theology, whether Christian or not, has as its most fundamental role the determination of the nature of true wealth. In Christian terms, it is applying the judgment of the God revealed in Jesus Christ to the fundamental question of power in the world, that is, determination of what is truly of value (pp. 4, 198).

IV. Economics and Theology in the University

Of the approaches that I have explored above, the third gets closest to the heart of the matter, not only because it is the most theologically rich, but also because it conforms most closely to the way that the economy and economics in fact function in the world. It is the model that is most empirically satisfying. In the wake of rolling blackouts that hit California's electricity supply in 2001, the architect of the deregulation that caused them was quoted in the *New York Times* expressing his conviction that "free" markets always work better than state regulation: "I believe in that premise as a matter of religious faith."[41] Jesus — as his comments on God and Mammon indicate — would not have been surprised. A sympathetic approach to this problem might be a kind of Augustinian awareness that in this temporal existence desire that is ac-

41. Philip Romero, quoted in Alex Berenson, "Deregulation: A Movement Groping in the Dark," *New York Times*, February 4, 2001, 4.6.

tually for God alights on all sorts of inferior objects. It becomes idolatry not when one consciously bows down and worships, but rather when it unconsciously takes the place of the divine in one's life. The role of theology in economics would be to mark when in fact God has been supplanted, to take note, that is, when money has gone from servant to master. But that need not always be the case. There is in fact room in the university for a more modest economics that does not necessarily stand in tension with theological convictions.

As Deirdre McCloskey has pointed out, although the official rhetoric of orthodox economics is positivist, in actual fact orthodox economics relies on metaphor, analogy, and appeals to authority in order to persuade.[42] There is no reason to conclude, as does the self-professed naturalist Tony Lawson, that "the whole project [of economics] is riddled with confusion and incoherence,"[43] unless one assumes that economics must conform to the standards of the natural sciences. The problem with orthodox economics is not that it uses metaphor and images, but that it denies that it does. Good economics, as Robert Solow says, is akin to storytelling. The true function of economics is "to organize our necessarily incomplete perceptions about the economy, to see connections that the untutored eye would miss, to tell plausible — sometimes even convincing — causal stories with the help of a few central principles, and to make rough quantitative judgments about the consequences of economic policy and other exogenous events."[44]

Solow still seems to view "the economy" as an object to be studied; I would want to question, as I do in chapter 2, how the story that there is a "the economy" to study gets told and the work that it does. A good economist must do more than apply ethical criteria to "the economy" as such, and must bring to light the kinds of theological stories that the practice and the study of economics construct. The economist must be a theologian, at least in some rudimentary way. The economist does not necessarily need to have a thorough grounding in the Nestorian controversies of the fifth century. The economist should, nevertheless, be attuned to the ways in which the *topoi* of economics can function like the *topoi* of theology. This is only to say that all economics supposes a

42. Deirdre McCloskey, *The Rhetoric of Economics* (Brighton: Wheatsheaf, 1986).

43. Tony Lawson, *Economics and Reality* (London: Routledge, 1997), p. 14, quoted in Beed and Beed, *Alternatives to Economics*, p. 263.

44. Robert Solow, "Economic History and Economics," *American Economic Review* 75, no. 2 (1985): 330.

particular articulation of what ultimate reality is like. Economics cannot — and, more to the point, does not — function without one.

Of course, at the university level there is no question of dissolving the economics department into the theology department. Economists have important work to do, not only in conducting empirical studies of people's behavior, but also in questioning the basic underpinnings of belief that motivate that behavior, and that of the economists themselves. To do so, a more flexible definition of orthodoxy than that institutionalized at most universities will have to prevail. Foundational arguments about what economics is all about should be allowed and encouraged, not avoided or stifled. Debate between "orthodox" and "heterodox" economists can reveal the true theological basis of economics. In the next chapter, I explore the intersection of theology and economics in the ends to which human persons are called.

CHAPTER FOUR

ACTUALLY, YOU *CAN'T* BE ANYTHING YOU WANT
(AND IT'S A GOOD THING, TOO)

T HE FOLLOWING QUOTATION is attributed to Abraham Lincoln: "You can be anything you want to be, do anything you set out to accomplish, if you hold to that desire with singleness of purpose." This message is constantly reinforced in education and entertainment directed at children. Disney movies often rely on a formula in which an anthropomorphized panda or plane or rat or monster or car believes in himself, overcomes his limitations and the restrictions of society, and fulfills his wildest dreams.[1] The protagonist along the way learns contempt for the unimaginative drudgery to which the majority of society remains captive; self-fulfillment is privileged over the common good. Disparagement of routine labor is accompanied by disregard for hard work and the development of good habits. As Luke Epplin's recent article in the *Atlantic* puts it, "Turbo and Dusty" — the protagonists of the animated movies *Turbo* and *Planes* — "don't need to hone their craft for years in minor-league circuits like their racing peers presumably did. It's enough for them simply to show up with no experience at the world's most competitive races, dig deep within themselves, and out-believe their opponents."[2] Customs, community, rules, habituation — all are ignored in favor of spontaneous gratification of one's wants.

What happens when young adults who have been marinated in this

1. I use male pronouns here because in most cases (but not always) the character is male.
2. Luke Epplin, "You Can Do *Anything:* Must Every Kids' Movie Reinforce the Cult of Self-Esteem?" *Atlantic,* August 13, 2013.

type of cultural messaging come to the range of questions surrounding vocation? They are often told not only that they can and must *choose* their life, but that they must maximize that choice and choose their *best* life. Furthermore, the choice of their best life consists of knowing what they want and then seeking to attain what they want. It is no wonder that many young adults find this demand paralyzing. How many times has panic flashed across the face of a student confronted by the seemingly innocent question, "What would you like to do when you graduate?" Many, no doubt, suspect that what Abraham Lincoln and Dusty the animated airplane say is simply not true: you actually can't be whatever you want to be. But even if they accept some realistic limitations on the fulfillments of their wants, the deeper problem remains: Do they even *know* what they want? How does anyone really know what kind of life one wants? Can people choose what sorts of lives are right for them before they have lived enough to know? The whole exercise of *choosing* one's vocation becomes fraught with anxiety.

This problem is not simply the way life has always been; rather, it has much to do with the peculiar type of economy and culture in which we live. Vocation must be understood against the cultural backdrop in which students are situated; in Western culture, vocation language has tended to center on individual choice. This chapter will offer a brief genealogy of some of the economic aspects of the problem of vocation to show that how we think about work and wants has changed. It will then examine some of the dynamics of choice in our culture. The chapter will conclude with a discussion of some resources for helping us think and act differently with regard to vocational reflection and discernment.

I. The Social Division of Labor

Sociologist Max Weber famously claimed that the way we think about vocation is integrally entwined with the rise of capitalism. Weber was right about this, but not necessarily for the reasons he offered. He argued that the rise of capitalism was facilitated in part by the Protestant development of the notion of a "calling" or vocation in one's everyday life. Weber contended that there was a significant shift from the medieval Catholic view, which associated God's call paradigmatically with the otherworldliness of monastic life, with the Reformation's emphasis on responding to God within the context of one's station in life, no matter how mundane. As Weber writes, "The effect of the Reformation as such was only that, as compared with the Catholic attitude, the moral emphasis on and the religious sanction of organized worldly labour in a calling was mightily increased."[3] With the elimination of the Catholic sacramental system in Protestant Europe, says Weber, the "magical" means of attaining God's grace were eliminated; this motivated the search for God's blessing in the success that one found in commerce and industry.[4] Here the Calvinist doctrine of predestination played a crucial role, but rather than encouraging resignation to fate or faith in God's sovereignty, Weber thought it produced an anxiety about whether or not one was chosen — an anxiety worked out through ceaseless activity, which was taken as a sign that God was busily overcoming sloth and idleness in one's life. Thus was born what Weber called a "worldly asceticism," whereby hard work, frugal living, saving, and investing were given spiritual sanction.[5]

ECONOMICS AND THEOLOGY INTERTWINED

Even those who question Weber's famous thesis begin the story of the development of vocation at roughly the same time as the development of capitalism. Catholic theologian Edward Hahnenberg's excellent book on vocation begins with the Reformation and credits the Protestant reformers with discovering the notion that the call to holiness extends to all people — laity included — and to all aspects of human life, even the most mundane and tedious jobs that must be done.[6] Martin Luther thought of vocation as being called to one's stations (in German, *Stände*) in life, and such stations were generally fixed. The Puritans, however, introduced the idea that "every person must *choose* a calling,"[7] one that most crucially enables the man to support himself and

---

3. Max Weber, *The Protestant Ethic and the Spirit of Capitalism*, trans. Talcott Parsons (New York: Charles Scribner's Sons, 1958), p. 83. Weber's view of the medieval period here is an overly broad caricature. The medieval guild system, for example, certainly fostered a strong link between one's worldly work and one's spiritual life.

4. Weber, *Protestant Ethic*, pp. 105-6.

5. Weber, *Protestant Ethic*, pp. 95-183.

6. Edward Hahnenberg, *Awakening Vocation: A Theology of Christian Call* (Collegeville, Minn.: Liturgical Press, 2010), pp. 5-27.

7. Hahnenberg, *Awakening Vocation*, p. 21.

his family. Puritans and Anglicans over the course of the seventeenth century contrasted the notion of vocation with the supposed idleness of medieval Catholic monasticism. Talk of vocation among Protestant writers and preachers was permeated by emphasis on productivity, and there arose a whole Christian literature distinguishing the "deserving poor," who were unable to work due to illness, age, and disability, from the "idle poor," who *were* able to work but chose not to.[8] The former were to be given Christian charity, the latter condemned and punished. "Vocation" became synonymous with "employment" or "work." The result, as Hahnenberg puts it, is that "The sacred and secular split apart and vocation landed on the side of the secular."[9] God became increasingly superfluous to the notion of vocation, as one's own choice took the place of God's calling.

Tracing the idea of vocation through the writings of the Reformers is interesting and important, but it can be misleading if it is done in isolation from a consideration of the actual economic conditions of the time. The notion that stations in life were relatively fixed was not just an idea that Martin Luther had; it was a reality of medieval life that carried over into early modernity. Men generally did what their fathers did, which for the majority was subsistence farming. Women generally married neither above nor below their station. The exception to this general reality for both men and women was the choice to enter religious life, which is perhaps why the language of vocation was tied to becoming a nun, priest, monk, or brother. Unless she were royalty, joining a religious order was generally the one chance a woman had of becoming a public figure.

Likewise, the notion of "choosing" one's line of work was not simply a brainstorm that occurred between the ears of Puritan thinkers; it marked a major shift in the economic reality of developing capitalist economies. The Industrial Revolution meant the massive displacement of people from subsistence farming and craft industries to large factories. We tend to narrate this movement as a positive liberation of people from the narrow bonds of a life over which they had very little individual control. And for a certain class of people, it was indeed a liberation. As a middle-class American, I enjoy tremendous freedom of choice that my ancestors in Ireland did not; I am glad that I am not trying to

8. Hahnenberg, *Awakening Vocation*, pp. 20-22.
9. Hahnenberg, *Awakening Vocation*, p. 23.

scratch out a living from a small plot of potatoes. Still, this economic liberation (in connection with which our modern discourse of vocation developed)[10] has a negative side, one that is rarely mentioned in the literature on vocation. Examining these shadowy, unacknowledged realities can help us understand why the choices that young people face today, when reflecting on vocation, might not always be experienced as liberation.

FORCED INTO CHOICE

People today are free to pursue various lines of work because the development of capitalism required the existence of a large class of laborers, freed from ties to the land, who could work in factories. Capitalists supplied the means of production (machinery, raw materials, and networks of distribution) and collected the profits. Laborers, who no longer owned land or small cottage industries, had nothing to sell but their labor — which they did, for wages. Why would a person choose factory work over subsistence farming? We tend to assume that they did so freely, looking for an improvement in income or an escape from the boredom and stasis of rural life. The truth, however, is that the separation of capitalists from wage laborers in the early modern period was accomplished with deliberate and shocking brutality. Coercion was necessary because no sensible person would voluntarily exchange a life of dignified subsistence for the dehumanization of the factory.

Subsistence farming was the occupation of the majority in England until the Industrial Revolution, and it was made possible by the existence of common lands. In historian Joan Thirsk's words,

> [P]eople had to work together amicably, to agree upon crop rotations, stints of common pasture, the upkeep and improvement of their grazings and meadows, the clearing of the ditches, the fencing of the fields. They toiled side by side in the fields, and they walked together from field to village, from farm to heath, morning, afternoon and evening. They all depended on common resources for their fuel, for bedding,

---

10. I am trying here to avoid causal language in either direction. I think it is misleading both to say that theological ideas caused the economic conditions and to say that economic conditions caused the theological ideas. The best we can do is to recognize their mutual influence, and try not to lose focus on either theology or economics.

and fodder for their stock, and by pooling so many of the necessities of livelihood they were disciplined from early youth to submit to the rules and customs of the community.[11]

Common lands were common by custom, not belonging to anyone by legal title. Beginning in the sixteenth century and carrying on into the nineteenth, common lands were "enclosed" or privatized. This happened in many ways, with legal sanction and without. In many cases, nobles simply declared a piece of land to be theirs and met any resistance with armed force. In the Scottish highlands, the heads of traditional clans began to think of themselves as owners of the clan's land, and drove off thousands of small tenant farmers by force in order to convert the land into sheep pastures. The duchess of Sutherland evicted thousands of families from their ancestral lands between 1811 and 1820. On seeing many of her former tenants starve, she wrote to a friend in England that "Scotch people are of a happier constitution and do not fatten like the larger breed of animals."[12] In other cases, a bill of enclosure was issued by the House of Lords. Where outright fraud was absent, common lands were distributed to landowners in the area in proportion to the amount of land they already possessed. Those who did not already own land were excluded, and enclosure was often ruinous for small landowners as well. Even if they could afford the legal fees and fencing required by the bill, they usually found that their small plot of land could not support a family without access to common pastures and woods. For many, their only remaining choice was to sell the land and find wage labor.

Two other sets of laws were instrumental in driving people off the land and into the factories. The Game Laws punished attempts to find food on property to which one did not have title; the severity of these laws increased over the course of the eighteenth century. Poachers were executed under the infamous Waltham Black Acts of 1722. A large proportion of those exiled to Australia had been convicted of poaching. What seems like a minor offense to us was a matter of survival for rural

11. Joan Thirsk, "Enclosing and Engrossing," in *The Agrarian History of England and Wales*, vol. 4, ed. Joan Thirsk (Cambridge: Cambridge University Press, 1967), quoted in Michael Perelman, *The Invention of Capitalism: Classical Political Economy and the Secret History of Primitive Accumulation* (Durham, N.C.: Duke University Press, 2000), p. 13.

12. Quoted in Janet Hilderly, *Mrs. Catherine Gladstone: "A Woman Not Quite of Her Time"* (Sussex: Sussex Academic Press, 2013), p. 191.

people accustomed to feeding their families from the produce of the land. As a journalist wrote in 1826, it was "difficult to make an uneducated man appreciate the sanctity of private property in game [when] ... the produce of a single night's poach was often more than the wages for several weeks' work."[13] Once traditional subsistence was made difficult, laws were enacted to ensure that people newly "liberated" from the land would not find other ways to avoid wage labor. Another set of laws was enacted against vagrancy; a typical 1572 law in England required flogging and branding for beggars over the age of fourteen. Repeat offenders over eighteen were to be executed if no one took them into indentured servitude.[14] Classical political economists were at one with Puritan theorists of vocation in waging a war on the "idle poor." The great theorist of liberty John Locke recommended starting work at the age of three. Adam Smith's teacher Francis Hutcheson wrote that "Sloth should be punished by temporary servitude *at least.*"[15] Jeremy Bentham recommended that children be put to work at age four instead of fourteen, so to avoid those "ten precious years in which nothing is done! Nothing for industry! Nothing for improvement, moral or intellectual!"[16]

All these measures were undertaken in the name of "modernization" and "improvement." Sheep replaced people on common lands because wool was needed to feed the growing Midlands clothing factories, and subsistence farming was seen as inefficient and not contributing to economic growth and national wealth. Most crucially, however, capitalism needed labor that was "free" to work for wages. As one observer in 1815 put it:

> Poverty is that state and condition in society where the individual has no surplus labor in store, or, in other words, no property or means of subsistence but what is derived from the constant exercise of industry in the various occupations of life. Poverty is therefore a most necessary and indispensable ingredient in society, without which nations and communities could not exist in a state of civilization. It is the lot of man. *It is the source of wealth,* since without poverty, there could be no labour; there

13. Quoted in Perelman, *The Invention of Capitalism,* p. 43.
14. Perelman, *The Invention of Capitalism,* p. 14.
15. Francis Hutcheson, quoted in Perelman, *The Invention of Capitalism,* p. 16.
16. Jeremy Bentham, quoted in Perelman, *The Invention of Capitalism,* p. 22.

could be *no riches, no refinement, no comfort,* and no benefit to those who may be possessed of wealth.[17]

The process by which some come to "be possessed of wealth" and others own nothing but their labor is known as "primitive accumulation." Karl Marx famously wrote that we are taught to think about this process through the lens of the theological notion of original sin. We tend to think that, way back in the misty past, some people were hardworking and frugal and others were lazy and dissolute; the former became the owners of capital, the latter were relegated to work for others. In actual historical fact, however, the process of primitive accumulation is, as Michael Perelman writes, "an uninterrupted story of coercion."[18] That story is not limited to England and Scotland, but played out similarly on the Continent and especially wherever colonization took place — including the *encomienda* system in Latin America, the theft of Indian land in North America, and the use of African slaves. Nor is primitive accumulation a long-ago phenomenon that characterized only the early modern period.[19] Fred Pearce's 2012 book *The Land Grabbers* documents the ongoing efforts of governments, corporations, and wealthy individuals around the world to push subsistence farmers off their plots and into wage labor, enclose common lands, and convert them into large-scale agribusinesses — again, always in the name of efficiency and modernization, and usually with devastating effects.[20] The destruction of small-scale farming in the United States took place over the course of the twentieth century, and was in significant part due to deliberate government policies that favored large-scale agriculture as more "efficient." Similarly, the home has ceased to be a place of production and is now almost exclusively a place of consumption. Such basic measures of self-sufficiency as preparing one's own food and raising one's own children have declined precipitously, as employment outside the home has come to occupy more of the average person's day. This in turn often

17. Patrick Colquhoun, quoted in Perelman, *The Invention of Capitalism,* p. 23.

18. Perelman, *The Invention of Capitalism,* p. 15.

19. Thomas Piketty's much-discussed book *Capital in the Twenty-First Century* (Cambridge: Harvard University Press, Belknap Press, 2014) shows how massive inequalities continue to be endemic in our economic system and are bound to get worse, barring decisive political action.

20. Fred Pearce, *The Land Grabbers: The New Fight over Who Owns the Earth* (Boston: Beacon Press, 2012).

compels people to spend their wages on prepared food, child care, and many other services they once provided for themselves.[21]

In sum, the modern notion of vocation and the rise of capitalism were intertwined, but not only in the way that Weber thought they were. True, one's vocation was no longer given; it became a choice. Ironically, however, this "freedom" developed as a result of an enormously coercive process by which wage labor replaced self-sufficiency. The result, of course, has had tremendous benefits, at least for the winners in the process. The abundance and availability of material goods have reached undreamed of levels in developed economies. Millions have been pulled out of poverty. Individuals have escaped the limitations of local cultures, and for those with access to good education there is an enormous range of different kinds of employment from which to choose.

At the same time, however, as efficiency has replaced self-sufficiency, people entering the market feel increasingly at the mercy of larger forces that are beyond their comprehension and control. People seeking employment must try to conform to the ever-shifting demands of the job market. American colleges prospered on the promise of providing graduates a ticket to the managerial classes, but the opportunity to work in a cubicle is no longer guaranteed. Even when it is achieved, it is not always experienced as liberation; it is certainly not an automatic ticket into the ownership class. The role of the managerial class is still instrumental; its role is to produce wealth for shareholders, the ownership class. As a result, the notion of vocation can become a rather lonely and anxiety-producing business. Individuals who have successfully negotiated the educational system are thrust into the job market with the expectation that they must invent their own lives without traditional markers of identity and custom. This marks an enormous change in the way human beings relate to one another. As Thirsk notes, "Common fields and pastures kept alive a vigorous co-operative spirit in the community; enclosures starved it. . . . [E]very household became an island unto itself."[22] The argument here is not that we should attempt to go back in time or that we would necessarily be better off without enclosure. The point is simply that enclosure happened, and we must deal with the consequences, both positive and negative.

21. Perelman, *The Invention of Capitalism,* pp. 34-35.
22. Thirsk, "Enclosing and Engrossing," quoted in Perelman, *The Invention of Capitalism,* p. 13.

II. The Tyranny of Choice

Choice was created by coercion, and it can also be experienced as coercive. Psychology professor Barry Schwartz has explored this theme in detail and concluded that choice is not to be equated simply with freedom. Having some choice is essential to freedom, but as choices proliferate — "You can do anything!" — they can be experienced as coercive rather than liberating.

Schwartz begins his analysis by surveying the range of choices open to consumers today. His local supermarket offers 285 varieties of cookies, 360 types of shampoo, 230 kinds of soup, 175 different salad dressings, and so on. The electronics store has 110 different models of television; with cable one can watch hundreds of channels. Modern universities — "intellectual shopping malls," as Schwartz puts it — have often jettisoned common curricula in favor of student choice from among a bewildering variety of unrelated courses. "There is no attempt to teach people how they should live, for who is to say what a good life is?"[23] In keeping with the mall motif, dining halls at universities now resemble food courts, with a tremendous variety of options. Beyond stores and universities, we choose our electricity supplier, phone provider, stocks for our retirement plan, religious affiliation, even our own face and body (there are one million cosmetic surgeries in the United States each year).[24] Work is a choice as well, and that choice is not made only once. The "dynamism" of the global economy demands a flexible workforce. People must be (and therefore are) willing to change jobs and change cities with increasing frequency. As Schwartz notes, this "means that the questions 'Where should I work?' and 'What kind of work should I do?' are never resolved. . . . The Microsoft ad that asks us 'Where do you want to go today?' is not just about web surfing."[25]

With all these choices open to us, we would expect to be happier, but Schwartz says that is not the case. By every major indicator — the doubling of the divorce rate since 1960, the tripling of the teen suicide rate and the quintupling of the prison population in the same period, the tenfold increase in clinical depression since 1900, to name a few —

23. Barry Schwartz, *The Paradox of Choice* (New York: Ecco, 2004), p. 15.
24. Schwartz, *The Paradox of Choice*, pp. 9-34.
25. Schwartz, *The Paradox of Choice*, p. 36.

more choice has not coincided with more happiness.[26] Schwartz offers a variety of reasons for thinking that more choice actually contributes to unhappiness. We have to devote enormous resources of time to sorting through the various choices before us. The stakes of our choices are thus increased, and we experience anxiety because we often lack the resources to separate good choices from less good choices. Even worse, the ideology of choice insists that we should strive to make not simply a *good* choice, but the *best possible* choice.

MAXIMIZERS AND SATISFICERS

Schwartz and other psychologists use the term "maximizer" to describe the person who tries to live up to this ideal of the sovereign chooser by making the optimal choice from the range of options. The ideal is a corollary of the notion that having more choices is always better; as choice expands, some *even better* options may come into play, thus increasing the range of candidates for the "best" possible choice. Maximizers do not stop looking for a sweater or a job when they find one they like; there is always one more store or one more Web site they need to check to make sure they don't settle for second best. The term "satisficer" is used to describe those who stop looking when they find what they are seeking. Maximizers are much less happy with life than satisficers, not because they make worse choices — after all, the maximizer might well end up getting a better deal on the same sweater — but because they can never be satisfied with the choices they make. Maximizers fantasize about living someone else's life, because the *best* life is always out of reach.[27]

The problem is not simply that we are limited in getting what we want; the problem is that we are limited in *knowing* what we want. Economic theory typically asserts that consumers are rational choosers who seek to maximize the fulfillment of their own wants; this claim, however, is increasingly questioned by psychologists. We base choices on previous experiences, but experiments have shown that people tend to judge their experiences in retrospect based disproportionately on how the experiences felt at their peak (either best or worst) and how

26. Schwartz, *The Paradox of Choice*, pp. 108-9.
27. Schwartz, *The Paradox of Choice*, pp. 77-89.

they felt at the end.[28] In addition, as Harvard psychologist Daniel Gilbert and his team have discovered, people are very bad at predicting how a future experience will impact their lives. We consistently overestimate how happy a positive choice — a new car, a new job, or a bigger house — will make us, and how long that happiness will last; this is called "impact bias." We likewise adapt more quickly to bad things that happen to us than we can predict. We get used to things, adjust to them, and start taking them for granted.[29] The proliferation of choices makes the problem of adaptation worse by increasing the amount of time and effort required to make a decision; if agonizing over a decision for months produced long-lasting results, that difficult process might be seen as worth the time and effort required, but such positive results are rarely forthcoming.[30] Moreover, evidence suggests that we are constantly surprised by our ability to adapt. We seem unable to anticipate adaptation and prepare for it. And so most people in our society stay on the "hedonic treadmill"; they continue to pursue novelty, new products, and new experiences — all of which promise happiness but inevitably disappoint.[31] Advertising and other kinds of cultural messaging exacerbate the problem by promising that we can exceed our limits and be anything we want to be.

BAD DECISIONS AND ANTICIPATED REGRET

Psychologists have suggested that, among other factors that adversely affect our ability to make rational choices, we suffer from an "empathy gap": the inability to predict how we will behave in "hot" emotional states when we are in a "cold" state. We not only make bad decisions in the heat of the moment, but we cannot consistently predict that we will do so and guard against the consequences.[32] When combined with the impact bias, we end up making all kinds of choices, small and large, that we will inevitably regret. Why did I think that working eighty hours a week at a law firm to earn more money would make me happy? Why did I think that taking a job far from my family would be a good idea?

28. Schwartz, *The Paradox of Choice,* pp. 48-51.
29. Jon Gertner, "The Futile Pursuit of Happiness," *New York Times Magazine,* September 7, 2003, p. 44.
30. Schwartz, *The Paradox of Choice,* pp. 176-77.
31. Schwartz, *The Paradox of Choice,* pp. 172-73.
32. Gertner, "Futile Pursuit of Happiness," p. 45.

"You know, the Stones said, 'You can't always get what you want,'" says Gilbert. "I don't think that's the problem. The problem is you can't always know what you want."[33]

Regret occurs only when people feel sole responsibility for their choices; it is impossible to regret decisions other people have made. Regret also depends on a person being able to imagine a counterfactual alternative that might have been better. As Schwartz points out, the availability of more choices exacerbates both of these conditions. More choices would seem to increase one's chances that a good option is out there; given enough effort, a person should be able to find it. When a choice proves disappointing or when the impact bias kicks in, we regret retrospectively. We can have "buyer's remorse" over a past decision, becoming convinced that some option we rejected would have been better, or imagining there are options out there that we have not yet encountered.

The proliferation of choices also produces what is called "anticipated regret," in which we already despair of our inability to make the right choice before the choice is even made. Anticipated regret is worse; it not only produces dissatisfaction, but can also affect decisions currently in process. Both types of regret raise the emotional stakes of decisions (i.e., they produce more "hot" emotional states). Anticipated regret in particular can produce paralysis, the inability to make a decision. People can put off choosing a major or a career, or making a commitment to a partner or spouse, because the stakes are just too high.[34] Anticipated regret can also have an undue influence on any decisions that are actually made. To use Schwartz's example, "If you're trying to decide whether to buy a Toyota Camry or a Honda Accord and your closest friend just bought an Accord, you're likely to buy one too, partly because the only way to avoid the information that you made a mistake is to buy what your friend bought and thus avoid potentially painful comparisons."[35] This applies not only to decisions about material purchases but to all sorts of major life choices.

One proposed solution to the problem of regret is to try to ensure that all choices are reversible. Leaving our options open would seem to guarantee that we never experience serious regret. If we can bring

33. Daniel Gilbert, quoted in Gertner, "Futile Pursuit of Happiness," p. 44.
34. Schwartz, *The Paradox of Choice*, pp. 147-64.
35. Schwartz, *The Paradox of Choice*, pp. 158-59.

our purchase back to the store and get our money back, then regret can always be fixed. But life does not work this way. Not only are the time, effort, and money invested in major choices (like college and career and marriage and children) nonrefundable, but leaving options open actually makes the problem of regret worse. If a decision is irreversible, we can stop thinking about it and get on with other things. If, on the other hand, we are always open to the possibility of dumping a spouse for another person, switching majors or jobs, or moving to another city, then we will always be considering the possibility that our choice of spouse or major or job or house was a mistake — or at least not the best decision we could have made. Our culture's ideology of choice is blind to this problem and thus makes it worse. We are constantly told that having more choices makes us happier; the more options open to us, the greater our freedom. But the opposite may often in fact be the case; for example, married people who consider their marriages reversible are less satisfied with their marriages than those who consider their vows irreversible.[36]

IMPLICATIONS FOR VOCATION

Any examination of the question of vocation requires taking a serious and critical look at the cultural context in which people are asked to discern their calling. Particularly when the word "vocation" is used without nuance, it can sometimes lead to a focus on individual choice. Since choices have proliferated in the modern era due to a massive restructuring of economy and society, the ideology of choice has spread as well. As we have seen, this ideology considers individuals to be rational choosers who benefit from the proliferation of choices; the more choices we have, the better chance we have of choosing our best life.

The preceding analysis should give us reason to question this ideology, which will in turn have significant implications for how we think about vocational reflection and discernment. Admittedly, for those with access to good education and other resources, our society offers tremendous opportunities to live a good life. Innovation is often a good, and some choice is of course necessary and beneficial for human flourishing. Constraints on choice due to race and gender and class are experienced as dehumanizing. The problems surrounding the matter of

36. Schwartz, *The Paradox of Choice*, pp. 144-46.

choice should not be used as an excuse to oppress others by artificially limiting their choices.

Still, we need to understand clearly why young people do not always experience the proliferation of choice as liberating. People who are in a position to make choices are often paralyzed by the choices they face. Which one of dozens of majors and thousands of careers is the right one for me? Where in the world should I live? Am I called to be married, and if so, who among millions is the right person for me? Given the mobility and flexibility of families, many young people cannot even count on family obligations to narrow down their options. The book *Quarterlife Crisis: The Unique Challenges of Life in Your Twenties* captures, through interviews, the anxieties of young people raised in a world where everything is up for grabs.[37] They experience intense self-doubt, in part because they are on their own when making decisions. In a world of individualized choosers, they have become convinced that, if their decisions disappoint, they will have no one to blame but themselves.[38]

III. Responses and Resources

There is no point to romanticizing the past or trying to re-create a lost world. Still, we can point to a number of resources — philosophical, literary, and theological — that can be of tremendous help when thinking about the process of vocational discernment under the cultural conditions of the present time. I will first discuss resources for making good choices, and then discuss resources for accepting the choices we have made.

THE LIMITATIONS OF HUMAN BEINGS

The first and most important resource is a realistic assessment of human limits. You cannot be anything you want. This does not sound at first like good news, and it poses a challenge for the marketing of our colleges and universities to prospective students. But it can be expe-

---

37. Alexandra Robbins and Abby Wilner, *Quarterlife Crisis: The Unique Challenges of Life in Your Twenties* (New York: Putnam, 2001); see the reference to this book in Schwartz, *The Paradox of Choice*, p. 142.

38. Schwartz, *The Paradox of Choice*, p. 211.

rienced by students as liberating, and it has the added advantage of being true. One of the most fundamental claims of Christianity, Judaism, and Islam is the notion that we are not God. This is established in the scriptures of all three faiths, wherein humans are created by God and therefore dependent on God for our being (Gen. 1 in the Hebrew Tanakh and Christian Old Testament; sura 2:30-34 in the Qur'an). This dependency is not understood to be a problem or a burden; indeed, having one God instead of many seems to be the solution to a problem. Many scholars believe these texts to have been written in response to the Babylonian creation myth *Enuma Elish,* in which creation results from a war among the gods. In contrast, all creation, including humans, is declared repeatedly in Genesis 1 to be good, and humans are created to live in harmony with God and with the rest of creation. Being finite creatures of a good God is not a fallen condition; the Fall occurs precisely when humans rebel against their limitations. They are tempted precisely by the (false) claim that if they eat of the tree, they "will be like God" (Gen. 3:5) or "become angels or such beings as live forever" (sura 7:30). The havoc that ensues shows how fruitless is any attempt to escape dependence on God and interdependence with other people, how self-deceptive it is to live as though one were self-sufficient. One need not consider these scriptural stories to be historical or scientific accounts of human origins to find here a compelling diagnosis of the human drama.

The human actors in these accounts are able to rebel because they are enough like God to have freedom. Like a child with a Chinese finger trap, however, the more they struggle to be free, the more they find themselves bound. They falsely imagine that freedom means being free from God, being the source of their own being. Sin and evil enter the world as a result of the freedom to choose to do what is against God's will. As Augustine explains, however, this type of freedom to choose anything at all, even what is bad, is not a strength but a weakness.[39] In an argument against the Pelagians, Augustine describes the freedom to do evil by using the metaphors of "slavery" and "sickness" — which, he notes, are hardly compatible with genuine freedom of choice.[40] True

39. Augustine, *Confessions,* trans. Henry Chadwick (Oxford: Oxford University Press, 1991), p. 199 (10.23.33).
40. Augustine, *The Spirit and the Letter* §52, in *Augustine: Later Works,* ed. John Burnaby (Philadelphia: Westminster, 1955), p. 236.

freedom, for Augustine, is not sheer indeterminacy; it is the fulfillment of what one is called to be.

In contrast, many current definitions of freedom are purely negative: freedom is defined as freedom from limits. In this sense, a heroin addict is free to shoot heroin if no one prevents him or her from doing so. Most people would recognize that this is not true freedom; they might in fact describe it using Augustine's language of weakness, sickness, or slavery to the drug. Negative freedom is a necessary ingredient for true freedom, but it is not sufficient. A positive account of freedom would define it as the ability to achieve a good goal. It is not enough to have negative freedom; it is not enough that, for example, no one is stopping you from playing the piano. Positive freedom is also necessary; you must learn how to play the piano, which requires a decision to pursue a particular goal, along with hours of practice to develop the necessary habits so that one's fingers move without thinking.

Augustine's intuitions on desire are remarkably similar to the findings of Schwartz, Gilbert, and other psychologists: the presence of more choices does not in itself make a person free, in part because people are not very good at knowing what they really want. Augustine describes this as a multiplicity within the self; in the *Confessions* he narrates the "struggle of myself against myself."[41] "I was neither wholly willing nor wholly unwilling. So I was in conflict with myself and was dissociated from myself."[42] Augustine intuits what true freedom might be, but finds himself unfree to choose it precisely because of the choices — *free* choices — that he has made. "I sighed after such freedom, but was bound not by an iron imposed by anyone else but by the iron of my own choice." Augustine explains the formation of this chain in this manner: "By servitude to passion, habit is formed, and habit to which there is no resistance becomes necessity. By these links, as it were, connected to one another (hence my term a chain), a harsh bondage held me under restraint. The new will, which was beginning to be within me a will to serve you freely and to enjoy you, God, the only sure source of pleasure, was not yet strong enough to conquer my older will, which had the strength of old habit."[43] For Augustine, sheer indeterminacy is not simply a bad way to live; it is impossible. Our choices inevitably

41. Augustine, *Confessions,* p. 152 (8.11.27).
42. Augustine, *Confessions,* p. 148 (8.10.22).
43. Augustine, *Confessions,* p. 140 (8.5.10).

dig a groove called habit, and habits color every choice we make. As Schwartz and Gilbert also recognize, the human person is never simply the sovereign consumer who stands back, surveys the options, and decides *ex nihilo* what path to take. The human person is a complex battleground of warring desires, and choices are constrained by human weakness and social forces that buffet the person from within and from without.

DEVELOPING GOOD HABITS

How does one find stability and vocation in such a conflicted condition? The goal cannot be to reject habit and seek indeterminacy. Habit is a way of relieving us from the burden of having to make choices. When we develop good habits — Thomas Aquinas called them "virtues" — we don't even need to spend time thinking about whether we might steal or commit adultery. For the person who has gotten into the habit of not doing these things, they rarely even come to mind. Habits are the way we achieve what is commonly called a "self," that is, the stable collection of characteristics that defines a person. The nature of the self, and the moral world it inhabits, is therefore not so much about *decisions* as it is about *formation.* If a person is well formed in the virtues, then action will come naturally, and without the anguished and groundless deliberation that characterizes choice in the absence of any ground for choosing. The process might be compared to trying to walk on ice: a smooth surface that allows one to "go anywhere" is also one where falling and injury are likely, but habit digs a groove in the ice to give the walker some traction. Admittedly, our habits limit our options; but if they are good habits, they also make it possible to achieve the options that really matter.

The real question, then, is how to cultivate good habits. To distinguish good habits (virtues) from bad habits (vices), there must be a way of distinguishing good goals from bad goals. This requires that we come to know ourselves, and to orient ourselves toward some goal that is truly worth pursuing. Given the ever-expanding range of choices and our relative lack of knowledge about them, our ultimate goals will need to be based on something other than subjective preference. Schwartz and Gilbert do not explain *why* humans are so bad at knowing themselves and orienting themselves toward good goals. Such explanations are offered by many faith traditions as a kind of estrangement from God, which they typically understand to be an estrangement from one's own self as well. For example, although Augustine says, "I find my own self hard to grasp,"[44] he also says that God is "closer to me than I am to myself" *(interior intimo meo).*[45] The healing of our weakness depends on recognizing the source of our being outside of ourselves, but this source is simultaneously within us; we find ourselves precisely by finding God. Thus, vocation is both a call from outside the self that draws one outside the confines of the small self and also, at the same time, a discovery of our deepest desires and our true self.

THE ROLE OF THE COMMUNITY

Learning to desire rightly is not merely an individual endeavor. Just as learning the piano is facilitated by a teacher, so the acquisition of virtue requires the guidance of people who have already mastered those virtues. The isolation felt by the individual chooser in a modern context can only be overcome by acknowledging the ways that our vocations are not simply a subjective choice, but a response to a call that comes from outside ourselves. The call is mediated by professors and pastors and friends who let the individual know that their lives belong, in some significant way, to others who expect and need the individual to give his or her talents in a particular way. In a university context, for example, students may need less "Do anything you want!" from their professors and counselors; they may need more "You don't seem happy with your major. Have you ever considered majoring in *x?*" Ultimately, the call is not merely a lifestyle choice; it evolves through an encounter with objective realities. Some of these realities will likely take the form of obstacles, and some of these obstacles will not be surmountable simply by believing that we can be anything we want. Moreover, discerning one's calling is a communal effort; it must involve the wisdom of others to break through the confines of the individual self. Churches can be this kind of community; so can colleges and universities. Indeed, one of the reasons for sending students to college is that they might enter

---

44. Augustine, *Confessions,* p. 193 (10.16.25).

45. Augustine, *Confessions,* p. 43 (3.6.11). Henry Chadwick's translation renders the passage rather woodenly as "more inward than my most inward part"; the translation offered here, using the word "closer," attempts to capture some of the resonance between the Latin *intimo* and the English "intimate."

into a community where what is being proffered by their professors and other mentors and friends is not only *knowledge* but also *wisdom.*

Vocational discernment, then, not only involves others; these others need to help us limit our choices. We need others to tell us what we can give to the world, which is a quite different question from what will give us pleasure. We need families to make demands upon us, to limit the places that we will consider living. We need to prepare one another for suffering, for running up against limitations, for caring for a special-needs child decade after decade. We need to make commitments to one another that are not reversible. Marriage vows and religious vows are closely linked to the question of vocation precisely because they move in the opposite direction of the common logic of choice. Making a unilateral and binding commitment to another cuts off a whole range of choices. But as Schwartz observes, "what seems to contribute most to happiness binds us rather than liberates us."[46] As we have already observed, such binding actually wards off rather than encourages regret.

TELLING OUR VOCATIONAL STORIES RIGHTLY

Yet, even when we enter into vocational discernment in a communal context and are attentive to our own limitations, the next step is of equal importance. Rather than focusing only on whether we have made the "right" choices, we need to learn to narrate the choices we have made in the light of our beliefs. What is perhaps most crucial is not so much making the right choices as telling the story of our choices rightly. We can encourage a step in this direction by noting the advantages of being a "satisficer" rather than a "maximizer." To be clear, being a satisficer is not the same as being lazy or weak, or accepting mediocrity; it is knowing what you want and stopping when you get it. This includes learning to accept "good enough" rather than judging our choices on the basis of what is "best." Even "good enough," however, is put in a different light when it is written as part of a larger story — God's story. Vocational discernment is not just a matter of choosing well enough, but of accepting the life you have; and this means learning to identify, retrospectively, the path that you did in fact choose as the right one. It may not be true that you can be anything you want to be, but you may find instead that you have become the person that God has called you to

46. Schwartz, *The Paradox of Choice,* p. 108.

be, even if you would not have chosen your life out of all the possibilities (had you even known what they were).

We must be careful here, because some choices are wrong choices, and we need others to help us discern when we need to repent and change. To tell the story of one's faults and failings and disappointments as "God's will" can also be turned into a resignation to cruel fate. There should be no question, for example, of staying in an abusive relationship because God wants it. Bad is not good enough; something must be good to be good enough. The point is not at all to give up one's agency and become passive before events beyond our control. Rather than simply accept the hand that fate has dealt us — "I should have married someone else or chosen a different career, but now I'm stuck with it, by God's will" — the idea is to recognize that our story is unfinished, and to hold to this view until we transform what we have been given from fate into destiny. As Samuel Wells puts it, "[O]ne says, 'How can this gift be understood or used in a faithful way? What does the way we accept this gift say about the kind of people we are and want to be? What can (or has) this gift become in the kingdom of God?'"[47] This is what Wells, borrowing a theatrical term, calls "overaccepting," which he defines as "accepting in the light of a larger story."[48] Wells displays this idea with a number of illustrations from improvisational theater, in which actors need to find ways of incorporating new ideas into a story line that is already in progress. He also uses the image of a concert pianist who is interrupted by a child who begins banging on the keyboard. Rather than either having the child removed, or simply letting the child make noise, the pianist puts her hands around the child's on the keyboard and begins to play music that weaves the child's discordant notes into a larger, harmonious whole.

One need not simply resign oneself to fate, nor must one refuse it and try vainly to assert one's negative freedom to choose. Rather, one can try to discern what God, like the concert pianist, is doing with one's life; one can ask how one's life might contribute to, and fit into, the much larger story of the world. A Christian seeks to interpret the fog of his or her own imperfect individual decisions through the lens of the much larger story of God's creation and redemption of the world

47. Samuel Wells, *Improvisation: The Drama of Christian Ethics* (Grand Rapids: Brazos, 2004), p. 130.

48. Wells, *Improvisation*, p. 131.

through the community known as Christ's body. Or, to return to the theatrical analogy, what I am describing involves seeing one's life ultimately as a comedy, not a tragedy; we are thereby relieved of the terrifying burden of imagining that we are alone responsible for our fates, that we need to make the best possible choices for our lives to come out "right."

We cannot be anything we want, in part because we cannot know what we want. We are not sovereign rational choosers but fragmented selves. Our hope is that, in the crucible of our encounters with others, the fragments of our lives will be gathered up and used to tell a story that is broader, more nuanced, and much more interesting.

II

DISPERSED POLITICAL
THEOLOGY

CHAPTER FIVE

THE MYSTICAL AND THE REAL:

PUTTING THEOLOGY BACK INTO

POLITICAL THEOLOGY

ONE OF THE most remarkable features of the recent interest in political theology is the sharp bifurcation of the field between those who do theology — that is, reflection on God — and those who do not. The bifurcation is, furthermore, asymmetrical. Theologians who do political theology — people like Stanley Hauerwas, Kathryn Tanner, and Graham Ward — read the likes of Giorgio Agamben, Slavoj Žižek, and Paul Kahn, but as far as I can tell, the reverse is not the case. Indeed, if there is one subject that is taboo in much political theology, it is theology. The introduction to a recent collection of essays entitled *Political Theology and Early Modernity* begins the volume with these words: "Let's get this straight. Political theology is not the same as religion. Instead, we take it to name a form of questioning that arises precisely when religion is no longer a dominant explanatory or life mode."[1] The introduction goes on to say that political theology "confronts its readers as crisis and not content,"[2] and later claims that "What is at stake for political theology is not the truth of religion but the status of theology as operative fiction."[3] We are warned that political theology is not a "turn to religion" because an attempted return to the past produces fundamentalist brutality, and even if we could return, "the religions of the past would fail to meet our expectations of coher-

---

1. Graham Hammill and Julia Reinhard Lupton, introduction to *Political Theology and Early Modernity* (Chicago: University of Chicago Press, 2012), p. 1.
2. Hammill and Lupton, introduction to *Political Theology and Early Modernity*, p. 3.
3. Hammill and Lupton, introduction to *Political Theology and Early Modernity*, p. 5.

ence and community. In effect, we have never been religious."[4] Despite the breakdown of the religious/secular dichotomy that political theology seems to recognize, "religion" nevertheless reappears as the Other from the past against which political theology must guard.

In this chapter, I want to explore this peculiarly modern anxiety to segregate political theology from theology. I will argue that, far from opening up liberating political possibilities beyond the modern religious/secular divide, this type of political theology tends to reinforce the homogenization of social space that is part of the modern project. I will trace the fiction/reality dichotomy in Ernst Kantorowicz and Paul Kahn, and show how Carl Schmitt and Henri de Lubac challenge that dichotomy. De Lubac, in particular, retrieves an early medieval view of sacramental action to challenge the immanent/transcendent and fiction/reality distinctions. I suggest that an incarnational and sacramental theology can open avenues for a radical democratic practice of postsecular politics, beyond the closure of the liberal state.

I. Mythmaking

Political theology in the last century can be appreciated in part as an attempt to understand secularization as something more than what Charles Taylor calls the "subtraction" of God from public life, but as itself theologically motivated. The first use of the term "secularization" in sixteenth-century France referred to the transfer of property from ecclesiastical to civil control.[5] The historical work of Ernst Kantorowicz in particular showed that modernity, at least in its early forms, was not the simple shedding of theological ways of handling the organization of society, but was rather marked by the migration of certain theological ideas from the church to the nascent state, a "secularization" of theological concepts, in the original sense of the term. Secularization is not then — at least not yet — marked by the mere absence of God. In Carl Schmitt's famous early exploration of political theology, however, he contends that "All significant concepts of the modern theory of the state are secularized theological concepts *not only because of their historical*

4. Hammill and Lupton, introduction to *Political Theology and Early Modernity*, p. 6.
5. Jan N. Bremmer, "Secularization: Notes toward a Genealogy," in *Religion: Beyond a Concept*, ed. Hent de Vries (New York: Fordham University Press, 2008), p. 433.

development — in which they were transferred from theology to the theory of the state, whereby, for example, the omnipotent God became the omnipotent lawgiver — but also because of their systematic structure, the recognition of which is necessary for a sociological consideration of these concepts."[6] I have highlighted the phrase "not only because of their historical development" because it seems to mark an important division in ways of approaching the task of political theology. One could make political theology the subject of a demythologizing genealogical narrative, whereby the modern state develops *out of* its theological past. One could, on the other hand, concentrate in the present on what Schmitt calls the "systematic structure" of political theology and argue that contemporary politics in the West are just as theological as they have ever been, whether that fact is recognized or occluded. We have never really *not* been theological.

Kantorowicz does not seem to fit neatly on either side of this distinction. In his foreword to Alain Boureau's biography of Kantorowicz, Martin Jay calls Kantorowicz both "mythmaker"[7] and part of a "larger movement of demythicization."[8] Jay suggests, as does Boureau, that Kantorowicz's later work, including *The King's Two Bodies*, is part of a repudiation of his early career, in which he fell under the influence of the romantic nationalism of Stefan George, wrote an overblown biography of Frederick II as charismatic spiritual leader of the German nation, and fought for Germany in World War I and as part of a right-wing militia against the Polish uprising immediately thereafter. Despite his ardent nationalism, the Nazi regime refused to see him as anything but a Jew, so he fled to the United States, where Jay and Boureau paint him as both disillusioned and yet nostalgic for the idea of a communion unavailable to modernity.[9]

Where mythmaker and demythicizer come together is in Kantorowicz's idea of fiction. Kantorowicz seemed to buy into the Weberian notion that the modern world had been disenchanted; his Oxford lectures in 1934 took the theme of the "secularization of the world" that had been accomplished by the profane requisition of Christian

6. Carl Schmitt, *Political Theology: Four Chapters on the Concept of Sovereignty,* trans. George Schwab (Cambridge: MIT Press, 1985), p. 36, italics added.

7. Martin Jay, foreword to *Kantorowicz: Stories of a Historian,* by Alain Boureau (Baltimore: Johns Hopkins University Press, 2001), p. viii.

8. Jay, foreword to *Kantorowicz,* p. x.

9. Boureau, *Kantorowicz,* pp. 86-87.

language.[10] At the same time, however, Weber's grim portrait of the iron cage of bureaucratic rationality, soaked in the acids of modernity, was contradicted by a Durkheimian strand of sociology that saw the sacred not as simply absent but as immanent to the social process. Religion marks out boundaries between the sacred and the profane, but those boundaries are man-made, not discovered. Religion is a society's representation of itself to itself. Kantorowicz seems to fit within this Durkheimian intellectual trajectory. The sacredness of the social bond is something to which Kantorowicz still aspires, but he sees it as an entirely immanent process, composed at least in part of the kinds of fictions and metaphors that he explores in *The King's Two Bodies*. Kantorowicz seeks to show how certain "vertical" theological terms were transmuted into "horizontal" terms; most especially, *corpus mysticum* "acquired a corporational character signifying a 'fictitious' or 'juristic' person."[11] The *corpus verum* was contrasted with the "*corpus fictum,* the corporate collective which was intangible and existed only as a fiction of jurisprudence."[12] To see social processes as fictions is to acknowledge their positive social function while simultaneously liberating them from being fixed and immutable; they are neither God-given — as the medievals thought — nor are they inscribed in nature, as in Nazi jurisprudence.[13] Kantorowicz saw the separation of the person of the king from the crown — what he calls "The Crown as Fiction" — as a way, in the long run, of undermining the divinity of the monarchy.[14] Kantorowicz is mythmaker in his appreciation of the social function of fiction, but demythologizer in his reduction of myth to something merely man-made, and therefore not "real" in any metaphysical sense.

The key distinction, then, is not between mythicizing and demythicizing political theology, but between seeing myth as God-given and seeing it as man-made. Kantorowicz's genealogy of political theology reinforces rather than questions the binaries of modern thought: fiction/reality, religion/secular, mysticism/politics, mysticism/reason.

10. Boureau, *Kantorowicz*, p. 88.

11. Ernst Kantorowicz, *The King's Two Bodies: A Study in Medieval Political Theology* (Princeton: Princeton University Press, 1957), p. 209.

12. Kantorowicz, *The King's Two Bodies*, p. 209.

13. Boureau, *Kantorowicz*, p. 106.

14. Kantorowicz, *The King's Two Bodies*, pp. 336-83. See also Victoria Kahn, "Political Theology and Fiction in *The King's Two Bodies*," *Representations* 106, no. 1 (Spring 2009): 84-85.

The introduction to *The King's Two Bodies* begins as follows: "Mysticism, when transposed from the warm twilight of myth and fiction to the cold searchlight of fact and reason, has usually little left to recommend itself."[15] Kantorowicz signals the havoc that political mysticism can wreak, and refers to "[t]hat kind of man-made irreality — indeed, that strange construction of a human mind which finally becomes slave to its own fictions — we are normally more ready to find in the religious sphere than in the allegedly sober and realistic realms of law, politics, and constitution."[16] Kantorowicz goes on to vindicate the kind of useful fictions borrowed from the mystical and religious realms, but he never questions the basic dichotomy between mystical and rational, according to which the church became a "rational monarchy on a mystical basis" while the state became a "mystical corporation on a rational basis."[17] Despite the borrowing back and forth across the divide, the church remains the realm of "religion" and the mystical, while the basis of the state, as "political" and "secular," remains reason.

Despite Kantorowicz's explicit disavowal of contemporary political relevance for his historical study as anything more than an "afterthought,"[18] recent commentators have seen Kantorowicz's work as a subtle attempt to undermine Carl Schmitt. Whereas for Schmitt the incarnation imposes a personal unity of divinity and humanity on the political form, for Kantorowicz the incarnation is a useful fiction by which the attributes of divinity were transferred to humanity. Kantorowicz's study ends with Dante as a representative of the new humanism whose divinized humanity would outlive a man's or woman's mortal body. In Victoria Kahn's view, Schmitt's personalist and decisionist view of political sovereignty is undercut by what she calls Kantorowicz's "constitutionalism," the idea that politics is about a people's self-representation. The idea that the crown was a fiction allowed for a kind of ideological critique of the divinity of kings, since the king's immortal body was in fact both a creation of and a representation of the body politic, that is, we the people.[19] Likewise, Richard Halpern sees in the fiction of the king's two bodies a constitutionalist rebuke to Schmitt's decisionism. The fiction is meant to provide continuity upon the death

15. Kantorowicz, *The King's Two Bodies,* p. 3.
16. Kantorowicz, *The King's Two Bodies,* p. 5.
17. Kantorowicz, *The King's Two Bodies,* pp. 193-94, 206.
18. Kantorowicz, *The King's Two Bodies,* p. viii.
19. Victoria Kahn, "Political Theology and Fiction," pp. 81-88.

of the king, and could also limit the power of the king; if lands belonged to the crown rather than to the king, the king could not sell them, since they belonged in a sense to all. Similarly, Kantorowicz traces the use of the fiction to turn royal taxation in times of emergency into a routine, annual guarantor of the crown's finances. According to Halpern, Kantorowicz thus "offers a kind of anti-Schmittian parable in which the sovereign's power to decide states of emergency cedes to bureaucratic regularity and continuity long before the modern era."[20] The bureaucratization of church and state required a deistic God, one who does not intervene with miracles but rules instead like the chairman of a corporate board. Halpern draws parallels between Kantorowicz's work and the genre of *Trauerspiel,* or bourgeois tragedy, where the sovereign cannot act decisively because access to transcendence and heterogeneity has been cut off, leaving only a natural world of meaning fabricated by creatures.[21]

Paul Kahn's recent book *Political Theology: Four New Chapters on the Concept of Sovereignty* is a much more explicit and appreciative appropriation of Carl Schmitt, but one that draws the fiction/reality dichotomy in much the same way that Kantorowicz does. Kahn's purpose is to show how even liberal nation-states like the United States have taken on the aura of the sacred and have perpetuated a theology and practice of blood sacrifice. For Kahn, the modern American nation-state occupies the place of the sacred for its citizens: the constitution carries "forward the religious concept of the covenant," "revolution is a secularized form of revelation," and so on.[22] Kahn attacks Mark Lilla's notion of the "Great Separation" between politics and theology in Western modernity on historical grounds. Lilla — whose work I discuss in detail in chapter 10 — thinks that secular, liberal government is a decisive break with political theology,[23] while Kahn contends that the break never happened; liberal government is the continuation of political theology under a different guise. "The serious claim of political theology today, however, is not that the secular should yield to the

20. Richard Halpern, "The King's Two Buckets: Kantorowicz, *Richard II*, and Fiscal *Trauerspiel*" *Representations* 106, no. 1 (Spring 2009): 71.

21. Halpern, "The King's Two Buckets," p. 72.

22. Paul Kahn, *Political Theology: Four New Chapters on the Concept of Sovereignty* (New York: Columbia University Press, 2011), p. 2.

23. Mark Lilla, *The Stillborn God: Religion, Politics, and the Modern West* (New York: Vintage, 2007).

church — whatever church that might be — but rather that the state is not the secular arrangement that it purports to be. A political life is not a life stripped of faith and the experience of the sacred, regardless of what we may believe about the legal separation of church and state."[24]

While thus apparently transgressing the religious/secular boundary to show that what is taken as a secular government really is religious, Kahn nevertheless goes to great lengths to reinforce the idea that political theology as he understands it is a purely secular discourse that can have nothing to do with theology proper, that is, theology as a discourse about the reality of God. "If political theology is about empowering theologians politically or theoretically, it has no future in the West" (pp. 3-4). Christian political theology must be kept quarantined from what Kahn considers political theology. Kahn insists, "The latter is an entirely secular field of inquiry, while the former expresses a sectarian endeavor that is no longer possible in the West" (p. 124). Similarly, "We are well past the era in which theology could draw upon reason to support the sacred. Indeed, that separation of reason from revelation may be a more important 'great separation' than that of which Lilla writes. We will not be convinced by any logical arguments for the existence of God, whether the god of politics or that of religion" (p. 25). For Kahn, the religious/secular divide stands as firmly as it does for Lilla. It is simply that Kahn and Lilla locate American liberal constitutional government on opposite sides of the divide. For Kahn, political theology does not question the religious/secular divide, but is rather a secular strategy of unmasking, a hermeneutics of suspicion, that spies religion still lurking where it is said to be banished. Using a functionalist understanding of "religion," the American political order is really religious, though it claims to be secular.

Though Kahn claims that his project is purely descriptive, he also makes clear that political theology in his sense is "part of the modernist project" insofar as it wants to ensure that "no religious authority has a privileged place in setting the political agenda" (p. 19). Political theology rejects the idea that the liberal conception of the state is in fact secular; "This difference at the level of theory, however, does not necessarily produce any tension between political theology and the political practices of liberalism" (p. 24). Christian theology has been

---

24. Paul Kahn, *Political Theology*, p. 18. Page references to this work have been placed in the following text.

banished from politics, and Kahn considers this a gain. He contrasts the "largely secular society" of western Europe with America, where we are "not yet released from the burdens of faith" (p. 17). Kahn fully embraces the modernist dichotomy between faith and revelation on the one hand and between faith and reason on the other. This, he maintains, is the crucial "great separation."

Nevertheless, it is faith in God, not faith as such, that Kahn would ban from political life. Against liberal theory, Kahn is not trying to establish politics on a rational basis: "Politics is not striving to be a perfect system of reason" (p. 157). As in Kantorowicz, there is something of the mythicizer in Kahn, who concludes that "Politics is a structure of the imagination" (p. 156). Kahn embraces Schmitt's decisionism, the idea that it is will, not reason, that characterizes the truly political. "A politics of the exception is one that relies on revelation and faith rather than argument and reason. It is, as Schmitt writes, a politics of the miraculous, but — and this is the most important point — it is also an experience of freedom" (p. 157). This is the most important point, because for Kahn "revelation" has nothing to do with something received from God. Revelation is something we construct out of our own human freedom. Freedom is precisely why the antiliberal Schmitt becomes a support for liberal political practice, though not liberal theory, in Kahn's view. For Kahn, the most important part of liberal politics is the freedom to make it all up on our own; this becomes the moment of sovereign decision.

Kahn draws the fiction/reality dichotomy in the same way Kantorowicz does. Political theology is all about unmasking theologies as human creations. "The point of a contemporary political theology must be just the opposite of those premodern political theologies of which Lilla writes: not the subordination of the political to religious doctrine and church authority, but recognition that the state creates and maintains its own sacred space and history" (p. 19). Not only the state's political theology but theology as a whole is fictional. Kahn has a thoroughly pragmatist view of truth. We decide among "models of order" not by their approximation to, or distance from, some "independent facts of the matter"; they become true as we use them to convince ourselves and others (p. 111). Kahn tells us that metaphysics is just a rhetorical device. "In a godless world, that is, a world with no normative significance whatsoever, there is nothing that nature has to teach us in thinking about how to order the political, except that it is entirely up to us" (pp. 116-17). The one thing forbidden — the one thing *not* entirely up to us to choose — is theology, that is, the kind that entertains the possibility of God. The price of admission to the modern and postmodern worlds is the banishment of theology to the medieval past. The immanent frame defines us, but Kahn does not think it confines us. It is rather the condition of our freedom to become convinced that we are making it all up.

II. Theology and Sociology

Interpreters of Schmitt today often read him as if he does not challenge the modern reduction of transcendence to a merely immanent sacrality. Paul Kahn's rereading of Schmitt for the American context, for example, opens the possibility of radically rethinking the religious/ secular divide, but then slams that door shut by circumscribing political theology into a purely "secular" field of inquiry that cannot allow the possibility of theology as theologians understand it. Kahn adopts Schmitt's "sociology of juristic concepts" as if sociology were exclusive of theology, describing a purely immanent social process. Schmitt, on the other hand, is considerably more nuanced. In his extensive comments on the sociology of concepts in chapter 3 of *Political Theology*, Schmitt dismisses both materialist (e.g., Marxist) reductions of metaphysics and theology to material causes and any attempt to create a sociology of concepts that is spiritual *as opposed to* material. Schmitt writes, "Both the spiritualist explanation of material processes and the materialist explanation of spiritual phenomena seek causal relations. At first they construct a contrast between two spheres, and then they dissolve this contrast into nothing by reducing one to the other. This method must necessarily culminate in a caricature."[25] Schmitt clearly rejects the "contrast between two spheres." His eschewing of causal relations here furthermore avoids the choice of either creator God or *homo faber*. Schmitt also rejects the fiction/reality dichotomy. "It is thus not a sociology of the concept of sovereignty when, for example, the monarchy of the seventeenth century is characterized as the real that is 'mirrored' in the Cartesian concept of God."[26] Sociology and theology or metaphysics are not dichotomized but rather united: "The presupposition of this kind of sociology of juristic concepts is thus a radical

25. Schmitt, *Political Theology*, p. 43.
26. Schmitt, *Political Theology*, p. 45.

conceptualization, a consistent thinking that is pushed into metaphysics and theology."[27]

When Schmitt gives examples of positivistic thinkers who ridicule their opponents with the charge of doing theology,[28] he never tries to defend himself from such charges, as Kahn does, by making clear that the kind of political theology he is doing is a purely "secular" exploration of certain myths that people create for themselves. A sociology that is properly radical, that has been properly pushed into metaphysics and theology, is an exploration of the "general state of consciousness"[29] of an epoch, but Schmitt carefully avoids any reductionist indication that any such state is simply man-made.

When Schmitt continues, "The metaphysical image that a definite epoch forges of the world has the same structure as what the world immediately understands to be appropriate as a form of its political organization,"[30] there is no warrant for the assumption that the metaphysical image is wholly and simply a product of human consciousness that forms a mirror of human consciousness. Such images are not necessarily man-made fictions. It is the "epoch" that forges the image, not "man" or any other such immanent causal agent.

When Schmitt returns to political theology in the generally neglected *Political Theology II*, published in 1970, he does not merely open a space for theology, but offers an idiosyncratic reading of incarnation and Trinity: "At the heart of the doctrine of Trinity we encounter a genuine politico-theological *stasiology*,"[31] where *stasis* indicates both rest and "uproar." The project of the book is both to resist Erik Peterson's attempted closure of political theology within Christian theology and to resist the external hominization that replaces the Christ-Adam figure with an "unplanned, arbitrary product of the process-progress of himself."[32] This process-progress, Schmitt claims, "is the opposite of creation *out* of nothing, because it is the creation *of* nothingness as the condition of possibility of the self-creation of an ever new worldliness."[33]

27. Schmitt, *Political Theology*, p. 46.
28. Schmitt, *Political Theology*, pp. 38-40.
29. Schmitt, *Political Theology*, p. 45.
30. Schmitt, *Political Theology*, p. 46.
31. Carl Schmitt, *Political Theology II: The Myth of the Closure of Any Political Theology*, trans. Michael Hoelzl and Graham Ward (Cambridge: Polity Press, 2008), p. 123.
32. Schmitt, *Political Theology II*, pp. 128-29.
33. Schmitt, *Political Theology II*, p. 129.

Carlo Galli has rightly seen that Schmitt's view of modernity is tragic because in modernity humanity must attempt the construction of a political form in the ruins of medieval society from nothing at all, an impossible task.[34] For Schmitt, the form of Christ's person was a *complexio oppositorum* that reconciled all antitheses: God and man, eternity and time, faith and reason, heaven and earth, and so on. With the collapse of the medieval order, the mediating reality of the person of Christ was lost, and politics has become a ceaseless reflection on conflict and the possibility of reconciliation. With Hobbes, the state begins anew, but power is based on no agreed good. The formal equality of all people before the law is insufficient to fund the social process of reconciliation formerly founded in the person of Christ. The personal decision of the sovereign and the identification of public enemies thus become an essential strategy of modern politics, but these are for Schmitt only a simulacrum of *complexio oppositorum* formerly located in Christ, who has been banished from secular politics. In Galli's reading, Schmitt's decisionism is tragic because it aims at the goal of reconciliation without being able to attain it, and Schmitt realizes this. For Galli, it is not that Schmitt is nostalgic for the medieval synthesis; he has simply identified the "blindspot in modern mediation." That blind spot is unseen because modern humanity has enclosed itself in an immanent box of its own making.

> [M]odern politics is structured like a game because its players are able to represent their most serious decisions *only* with reference to rules that are at once self-enclosed yet arbitrary, totalizing yet lacking any reference to a "transcendental signified." What is unthinkable and unspeakable in these terms is that the very *keystones* of modern politics — peace on earth, reconciliation, order — are genealogically derived from a mode of representation (the *complexio*) that, precisely because it *is* grounded in a "transcendental signified," is fundamentally incommensurable with modern mediation, indeed, is mutually exclusive with it.[35]

Pace Kantorowicz and Kahn, the "discovery" that we are making it all up is limiting rather than liberating. Kahn's declarations of the

---

34. This summary of Galli's thought on Schmitt is taken from Adam Sitze, "The Tragicity of the Political: A Note on Carlo Galli's Reading of Carl Schmitt's *Hamlet or Hecuba*," in *Political Theology and Early Modernity*, pp. 48-59.

35. Sitze, "Tragicity of the Political," p. 56.

impossibility of theology appear as an unnecessary and unwarranted self-confinement.

What is potentially liberating about the critical process of political theology carried out in Schmitt's wake is the way it undoes the religious/secular dichotomy that modernity has constructed for itself. Secular political theology claims boldly to transgress that dichotomy by identifying the deeply theological structures of supposedly secular politics. But at the same time, much secular political theology reinforces that dichotomy by claiming adamantly that it is a secular, not religious, discourse. The secular reappears as a neutral standpoint from which to carry out ideological critique, the unmasking of politics as deeply theological, and the unmasking of theology as fiction. But the identification of fictions is a two-edged sword. Is the reality/fiction dichotomy not itself a fiction? If secular discourse must insist that all myth is man-made, are not the secular/religious and immanent/transcendent divides equally capable of being unmade? Kahn's apparently flexible and pragmatic conception of truth becomes perfectly inflexible on this point: we have discovered the objective truth that we are making it all up, and there is therefore no way to return to theology proper. But a truly critical genealogy can and should unmask the dichotomies on which Kahn relies as themselves products of a political process. The religious/secular dichotomy is a thoroughly contingent set of affairs that arises in the process of the creation of the modern state; it is not simply the way things are.

Any critical political theology needs to be aware of all the work done over the last few decades on the genealogy of the religious/secular divide, work I will discuss in more detail in chapter 9.[36] The concept of religion as something essentially distinct from secular aspects of human life such as politics and economics is a modern Western concept. There simply was no such divide before modernity — religious and secular named two different kinds of priests in the medieval period — nor is there any such divide in cultures that have not been significantly Westernized. Kahn's "great separation" between reason and faith, secular and religious, is not akin to the European "discovery" of America, as if

36. For a compendium of such scholarship, see chapter 2 of my book *The Myth of Religious Violence: Secular Ideology and the Roots of Modern Conflict* (New York: Oxford University Press, 2009), or more recently, Brent Nongbri, *Before Religion: A History of a Modern Concept* (New Haven: Yale University Press, 2012).

it were something that one simply bumps into when trying to get somewhere else. The "great separation" was a political effect of the triumph of state power over ecclesiastical power in the early modern period.

A functionalist reading of secular politics — say American nationalism — as a religion is inadequate because, as Talal Asad puts it, "it takes as unproblematic the entire business of defining religion."[37] A functionalist expands the definition of religion beyond the usual suspects (Christianity, Islam, Buddhism, etc.) and uses it to encompass things that are normally considered "secular" (American nationalism, Marxism, capitalism, etc.). The problem is that functionalism is still searching for religion as an essential human phenomenon. It is more profitable and critically aware to see religion and the secular as phenomena constructed by and for certain political arrangements. A constructivist approach does not go searching for signs of religion in the secular, but asks why and under what conditions certain phenomena are labeled "religious" and others "secular." Why is American nationalism considered "secular" in constitutional law, and yet American presidents can speak of patriotism as a "living faith"? The answer is not that religion sometimes escapes its cage and runs amok in the secular. As Asad writes, "'the secular' should not be thought of as the space in which *real* human life gradually emancipates itself from the controlling power of 'religion' and thus achieves the latter's relocation. It is this assumption that allows us to think of religion as 'infecting' the secular domain or as replicating within it the structure of theological concepts. The concept of 'the secular' today is part of a doctrine called secularism."[38] Secularism is an ideology that constructs "the secular" as a neutral, rational location from which to position "religion." "In the discourse of modernity 'the secular' presents itself as the ground from which theological discourse was generated (as a form of false consciousness) and from which it gradually emancipated itself in its march to freedom. On that ground humans appear as the self-conscious makers of History ... and as the unshakable foundation of universally valid knowledge about nature and society."[39] When the political history of this ideology is traced, however, it becomes apparent that "secular" discourse is no

---

37. Talal Asad, *Formations of the Secular: Christianity, Islam, Modernity* (Stanford: Stanford University Press, 2003), p. 189.

38. Asad, *Formations of the Secular,* p. 191.

39. Asad, *Formations of the Secular,* pp. 192-93.

more grounded than "religious" discourse; the myth of *homo faber* is no more grounded than the myth of the creator God.

The task of political theology, then, is not only to expose the hidden theology behind so-called secular forms of power, but also to ask what kinds of political power are being established and reinforced by the banishment of theology from respectable discourse. Many practitioners of political theology as secular critique simply assume that appeal to any transcendent realm beyond the immanent is an ideological ploy that must be contrary to any truly progressive politics. But the rigid insistence on the inviolability of the transcendent/immanent or religious/secular divides ignores the ways those divides were constructed by exactly the kinds of liberal politics that most practitioners of secular political theology seek to overcome.

III. Radical Politics and the Incarnation

There is a long tradition of leftist thought that assumes that any attempt to link politics to transcendence must be an exercise in heteronomy, the alienation of rule to a fictional force beyond humanity that can only frustrate humanity's efforts to control its own affairs. Cornelius Castoriadis, for example, thought that the self-constitution of a people that rules itself — a democracy — must be acknowledged as without ground, and it is religion that mystifies this groundlessness by trying to supply a transcendent ground. Castoriadis thus rejected any attempt to maintain a positive role for theology or religion for a democratic politics.[40] Other democratic theorists have retained the notion of positive theopolitical fictions underlying political formations, while also insisting that such fictions do not transgress the plane of immanence. Thus Clayton Crockett: "A radical democracy that insists upon the immanence of our common life together and the generative power that comes from our modes of cooperation, both already present and still to come, this is a project that is theopolitical as well."[41] What Castoriadis and Crockett

40. Cornelius Castoriadis, "Institution of Society and Religion," *Thesis Eleven* 35, no. 1 (May 1993): 1-17.
41. Clayton Crockett, *Radical Political Theology: Religion and Politics after Liberalism* (New York: Columbia University Press, 2011), p. 191, quoted in Annika Thiem, "Schmittian Shadows and Contemporary Theological-Political Constellations," *Social Research* 80, no. 1 (Spring 2013): 24.

have in common with Schmitt is the assumption that democracy confines itself to immanence. Schmitt thought that this was precisely what was wrong with democracy. Without any authority above the enclosed circle of democratic self-creation — without any authority above the law to decide on the exception and therefore establish people's obligation to the law as to something outside of themselves — there could be no politics. Schmitt's theological account of sovereignty thus opens up the possibility of a critique of any system of law that aspires to be closed, comprehensive, and final. The problem with Schmitt is that he identifies sovereignty so closely with a vertical and this-worldly power that he ends up endorsing a dangerous and idolatrous view of state sovereignty.[42]

The usefulness of Schmitt is limited by the taint of authoritarian state politics. Is it not possible, however, that refusal to be enclosed in an immanent box of our own making can have liberating political effects? If such a political theology is not to be an exercise in Catholic nostalgia or authoritarian state politics, however, it will have to show how an opening to transcendence can facilitate an opening to a kind of personalist and democratic politics that escapes the bureaucratic closure of the modern state without concentrating power in sovereign authority. If there is a theological politics that can open up such avenues, it would have to resist both the closed immanentism of Kantorowicz and the vertical authoritarianism of Schmitt.

The figure of Henri de Lubac looms large in Catholic theology in the twentieth century, and his thought has begun to be explored as a source for a radical political theology.[43] De Lubac is known especially for his attempts to overcome neoscholastic extrinsicism that — in an attempt to protect the gratuity of God's grace over against a materialistic reductionism — defended a concept of "pure nature" to which God's grace was then superadded. De Lubac's careful historical studies showed that neo-scholasticism was a modern misreading of a more subtle patristic and early medieval attempt to see nature as already "graced," thus

---

42. See Ted A. Smith, *Weird John Brown: Divine Violence and the Limits of Ethics* (Stanford: Stanford University Press, 2014), chap. 3.

43. See, for example, William T. Cavanaugh, *Torture and Eucharist: Theology, Politics, and the Body of Christ* (Oxford: Blackwell, 1998); William T. Cavanaugh, "The Church in the Streets: Eucharist and Society," *Modern Theology* 30, no. 2 (April 2014): 384-402; John Milbank, *The Suspended Middle: Henri de Lubac and the Debate concerning the Supernatural* (Grand Rapids: Eerdmans, 2005).

putting transcendence and immanence in a dynamic and intrinsic relation to one another. Most of this controversy was played out in intramural Catholic battles over systematic theology, reform of the liturgy, the role of the laity, and so forth. De Lubac himself mostly avoided political theology. But, as David Grumett writes, "It is now clear ... that the context, motivation and implications of de Lubac's theology are profoundly political."[44] De Lubac was active in the publication of an underground journal for Catholic resistance to the Vichy regime, and he fought a theological battle on two fronts: both against the politicization of the church for the support of the authoritarian state (as in Action Française and Vichy) and against the removal of the church from the social and political realms by the individualization of Catholic faith, whereby the Eucharist, for example, was a miraculous and extrinsic transaction between God and the individual believer but its social effects were bypassed.

One of de Lubac's most important works was *Corpus Mysticum*, finished in 1939 and published in 1944. With an impressive grasp of the patristic and medieval sources, de Lubac shows how the dynamic relationship between the liturgical action of the Eucharist and the formation of the church community was gradually reduced until the community-forming power of the sacrament was borrowed by the nascent state and the Eucharist became an individualized, miraculous spectacle that served to reinforce clerical power. Whereas the early church saw Christ's *corpus mysticum* as the sacrament on the altar that gathered Christ's *corpus verum*, the church, by the twelfth century the terms had been inverted, so that the real body was the miracle on the altar, and the community became the mystical body, where "mystical" indicated something less than real. The mystical as corporative fiction then made its way into the legitimation of the modern state.

Both Schmitt and Kantorowicz understood that the use of the *corpus mysticum* was not just an intramural church affair, but had profound effects on the development of modern politics. For Schmitt, the church as *corpus mysticum* was a Protestant heresy, the reduction of Christianity to the interior and the spiritual, and the consequent reduction of the church to a horizontal fellowship instead of a visible institution with hierarchy and laws. Schmitt saw "mystical," in other words, as a

---

44. David Grumett, *De Lubac: A Guide for the Perplexed* (London: T. & T. Clark, 2007), p. 25.

diminishment of "real." "One cannot believe God became man without believing there will also be a visible Church as long as the world exists. Every religious sect which has transposed the concept of the Church from the visible community of believing Christians into a *corpus mere mysticum* basically has doubts about the humanity of the Son of God. It has falsified the historical reality of the incarnation of Christ into a mystical and imaginary process."[45] The reason this matters politically is that Schmitt sees the Catholic Church as a crucial source of legitimation for the state, based on the church's "absolute realization of authority."[46] In democracy, says Schmitt, "the people hover above the entire political life of the state, just as God does above the world, as the cause and end of all things."[47] The only way to resist this immanentization of political authority was to emphasize vertical, personal, transcendent authority, which Schmitt tended to see incarnated in the authoritarian sovereign.

For Kantorowicz, on the other hand, the horizontalization of political authority through the harnessing of the *corpus mysticum* fiction is not a declension narrative. Though he rejected German nationalism, Kantorowicz remained "a patriot without a country," as Boureau writes, and embraced the horizontal and man-made bonds of liberal constitutionalism. Kantorowicz is clearly indebted to de Lubac's work as inspiration for his own, and he cites de Lubac's *Corpus Mysticum* directly. Nevertheless, Kantorowicz distorts de Lubac's work in crucial ways. For Kantorowicz, the term *corpus mysticum* goes from being purely liturgical or sacramental in the early Middle Ages — and not referring at all to either church or society — to being sociological and becoming the fictive glue for the nascent state. The mystical becomes the fictional when it is transferred from the liturgical to the political realm. As Jennifer Rust comments, "As theological tropes become sociological in *The King's Two Bodies,* they tend also to be tamed into pliable fictional material for representing specific political, very human, interests, evacuated of all but the barest hint of transcendent content."[48] For de Lubac, on the other hand, "liturgical" and "sociological" were

---

45. Carl Schmitt, *Roman Catholicism and Political Form,* trans. Gary Ulmen (Westport, Conn.: Greenwood Press, 1996), p. 52.

46. Schmitt, *Roman Catholicism,* p. 18.

47. Schmitt, *Political Theology,* p. 49.

48. Jennifer Rust, "Political Theologies of the *Corpus Mysticum:* Schmitt, Kantorowicz, and de Lubac," in *Political Theology and Early Modernity,* p. 114.

not located in a dichotomy in the early church, and it was precisely his project to overcome modern dichotomies between transcendence and immanence that the High Middle Ages' inversion of the *corpus verum* and the *corpus mysticum* had instantiated.

For Kantorowicz, the *verum* and the *mysticum* tracked the real and the fictional; the *corpus mysticum* supplied metaphorical material for the legal fictions that created the modern state in opposition to what he called "the horrifying experience of our own time in which whole nations, the largest and the smallest, fell prey to the weirdest dogmas and in which political theologisms became genuine obsessions defying in many cases the rudiments of human and political reason."[49] De Lubac, on the other hand, is trying to move behind the modern inversion in order to recapture a sense of the mystical that is not opposed to the real, to overcome "the temptation of no longer seeing anything in this metaphor except the metaphor itself, and of considering 'mystical' as a watering-down of 'real' or of 'true.'"[50] As Rust writes, "De Lubac's interpretation of the *corpus mysticum* as a dynamic paradox — simultaneously transcendent and immanent — offers a theological perspective that elucidates the potential inadequacy of both the vertical orientation of Schmitt's account of sovereignty (as personal and transcendent) and Kantorowicz's emphasis on horizontal bureaucracy as a mysticized 'body politic.'"[51]

De Lubac's slogan "The Eucharist Makes the Church" was an attempt to emphasize the social body of the church as an action, a dynamic calling together of a group of people by the living God. "A mystery," as he famously wrote, "is more of an action than a thing."[52] In the High Middle Ages, the Eucharist had become more of a spectacle of a presence than an action, while the church simultaneously became an institution, increasingly rationalized, centralized, and bureaucratized. In the early tradition, the Eucharist was the "mystery of unity," a social action binding people to one another. "Being in communion with someone means to receive the body of the Lord with them."[53] As the sacramental presence was emphasized, eucharistic devotion became

---

49. Kantorowicz, *The King's Two Bodies*, p. viii.

50. Henri de Lubac, *Corpus Mysticum: The Eucharist and the Church in the Middle Ages*, trans. Gemma Simmonds with Richard Price and Christopher Stephens (Notre Dame: University of Notre Dame Press, 2006), p. 249.

51. Rust, "Political Theologies," p. 104.

52. De Lubac, *Corpus Mysticum*, p. 49.

53. De Lubac, *Corpus Mysticum*, p. 21.

more individualized, and the process of binding people one to another was left to the state, the new form of social integration that would eventually mark the passage from the medieval to the modern.

For de Lubac this was more than history. He thought that the inability of many Catholics to resist the fascism of the Vichy regime was based on the individualism of their sacramental piety and the separation of the natural from the supernatural that was encouraged by neo-scholasticism but had its roots in the medieval separation of the mystical from the real. De Lubac's politically aware theology was situated against both the collectivist fascisms and the secular individualisms of his age. De Lubac's emphasis on the horizontal communion of Catholics across national boundaries was made possible by the action of Christ, not the action of any earthly decisionist sovereign. At the same time, de Lubac wrote that "our main temptation is to make of God a symbol for man, the objectified symbol of himself."[54] It was only the continuing action of the God-man in human history that could overcome the alienations of our self-imposed fictions. Although de Lubac himself never worked it out in a systematic way, he offers us a vision of the church as a political *tertium quid,* a type of social action that both finds its transcendent source above the state and gathers people below the level of the state in a performance of communion and solidarity.

Perhaps the best way to flesh out this kind of incarnational politics is to look at the Catholic radical Ivan Illich's comments on the parable of the Good Samaritan, to which Charles Taylor points near the end of his sprawling work *A Secular Age.* According to Illich, Western secularism is neither the fulfillment nor the negation of Christianity, but rather its corruption. The parable of the Good Samaritan is commonly read today as a tale of universalizing the care of people; the bounds of group identity are broken open, and the neighbor becomes all our fellow human beings. This universalization becomes the basis of the modern welfare state and the impulse to regularize and institutionalize a code of ethics. Christianity is the basis on which the institutionalization of a horizontal and universalist moral consciousness is built, a consciousness that seeks to care for all *without exception.* For Illich, however, this state of affairs is a corruption of the Good Samaritan parable, which is based on spontaneity and freedom, and not on norms or a universal sense of

54. Henri de Lubac, *Scripture in the Tradition,* trans. Luke O'Neill (New York: Crossroad, 2000), p. 70.

"ought." The Good Samaritan cared for the wounded Jew not because he recognized some shared property with him, some common national identity or universal human rights. He cared for him simply because, as the Gospel says, he "felt moved in his belly," in Illich's translation.[55] He was thrown into the situation by pure contingency, and he responded as an enfleshed being to another being of the same flesh. His response furthermore enabled what Taylor calls a "skein of relations which link particular, unique, enfleshed people to each other."[56] Those relations could only be established if the wounded Jew could recognize that the action was gratuitous, not obligatory.

For Illich, this skein of relations is not established on the basis of some universal, horizontal, and fictional account of what we share in common; it is established by the incarnation of God in human flesh. According to Illich, Christianity establishes contingency, because it recognizes the sheer gratuity of both God's creation of the world and God's incarnation in the form of Jesus Christ.[57] It is the vertical or transcendent axis that allows for the possibility of something new and something free in the space of human relations. Furthermore, the enfleshment of God is precisely what establishes the possibility of relations that begin with the lived body. Illich says,

> I believe, as I hope you do, in a God who is enfleshed, and who has given the Samaritan, as a being drowned in carnality, the possibility of creating a relationship by which an unknown, chance encounter becomes for him the reason for his existence, as he becomes the reason for the other's survival — not just in a physical sense, but a deeper sense, as a human being. This is not a spiritual relationship. This is not a fantasy. This is not merely a ritual act which generates a myth. This is an act which prolongs the Incarnation. Just as God became flesh and in the flesh relates to each one of us, so you are capable of relating in the flesh, as one who says ego, and when he says ego, points to an experience which is entirely sensual, incarnate, and this-worldly, to that other man who has been beaten up.[58]

55. Ivan Illich, *The Rivers North of the Future: The Testament of Ivan Illich,* ed. David Cayley (Toronto: Anansi, 2005), p. 222.

56. Charles Taylor, *A Secular Age* (Cambridge: Harvard University Press, 2007), p. 739.

57. Illich, *Rivers North,* p. 74.

58. Illich, *Rivers North,* p. 207.

Unlike Schmitt, for whom the incarnation establishes the visibility and institutionality of the church, Illich sees the incarnation of God as that which brings people together into one flesh, an act he traces directly to the Eucharist.[59] To care for the stranger is to care for Christ (Matt. 25:31-46), which is also to care for a member of one's own body, for the Eucharist gathered all into the body of Christ (I Cor. 12). The flesh is precisely where the transcendent and immanent become inseparable.

Illich's declension narrative begins in the same place as de Lubac's: with the controversy over Berengar of Tours's theology of the Eucharist in the eleventh century. Illich traces the history of Western excarnation, the distancing of our selves from our bodies, to Berengar's questioning of how the bread and wine shared by the community could really be the body and blood of Christ. The official church's response — the inversion of which de Lubac writes — only made matters worse by confining the *corpus verum* to the altar, thus increasingly limiting the Eucharist to an extrinsic miracle that is not enacted in face-to-face encounters with other people. Increasingly over the later Middle Ages, care for others becomes institutionalized and bureaucratized. As Taylor writes, "Here's where the corruption comes in: what we got was not a network of agape, but rather a disciplined society in which categorical relations have primacy, and therefore norms."[60] While Illich begrudgingly and Taylor more willingly recognize the necessity of institutions and the good in the universal expansion of care for others, they warn of a world in which contingency can only be seen as an obstacle. The loss of transcendence entraps us in an immanent and bureaucratized box of our own making. As Taylor writes, "[W]e are now living caricatures of the network life. We have lost some of the communion, the 'conspiratio,' which is at the heart of the Eucharist. . . . The spirit is strangled."[61] This is not just another complaint about the lifelessness of the iron cage. While we might be tempted to think that the regularity of the modern world has tamed the violence of "religion," Taylor warns that "The code can rapidly become the crutch for our sense of moral superiority."[62] The poor become a problem to be managed rather than a call to solidarity. Indeed, history itself — as a product entirely of human

---

59. Illich, *Rivers North*, p. 208.
60. Taylor, *A Secular Age*, p. 158.
61. Taylor, *A Secular Age*, p. 739.
62. Taylor, *A Secular Age*, p. 743.

making — must also be managed and controlled, by the most powerful means at our disposal. Illich puts the point dramatically:

> Take away the fleshly, bodily, carnal, dense, humoural experience of self, and therefore of the Thou, from the story of the Samaritan and you have a nice liberal fantasy, which is something horrible. You have the basis on which one might feel responsible for bombing the neighbour for his own good. This use of power is what I call the *corruptio optimi quae est pessima*. What is most glorious but remains, as a possibility of thinking and experiencing, always somewhat in the shadow, somewhat in the clouds, is corrupted into a very clear and powerful ideal of democracy.[63]

Conclusion

A theological politics based on the incarnation of God, of course, will not be convincing to everyone, nor should it have to be. It should go without saying that there is no returning to Christendom. Indeed, it is precisely the calcifying of Christianity into a way to govern civilization that brings about the domestication of transcendence. But to acknowledge this is not at all to imply that theology is no longer possible for us. I have suggested that a political theology of the body of Christ is not only still possible in modernity but may be more relevant to a postsecular age than political theologies that attempt to reinforce the very religious/secular boundaries that the idea of political theology undermines. There is no good reason to demand that political theology police the border between the transcendent and the immanent, and a political theology that refuses to do so may in fact be much more useful for imagining a better world. In the next chapter, I continue the search for a political theology that crosses these boundaries.

[This chapter is also published in Jaume Aurell and Montserrat Herrero, eds., *Theopolitical Discourses, Rites, and Representations in Medieval and Early Modern Europe* (Turnhout: Brepols, 2016).]

63. Illich, *Rivers North*, p. 207.

CHAPTER SIX

"DISPERSED POLITICAL AUTHORITY":

SUBSIDIARITY AND GLOBALIZATION

IN *CARITAS IN VERITATE*

THERE IS A brief sketch in an episode of *Monty Python's Flying Circus* called "How to Do It." In the segment, three very enthusiastic presenters breathlessly explain to the audience such things as how to play the flute, how to split an atom, and how to reconcile the Russians and the Chinese. Here's Jackie to explain how to rid the world of all known diseases: "Well, first of all become a doctor and discover a marvelous cure for something and then when the medical profession really starts to take notice of you, you can jolly well tell them what to do and make sure they get everything right so there'll never be any diseases ever again."

I sometimes think of this sketch when reading papal social encyclicals, because of the enormity of the problems addressed and the brevity and generality with which the solutions to such problems are treated. It is easy to fault papal social encyclicals for their generality, but it is good to remember that these encyclicals are not meant to be blueprints for the reconstruction of the world order. They are not really about How to Do It, but rather they open up different ways of imagining the world. It is helpful to think of them not as wishing to impose a preconceived model on society from the top down, but rather as seeking to imagine new spaces for a more human society to be enacted.

In this chapter I want to explore how *Caritas in Veritate* seeks to open up such alternative social spaces. I will first do an exegesis of the document and show how it attempts to get beyond the binary of state and market by imagining the possibility of other types of social space. I will then show how the related theme of subsidiarity has been interpreted in two ways, one more state centered, the other more critical of the state. Finally, I will argue that *Caritas in Veritate* fits into the latter trajectory, and show how it can be connected to a Christian tradition of advocacy for a more complex and decentralized social space in the late nineteenth and early twentieth century.

I. Beyond the State/Market Binary

Caritas in Veritate is marked by a profound sense that economic development cannot be left to market forces if the goal of integral human development is to be achieved. This is not because the market is an evil in and of itself. The market is simply an instrument that facilitates encounters and exchanges between persons. As I have argued elsewhere,[1] there is no point in blessing or damning "the free market" as such. The real question is, "When is a market free?" In other words, under what conditions do exchanges happen that contribute to the flourishing and integral freedom of the parties involved? To answer this question requires a substantive account of the true ends of the human person, and Benedict XVI assumes such an account in *Caritas in Veritate*. As the first paragraph makes plain, it is only in truth that a person becomes free (1).[2] This truth is not any generic truth; Christ himself is the Truth (John 14:6 is cited). Charity appears in the document as the driving, "erotic" force that unites us to God and to one another. In order that charity not degenerate into "sentimentality" and "emotionalism," it must always remain united with the truth (3). True freedom is freedom in truth. It is truth that frees us from mere subjective opinions and cultural limitations to unite in an objectively valid understanding of the value of things (4). Truth is where true communion is made possible.

The fact that truth is bigger than subjective preferences at the same time liberates charity from being confined to a private realm of preferential giving to the less fortunate. Charity, as Pope Benedict makes clear, is "the principle not only of micro-relationships (with friends, with

1. William T. Cavanaugh, *Being Consumed: Economics and Christian Desire* (Grand Rapids: Eerdmans, 2008), chap. 1.

2. I have used the English version of *Caritas in Veritate* posted on the Vatican Web site at http://w2.vatican.va/content/benedict-xvi/en/encyclicals/documents/hf_ben -xvi_enc_20090629_caritas-in-veritate.html. I will cite the document by paragraph number in parentheses in the text of this chapter.

family members or within small groups) but also of macro-relationships (social, economic, and political ones)" (2). This is one of the most significant emphases in the document. The key third chapter, "Fraternity, Economic Development, and Civil Society," begins with a reflection on the experience of gift. Charity in truth is "the absolutely gratuitous gift of God," and it also manifests the essence of gift itself. Gift by its nature is excessive and ecstatic; it goes beyond merit to superabundance. Applying this kind of language to economics would seem to have a profoundly destabilizing effect on a discipline that treats scarcity as axiomatic and merit as crucial to the just distribution of goods. Benedict makes clear in the same paragraph, nevertheless, that any appeal to the autonomy of the economy, any attempt to shield economics from moral influences stemming from the language of gift, can only lead to abuses of the economic process. "In addressing this key question, we must make it clear, on the one hand, that the logic of gift does not exclude justice, nor does it merely sit alongside it as a second element added from without; on the other hand, economic, social, and political development, if it is to be authentically human, needs to make room for the *principle of gratuitousness* as an expression of fraternity" (34).

The relationship between justice, the rendering of *suum cuique* — to each his or her own — and gift, which calls into question the distinction between mine and thine, is spelled out more closely in paragraph 6. Charity goes beyond justice, because it offers "what is 'mine' to the other," but it also demands first that justice be done, so that the other gets first what is rightfully his or hers. The earthly city should be built according to law and justice, but charity transcends and completes justice in giving and forgiving. Benedict seems to indicate that charity is not simply superadded to justice in the earthly city. "The *earthly city* is promoted not merely by relationships of rights and duties, but to an even greater and more fundamental extent by relationships of gratuitousness, mercy and communion" (6). In this way the earthly city can be "to some degree an anticipation and a prefiguration of the undivided *city of God*" (7).[3] What is remarkable about this formulation

3. Benedict here seems to be using "earthly city" in a different way than does Saint Augustine, for whom the *civitas terrena* is an essentially negative phenomenon, marked by "self-love reaching the point of contempt for God"; Augustine, *The City of God*, trans. Henry Bettenson (Harmondsworth: Penguin, 1972), p. 593 (14.28). For Augustine, it is usually the *civitas Dei* on earth, not the *civitas terrena*, that is the prefiguration of the undivided city of God in heaven, though in 15.2 he allows, in interpreting Old Testament

is the way in which it radically destabilizes the modern boundaries between "secular" and "religious" phenomena. Theology does not face economics and politics across a wide divide; to the contrary, economics and politics are radically incomplete without theology. And theology does not complete them merely by adding on to the foundation they establish; the grace of God of which theology speaks transforms justice, transforms the economic and the political, into anticipations of the city of God.

Pope Benedict gives this destabilization more specificity by criticizing what he calls "the continuing hegemony of the binary model of market-plus-state" (41). Both market and state as they are currently envisioned exclude the kinds of gratuitousness and charity that make for a humane politics and economy. "The market of gratuitousness does not exist, and attitudes of gratuitousness cannot be established by law" (39). Benedict acknowledges that *Rerum Novarum* was ahead of its time by advocating for state intervention in the market for the purposes of redistribution. In a mild gesture of discontinuity with his papal predecessor, however, Benedict writes, "Not only is this vision threatened today by the way in which markets and societies are opening up, but it is evidently insufficient to satisfy the demands of a fully humane economy" (39).[4] We can no longer trust the economy to create wealth and the state to distribute it, because economic activity has overrun all territorial boundaries, while state authority remains within national borders (37).

Neither the market nor the state is able to accommodate the kinds of charity in truth that Benedict envisions as fundamental to a truly human social order. Furthermore, and crucially, Benedict comes close to grasping the way in which the choice we commonly face between the state and the market is not really a choice at all, because the state and the market work together. In the United States, political party lines are most commonly drawn between the party of the market — Republicans — and the party of the state — Democrats. What is becoming increasingly apparent, however, and may be behind the general disgust with both parties and cynicism about the political elites, is that

figures like Hagar, that "One part of the earthly city has been made into an image of the Heavenly City, by symbolizing something other than itself, namely that other City."

4. Benedict very quickly returns to a hermeneutic of continuity. The next sentence reads, "What the Church's social doctrine has always sustained, on the basis of its vision of man and society, is corroborated today by the dynamics of globalization" (39).

the state and the market are not opposed forces but collaborate much more often than they contradict one another. In the economic crisis that broke in 2008, government bailouts of financial institutions that are "too big to fail" brought this reality home. Free market ideology protects corporations from state curbs on corporate power while corporations simultaneously avail themselves of massive state subsidies and state protection from having to face the discipline of the market for reckless behavior. Benedict hints at the collaboration of state and market in terms of their mutual agreement to exclude true conditions of charity and gratuitousness.

> When both the logic of the market and the logic of the State come to an agreement that each will continue to exercise a monopoly over its respective area of influence, in the long term much is lost: solidarity in relations between citizens, participation and adherence, actions of gratuitousness, all of which stand in contrast with *giving in order to acquire* (the logic of exchange) and *giving through duty* (the logic of public obligation, imposed by State law). In order to defeat underdevelopment, action is required not only on improving exchange-based transactions and implanting public welfare structures, but above all on gradually *increasing openness, in a world context, to forms of economic activity marked by quotas of gratuitousness and communion.* The exclusively binary model of market-plus-State is corrosive of society, while economic forms based on solidarity, which find their natural home in civil society without being restricted to it, build up society. (39)

As this passage indicates, Benedict's preferred solution to the market-state binary is to encourage the formation of alternative spaces that outwit the logic of both market and state. A key role here is played by "intermediate groups" that, together with individuals and families, make up society (7). "To take a stand for the common good is on the one hand to be solicitous for, and on the other hand to avail oneself of, that complex of institutions that give structure to the life of society, juridically, civilly, politically and culturally, making it the *pólis,* or 'city'" (7). The pope urges us to think beyond the "private business leader of a capitalistic bent on the one hand, and the State director on the other," and develop both business and political institutions in a complexly "articulated way" (41). Business should overcome the "simple distinction between 'private' and 'public'" and between nonprofit and for-profit enterprise (41). In the realm of politics, we should "promote a dispersed political authority" (41). This does not mean the elimination of the state, and the pope acknowledges the existence of weak states where the rule of law needs to be strengthened. However, "the support aimed at strengthening weak constitutional systems can easily be accompanied by the development of other political players, of a cultural, social, territorial or religious nature, alongside the State. The articulation of political authority at the local, national and international levels is one of the best ways of giving direction to the process of economic globalization. It is also the way to ensure that it does not actually undermine the foundations of democracy" (41). It is this emphasis on a "dispersed political authority" and "other political players" besides the state that I find intriguing about the encyclical.

The encyclical has more to say about creating economic spaces that neither are state-run enterprises nor obey market logic. The market tends to bifurcate businesses into for-profit and not-for-profit enterprises. *Caritas in Veritate*, however, encourages the emergence of "hybrid forms of commercial behavior" (38) that are neither ruled by the acquisitive logic of market exchange nor confined to the merely private realm of what is commonly considered "charity." "Space also needs to be created within the market for economic activity carried out by subjects who freely choose to act according to principles other than those of pure profit, without sacrificing the production of economic value in the process. The many economic entities that draw their origin from religious and lay initiatives demonstrate that this is concretely possible" (37). Here the pope presumably has in mind businesses like Spain's Mondragón Cooperative, founded by Basque priest José Maria Arizmendiarrieta, a multibillion-dollar company that is entirely worker-owned and worker-governed, and the Focolare Movement's Economy of Communion, whose founder Chiara Lubich describes it as "an economy of giving."[5] It would be possible to write such businesses — along with fair trade and other kinds of socially oriented enterprises — into the larger market narrative as niches that appeal to certain persons' preferences. The pope might seem to be doing so by simply juxtaposing them with other, more typical enterprises of market and state. "Alongside profit-oriented private enterprise and the various types of

5. Chiara Lubich, quoted at www.edc-online.org/uk/_idea.htm. For more information on the Mondragón Cooperative, see www.mondragon.mcc.es.

public enterprise, there must be room for commercial entities based on mutualist principles and pursuing social ends to take root and express themselves" (38). However, Pope Benedict continues on to indicate that such entities are not meant to remain confined to niches, but are rather meant to evangelize the economy as a whole: "It is from their reciprocal encounter in the marketplace that one may expect hybrid forms of commercial behaviour to emerge, and hence an attentiveness to ways of *civilizing the economy*" (38). Clearly the effect of such enterprises is not meant to be limited to satisfying the preferences of a few.

To say this, however, is not therefore to say that scale is unimportant, or that such enterprises are meant to grow large. There are many indications in *Caritas in Veritate* that scale is important, and, while not wistfully wishing to ignore or turn back the clock on globalization, the pope indicates that local enterprises must be considered afresh as offering important advantages for the civilization of the economy. For example, in paragraph 27 the pope discusses food insecurity and points to the necessity of local communities being involved in any decisions having to do with the use of the land. In this vein, Pope Benedict also recommends the proper use of traditional farming techniques, alongside innovation, as an apparent contrast to the ways in which globalized agribusiness has imposed its solutions on local economies. The encyclical similarly warns in paragraph 40 that the "growth in scale" of business has made it increasingly rare that corporations remain loyal to any particular territory or remain in the hands of a "stable director who feels responsible in the long term, not just the short term." Thus has emerged a "new cosmopolitan class of managers" (40) that are beholden only to the shareholders of anonymous funds. Forgotten in this cosmopolitan atmosphere are the other stakeholders in particular geographical areas that have to live with the consequences of corporate behavior. "[T]he so-called outsourcing of production can weaken the company's sense of responsibility towards the stakeholders — namely the workers, the suppliers, the consumers, the natural environment and broader society — in favour of the shareholders, who are not tied to a specific geographical area and who therefore enjoy extraordinary mobility" (40). The pope does not wish to shut down all international investment, but thinks that it must be undertaken only while considering the "real contribution to local society" (40) that such investments can make. When discussing development projects, he also emphasizes that "the people who benefit from them ought to be directly involved in their planning and implementation," and recommends "micro-projects" alongside "macro-projects" (47).

While it cannot be said that Pope Benedict is simply adopting a "small is beautiful" approach to the economy, it is clear that an approach that seeks to prioritize charity must also give priority to face-to-face encounters between human beings. As the pope writes, "In a climate of mutual trust, the *market* is the economic institution that permits encounter between persons. . . . And today it is this trust which has ceased to exist, and the loss of trust is a grave loss" (35). The larger the scale of the state and corporation becomes, the more difficult trust becomes, because it is difficult to trust people you cannot see. The anonymous nature of global finance, to which the pope refers, is one symptom of the magnification of scale that has attended globalization. In response, Pope Benedict recommends microcredit in particular and microfinance more generally (45, 65). Again, however, microfinance is not meant to create niches: "Efforts are needed — and it is essential to say this — not only to create 'ethical' sectors or segments of the economy or the world of finance, but to ensure that the whole economy — the whole of finance — is ethical, not merely by virtue of an external label, but by its respect for requirements intrinsic to its very nature" (45).

Pope Benedict's emphasis on the local is clearly indebted to the principle of subsidiarity articulated by his predecessors. According to *Caritas in Veritate*, "Subsidiarity is first and foremost a form of assistance to the human person via the autonomy of intermediate bodies" (57). The word "autonomy" is interesting here, because it indicates something more than intermediate bodies as a simple stepping-stone between the individual and the state, something more than the way individuals present themselves in groups before the state, or the way the state's will is mediated to individuals. Intermediate bodies have their own life and proper autonomy. In them, subsidiarity "fosters freedom and participation through assumption of responsibility," something that a large bureaucratic state cannot foster. "By considering reciprocity as the heart of what it is to be a human being, subsidiarity is the most effective antidote against any form of all-encompassing welfare state" (57). It is worth noting that here the main target of subsidiarity is not, as it was in previous papal encyclicals, the totalitarian state, less a threat since the fall of the Berlin Wall. The welfare state is a First World, not a Second World, phenomenon. Subsidiarity should be used, according to *Caritas in Veritate*, to create better welfare systems, eliminating waste and fraudulent claims (60), by including individuals and intermediate groups. "A more devolved and organic system of social solidarity, less bureaucratic but no less coordinated, would make it possible to harness much dormant energy, for the benefit of solidarity between peoples" (60). Although the prescriptions here are vague, Pope Benedict does recommend, in the sentence immediately following this one, the possibility of "allowing citizens to decide how to allocate a portion of their taxes they pay to the State" (60).

This devolution of political authority to individuals and groups seems hard to square with Pope Benedict's call in paragraph 67 for "a true world political authority." What exactly the pope has in mind is hard to say, but he envisions a regulatory body with more power than the United Nations. "[S]uch an authority would need to be universally recognized and to be vested with the effective power to ensure security for all, regard for justice, and respect for rights. Obviously it would have to have the authority to ensure compliance with its decisions from all parties, and also with the coordinated measures adopted in various international forums" (67). At the same time, Pope Benedict recognizes that such an authority would need to be "organized in a subsidiary and stratified way" in order that it not produce "a dangerous universal power of a tyrannical nature" (57). How exactly this balancing act is to work is not spelled out. What is clear, however, is that the pope is pointing to models both below the state — intermediate associations and cooperative forms of business — and above the state — transnational political authorities — in advocating a more dispersed and articulated political authority.

II. Interpreting Subsidiarity

How one reads *Caritas in Veritate* will have a lot to do with how one interprets the principle of subsidiarity more generally. It can be viewed as a procedural principle that takes current political and social structures for granted but states that social problems should be addressed at the lowest level at which they can be addressed effectively. Applying the principle would then be a matter of empirical tests of effectiveness at the various levels of social authority. We might disagree over the results of those tests and how to conduct them, but who could disagree that families, neighborhoods, businesses, and social groups should be allowed to resolve their problems themselves, insofar as they can, and the state should only step in when needed? If, in this sense, both the European Union and the George W. Bush administration embraced the principle of subsidiarity, who could be against it?[6] On the other hand, the principle of subsidiarity can be read as more than a procedural principle, as rooted in a theological anthropology that is deeply subversive of the modern state's tendency to reduce social relations to an oscillation between the state and the individual.

Bryan Hehir can serve as an example of the first type of approach. In an essay on subsidiarity in a volume on religion and the welfare state in America, Hehir argues that subsidiarity is a "second-order principle" that only makes sense within a broader framework that moves from interpersonal relations, to citizen-state relations, to state-state relations, then to the international system.[7] Subsidiarity is a "procedural guideline not an independent substantive concept" that helps determine at which level problems should be addressed.[8] According to Hehir, subsidiarity does not begin with a defensive posture against the size or intrusiveness or expansion of the state, but with a consideration of the normative responsibilities of the state for the common good. In this respect, says Hehir, we should not overemphasize the differences between Catholic and liberal views of the state.[9]

According to Hehir, the story of subsidiarity belongs within the shift from papal support under Gregory XVI and Leo XII for an organic "ethical state" that monitored moral and religious activity in society to the post–Vatican II acceptance of a "constitutional state" that recognized religious liberty and pluralism within civil society. Hehir adopts John Courtney Murray's narration of this shift, and fits the rise of the principle of subsidiarity, first articulated by Pius XI, within it.[10] According to Hehir, subsidiarity is part of the process of "shrinking the state" in Catholic social thought insofar as Catholic social thought assumes that

6. Robert K. Vischer, "Subsidiarity as Subversion: Local Power, Legal Norms, and the Liberal State," *Journal of Catholic Social Thought* 2, no. 2 (Summer 2005): 277-78.

7. J. Bryan Hehir, "Religious Ideas and Social Policy: Subsidiarity and Catholic Style of Ministry," in *Who Will Provide? The Changing Role of Religion in American Social Welfare,* ed. Mary Jo Bane, Brent Coffin, and Ronald Thiemann (Boulder, Colo.: Westview Press, 2000), p. 101.

8. Hehir, "Religious Ideas," p. 101.

9. Hehir, "Religious Ideas," pp. 101-2.

10. Hehir, "Religious Ideas," p. 102.

the state will no longer be in charge of religious and moral hygiene. While Leo XIII assumed that the state was responsible for the whole of the common good, his successors would limit that role and recognize other actors such as unions and professional groups as contributing to the common good.[11] At the same time, however, Hehir claims that the fundamentally positive view of the state carries over into subsidiarity from the older conception of the state.

> Murray specifies the socio-economic teaching of Leo XIII and Pius XI as the initial point of divergence from the ethical to the constitutional notion of the state's role in society. Subsidiarity fits into this process of development. It does set limits to the state's role, but it does so from a starting point of a conception of state power that gave it *primary* responsibility for the achievement of the common good. Contemporary conservative discourse *begins* with a highly restricted conception of the state's social role and then seeks to use subsidiarity to maintain or even tighten these restrictions. But the background from which the principle emerged began with a quite positive conception of the state's role, and then sought to assess how that conception should function vis-à-vis socio-economic policy.[12]

Hehir manages to situate subsidiarity both within a narrative of "shrinking the state" and within a narrative of a fundamentally positive view of the state that looks benignly on the state's expansion. According to Hehir, the key figure in the "evolution" of subsidiarity toward a greater role for the state is John XXIII, whose 1961 encyclical *Mater et Magistra* recognized subsidiarity but treated it within the context of a recognition of increasing "socialization." Socialization, says Hehir, is a "descriptive term identifying growing levels of complexity in modern society which have moral consequences."[13] Socialization justifies state intervention in social and economic life to guarantee basic human rights and fulfill human needs. In fact, it provides the warrant for John XXIII and his successors to reinterpret and even override subsidiarity. "The reinterpretation maintains subsidiarity as a key functional principle in

11. Hehir, "Religious Ideas," p. 105.
12. Hehir, "Religious Ideas," pp. 102-3.
13. Hehir, "Religious Ideas," p. 106. The word "socialization" does not actually appear in the text of *Mater et Magistra,* nor does "socialize" or "socialized."

Catholic social teaching and continues to give it primacy as a norm for assessing the appropriate role of the state and its relationships to other social institutions. But the character of socialization and its impact on the rights and duties of individuals provides a rationale for overriding the limit subsidiarity places on the state."[14] Hehir does not ignore the role of intermediate associations in this scheme, but he locates them within a story of how Catholic institutions, such as hospitals, evolved in the United States from a parallel presence with regard to existing social institutions to a collaborative presence fully engaged with the federal government at all levels. Though acknowledging problems of identity and integrity of mission, Hehir thinks the collaborative model best exemplifies the positive Catholic view of the expansive state.[15]

In contrast to Hehir, a second type of reading of subsidiarity emphasizes its critical edge with regard to state power. Robert Vischer's article "Subsidiarity as Subversion: Local Power, Legal Norms, and the Liberal State" is one example of this type of reading. Vischer begins not with an abstract ideal of the "role of the state" as such. He begins instead with an empirical analysis of the way liberal states actually function to weaken intermediate forms of human association. He cites Bertrand de Jouvenel's work *On Power* to argue that, despite our normal assumption that individual rights act as a check on state power, the opposite is the case. The democratic state grows ever larger and more powerful in an attempt to liberate the individual from the tyranny of social ties, that is, from forms of norm-setting common life below the state.[16] Legal decisions in the liberal state tend to view not social groups but only the individual and his or her consumer preferences as the subject of rights. As an example, Vischer cites a case in which the California Supreme Court compelled Catholic Charities to subsidize contraception to its employees despite the fact that to do so would violate Catholic teaching. (More recent clashes over the Obama administration's health-care mandate raise similar issues.)[17] As Vischer points out, in refusing to exempt Cath-

---

14. Hehir, "Religious Ideas," p. 106.

15. Hehir, "Religious Ideas," pp. 106-13.

16. Vischer, "Subsidiarity as Subversion," pp. 279-81. Robert Nisbet's work is excellent in making the same point. Nisbet shows, from a sociological point of view, that "The real conflict in modern political history has not been, as is so often stated, between State and individual, but between State and social group"; Robert Nisbet, *The Quest for Community* (London: Oxford University Press, 1953), p. 109.

17. Regardless of what one thinks of the official Vatican position on contraception,

olic Charities from a state law mandating the coverage of contraception under employer prescription drug plans, the court recognized not only a negative liberty of the individual to practice contraception regardless of his or her employer, but a positive liberty to compel the employer to pay for that practice.[18] Vischer is consequently much less sanguine than Hehir about the "collaboration" of the Catholic health system with the state. Vischer sees "conscience clauses" as a necessary but desperate rearguard action against a wider trend toward state enforcement of the availability of morally objectionable procedures such as abortion in all health-care facilities that receive state funding.[19]

The principle of subsidiarity for Vischer is much more than a procedural guideline for governments, but is rather deeply rooted in a Christian anthropology of the person as essentially in relationship with others. Subsidiarity works against both individualism and collectivism by establishing the priority of deep forms of face-to-face community. The person is only a person in communion with others, and this cannot be replaced either by more abstract forms of collectivity like the nation-state or more isolating forms of individualism based on consumer preference. Subsidiarity is therefore subversive of the reigning paradigm of the state. When the state in actual practice seeks "either to marginalize intermediate associations or remake them in the state's own image," subsidiarity's support for the integrity and autonomy of such associations can serve as a "subversive wrench in the collective enthronement of individualism."[20] Vischer does not wish to do away with all centralized authority. "Subsidiarity does, however, reframe our image of the modern state, envisioning it as a resource for localized empowerment and coordination, rather than as the arbiter and provider of the social good."[21] The goal should be carving out a plurality of public spaces where different visions of the good can flourish. According to Vischer, this does not at all mean the abandonment of the notion of truly objective common goods; it only means a reluctance to impose them through state coercion.[22]

---

the state's power to override church teachings in church institutions should be troublesome to Christians on both ends of the ideological spectrum. For a more detailed discussion of this problem, see chapter 12.

18. Vischer, "Subsidiarity as Subversion," p. 281.

19. Vischer, "Subsidiarity as Subversion," p. 282.

20. Vischer, "Subsidiarity as Subversion," p. 288.

21. Vischer, "Subsidiarity as Subversion," p. 288.

22. Vischer, "Subsidiarity as Subversion," pp. 305-11. Vischer thinks that state co-

III. Alternative Social Spaces

My intention here is not to undertake a thorough exposition of Hehir's and Vischer's own views, but to use them to show two distinct trajectories in the interpretation of subsidiarity, one with a fundamentally positive view of the modern state, and one with a more critical view of state power. To which trajectory does *Caritas in Veritate* belong? Though not without ambiguity, the document, I think, belongs in the latter camp. In it, subsidiarity seems to be more than a procedural guideline for political leaders but fits within Benedict's attempt to promote charity, gratuitousness, and obedience to truth in social relations. Benedict sees that state coercion cannot enforce love and the market cannot leave truth to the individual's consumer preferences. *Caritas in Veritate* thus gropes for a way to move beyond the state-and-market binary by encouraging the proliferation of alternative political and economic spaces, intermediate associations and hybrid forms of business, a dispersed political authority and economies infused with charity. It is primarily in those kinds of spaces that true human encounters can take place, and charity in truth can flourish. The point, however, is decidedly not to restrict charity in truth to enclaves, but to disperse such gifts throughout the whole precisely by dispersing the state-and-market binary that would confine and marginalize them.

Caritas in Veritate can be connected to a tradition of Catholic social thought and practice in the early twentieth century that emphasized the importance of decentralized forms of social life. The *Compendium of the Social Doctrine of the Church* traces the principle of subsidiarity back to *Rerum Novarum*.[23] Though it is not explicitly articulated there, Leo XIII does write of state interference in lesser associations, the "principle being that the law must not undertake more, nor proceed further, than is required for the remedy of the evil or the removal of the mischief."[24] The state has a negative duty to prevent such associations

---

ercion is justifiable in a case like abortion, where the matter to be decided is the unavoidably collective matter of who is to be included as a person. He thinks, on the other hand, that legally discouraging the use of contraception would not be a legitimate use of state coercion.

23. Pontifical Council for Justice and Peace, *Compendium of the Social Doctrine of the Church* (Washington, D.C.: USCCB Publishing, 2004), p. 81 (§185).

24. Leo XIII, *Rerum Novarum;* http://www .vatican .va/holy_father/leo_xiii/ encyclicals/documents/hf_l-xiii_enc_15051891_rerum-novarum_en.html, §36.

from spreading evil, but the state is not prior to such associations and is not responsible for their genesis. Society, for Leo XIII, is not an aggregate of individuals but a society of societies that, at least in the case of families and religious confraternities and societies, spring directly from the law of nature.[25] Though he does not question the designation of intermediate societies as "private,"[26] as Benedict XVI perhaps would, Leo XIII nevertheless emphasizes that such associations are "real societies."[27] His vision of the social order is based on the proliferation of organisms like the "artificers' guilds of olden times,"[28] unions, mutual aid societies, confraternities, and a host of other, organically related forms of social life.[29] Leo XIII expresses his concern that, since the final destruction of guilds in the eighteenth century, workers have remained isolated and defenseless.[30]

The origin of an explicit principle of subsidiarity is commonly traced to paragraph 79 of *Quadragesimo Anno:* "Still, that most weighty principle, which cannot be set aside or changed, remains fixed and unshaken in social philosophy: Just as it is gravely wrong to take from individuals what they can accomplish by their own initiative and industry and give it to the community, so also it is an injustice and at the same time a grave evil and disturbance of right order to assign to a greater and higher association what lesser and subordinate organizations can do."[31] Subsidiarity was articulated by Pius XI as part of his vaguely corporatist scheme to revitalize guild-like associations to break the monotonous relationship of state and individual. As he says in paragraph 78 of *Quadragesimo Anno,* "When we speak of the reform of institutions, the State comes chiefly to mind, not as if universal well-being were to be expected from its activity, but because things have come to such a pass through the evil of what we have termed 'individualism' that, following upon the overthrow and near extinction of that rich social life which was once highly de-

25. Leo XIII, *Rerum Novarum,* §13-14, 53.

26. Leo XIII, *Rerum Novarum,* §51.

27. Leo XIII, *Rerum Novarum,* §50.

28. Leo XIII, *Rerum Novarum,* §49.

29. Leo XIII, *Rerum Novarum,* §48-54. In paragraph 30, Leo XIII makes clear, as does Benedict XVI, that state welfare is not an adequate substitute for Christian charity.

30. Leo XIII, *Rerum Novarum,* §3.

31. Pius XI, *Quadragesimo Anno;* http://www.vatican.va/holy_father/pius_xi/encyclicals/documents/hf_p-xi_enc_19310515_quadragesimo-anno_en.html, §79.

veloped through associations of various kinds, there remain virtually only individuals and the State."[32] Bryan Hehir is right that Pius XI came out of a Thomist tradition that had a positive view of the state in the abstract, but Pius was clearly alarmed by the actual form of the modern state that had absorbed the authority that "the wrecked associations once bore."[33]

Pius XI was concerned that economic life not be left to the competition of the market or directed by an all-embracing state.[34] The remedy was largely entrusted to self-governing guilds and associations that would bring workers and owners of industry together, and in which the interests of the whole industry or profession would hold first place.[35] Even more explicitly than Leo XIII, Pius XI emphasized that all such social organisms were not dependent upon the state for recognition, but were derived from a "natural right to form associations" by "those who needed it most to defend themselves from ill treatment at the hands of the powerful."[36]

As the language of guilds makes clear, both Leo XIII and Pius XI looked to the medieval past for models of a proper social order. "For there was a social order once," writes Pius XI, "which, although indeed not perfect or in all respects ideal, nevertheless, met in a certain measure the requirements of right reason."[37] If it has perished, he goes on to say, it is not because it could not have been adapted to changing conditions, but because modernity has been too much tainted by love of self. Both popes were heavily influenced by the corporatist romanticization of the Middle Ages so popular in Catholic circles in the late nineteenth and early twentieth centuries.[38] Figures such as Karl von Vogelsang in Austria, Friedrich von Schlegel and Adam Müller in Germany, and René de la Tour du Pin in France advocated replacing the current capitalist system with guilds that would include both workers and employers. These guilds or corporations would be semi-autonomous with regard to the state and would exercise the right to set prices, wages, and working

32. Pius XI, *Quadragesimo Anno*, §78.
33. Pius XI, *Quadragesimo Anno*, §78.
34. Pius XI, *Quadragesimo Anno*, §88.
35. Pius XI, *Quadragesimo Anno*, §85.
36. Pius XI, *Quadragesimo Anno*, §30. See also §37 and §87.
37. Pius XI, *Quadragesimo Anno*, §97.
38. For example, James J. Walsh's book *The Thirteenth: Greatest of Centuries* (New York: Catholic Summer School Press, 1913).

conditions based on principles of justice and charity.[39] Leo XIII did not adopt the corporatist position in its extreme form, but was more directly influenced by Bishop Wilhelm von Ketteler of Mainz, who did not wish to abolish capitalism but wanted to reform it piecemeal with corporatist ideas and structures.[40] Pius XI's posture was similar, though the advent of totalitarianism gave him even more reason to be wary of centralized state control.

Corporatism in Europe was ultimately a failure. The term was adopted by right-wing regimes in Catholic countries such as Austria, Italy, Portugal, and Spain. In these countries corporatism was little more than a facade for bringing workers to heel under associations dominated by capitalists and totalitarian regimes. Corporatism was recruited into the very kind of state centralization that the original corporatists had tried to counteract.[41] Despite this hijacking of corporatist language, I want to argue, nevertheless, that there was something valuable in the emphasis of the earlier tradition on the dispersal of political and economic authority through the proliferation of semi-autonomous associations of the kind I discussed in chapter 2. I think such ways of resisting the centralizing tendencies of state and market are very relevant today, and have affinities with the vision of *Caritas in Veritate.*

In addition to the Continental Catholic corporatist tradition that the popes drew on, there was an English tradition of pluralist social thought in the same period that, in some ways, has better stood the test of time. Although some of it was steeped in a romanticized and nostalgic view of the medieval period,[42] interesting work was being done in legal and political theory that attempted to resist the growth of the sovereign state in modernity by calling on an earlier tradition of dispersed political authority. The publication of Otto von Gierke's *Political Theories*

39. Richard L. Camp, *The Papal Ideology of Social Reform* (Leiden: Brill, 1969), pp. 26-27.

40. Camp, *Papal Ideology,* pp. 27-29. See also John E. Kelly, "The Influence of Aquinas' Natural Law Theory on the Principle of 'Corporatism' in the Thought of Leo XIII and Pius XI," in *Things Old and New: Catholic Social Teaching Revisited,* ed. Francis P. McHugh and Samuel M. Natale (Lanham, Md.: University Press of America, 1993), pp. 104-43.

41. Camp, *Papal Ideology,* p. 37.

42. For an overview of Catholic medievalism in the late nineteenth and early twentieth centuries, see Philip Gleason, "Mass and Maypole Revisited: American Catholics and the Middle Ages," *Catholic Historical Review* 57, no. 2 (July 1971): 249-74.

of the Middle Age in English in 1900[43] gave impetus to Anglo-Catholic pluralists like John Neville Figgis and to English Catholic distributists like G. K. Chesterton and Hilaire Belloc. Gierke shows how, with the growing hegemony of Roman law in the High Middle Ages, the idea that associations or "corporations" were organic and natural entities — as they clearly are in modern papal social tradition — was replaced by the idea that a corporation is a *persona ficta,* that is, a person by fiction only. And this fiction is a creation of the sovereign power; "Fiction Theory" leads to "Concession Theory." As F. W. Maitland put it in his introduction to the English version of Gierke's work, for modernity "The corporation is, and must be, the creature of the State. Into its nostrils the State must breathe the breath of a fictitious life, for otherwise it would be no animated body but individualistic dust."[44] No body exists naturally between the state and individual unless the state recognize its existence. A corollary of this concentration of power in the state is, as Gierke says, the "tendency to emancipate the Individual from all bonds that are not of the State's making."[45]

In the medieval view, by contrast, the whole was not simply a collection of individuals, but each part was a microcosm of the whole, and possessed its own intrinsic value. Each part reflected the order of God's rule of the whole within it.[46] Furthermore, the image of the commonwealth as the body of Christ facilitated what Gierke calls a "Mediate Articulation"[47] whereby each member is not joined directly to the head: "otherwise there would be a monstrosity; finger must be directly joined, not to head but to hand; then hand to arm, arm to shoulder, shoulder to neck, neck to head."[48] In other words, to call the organic associations of human social life "intermediate associations" is inadequate, because it assumes that such associations merely stand directly between the individual and the state and mediate power between those two poles.

The English pluralists active in the early decades of the twentieth century drew on Gierke and others to put forward a vision of society not

43. The book in English was a translation of just one section of a much larger work, *Das deutsche Genossenschaftsrecht (The German Law of Associations).*

44. Frederic William Maitland, translator's introduction to *Political Theories of the Middle Age,* by Otto Gierke (Boston: Beacon Press, 1958), p. xxx.

45. Gierke, *Political Theories,* p. 94.

46. Gierke, *Political Theories,* pp. 7-8.

47. Gierke, *Political Theories,* p. 28.

48. Gierke, *Political Theories,* p. 135 n. 89.

as a monolithic aggregate of individuals, but as a complexly articulated association of associations. Unlike the American pluralism of Robert A. Dahl, English pluralism did not see intermediate associations as conflicting competitors for influence over the state. Associations were seen rather as public spaces in their own right, bodies in which people pursued truly common purposes and to which people owed loyalties that were not simply trumped by allegiance to a sovereign state. In a way similar to Pius XI, the English pluralists advocated a conception of society based on self-governing associations of producers and workers. The specific problems of the railways would be dealt with by a governing body of the railway industry, outside the government's active control, but still under its formal legal power to intervene. The state would still be necessary to coordinate, but it would be a minimal state whose primary task would be the creation of the conditions necessary for associations to flourish.[49]

I cannot begin to unpack the full proposals of the English pluralists here, nor is it my intention to do so. I only mean to suggest that *Caritas in Veritate*'s call for a "dispersed political authority" can be located within a longer trajectory of Christian social thought for whom subsidiarity meant more than simply delegating tasks to the lowest part of the social pyramid that stretches from individuals through intermediate associations to the sovereign state. I am not arguing that Benedict XVI necessarily consciously locates himself within this trajectory. I do think, however, that reading this encyclical within that trajectory can not only connect *Caritas in Veritate* to an earlier tradition in Catholic thought, but it can also connect Catholic social thought to some of the interesting work being done by "radical democrats" like Sheldon Wolin and Romand Coles. *Caritas in Veritate* puts forth a breathtakingly ambitious vision of a political economy that is based in love and truth. This vision cannot be realized within a larger resignation to the state and market binary, but requires a more radical reconfiguration of social space. In the next chapter, I explore resources for a radical democracy in Augustine's thought.

---

49. Paul Q. Hirst provides an excellent introduction to the English pluralists in *The Pluralist Theory of the State: Selected Writings of G. D. H. Cole, J. N. Figgis, and H. J. Laski* (London: Routledge, 1989), pp. 1-41.

CHAPTER SEVEN

A POLITICS OF MULTIPLICITY:

AUGUSTINE AND RADICAL DEMOCRACY

LTHOUGH AUGUSTINE NEVER quite goes out of style, there is something about Thomist thought that seems to have fit the mood of early- and mid-twentieth-century Catholic reflection on the political. It seemed easy to mine the thought of Aquinas and his teacher Aristotle for reflection on rights guaranteed by a state, conceived as the natural political unit whose job was to protect the common good. Now that the boundaries of the state have been so thoroughly penetrated by other global forces, however — especially global finance and transnational corporations — there is something about the present condition that is perhaps better captured in an Augustinian frame. The revival of Augustinian political thought by such diverse figures as Rowan Williams, Oliver O'Donovan, John Milbank, Jean Bethke Elshtain, Eric Gregory, and Charles Mathewes[1] seems warranted not simply on the basis of some supposed Augustinian "pessimism," but on the way Augustine refuses to give us anything like a theory of the state.

1. See, for example, Rowan Williams, "Politics and the Soul: A Reading of the *City of God*," *Milltown Studies* 19/20 (1987); Oliver O'Donovan, "The Political Thought of *City of God* 19," in Oliver O'Donovan and Joan Lockwood O'Donovan, *Bonds of Imperfection: Christian Politics, Past and Present* (Grand Rapids: Eerdmans, 2004), pp. 48-72; John Milbank, *Theology and Social Theory: Beyond Secular Reason* (Oxford: Blackwell, 1990), pp. 380-438; Jean Bethke Elshtain, *Augustine and the Limits of Politics* (Notre Dame: University of Notre Dame Press, 1998); Eric Gregory, *Politics and the Order of Love: An Augustinian Ethic of Democratic Citizenship* (Chicago: University of Chicago Press, 2010); Charles Mathewes, *The Republic of Grace: Augustinian Thoughts for Dark Times* (Grand Rapids: Eerdmans, 2010).

Politics for Augustine is not an analysis of certain natural, God-given, structures for the organization of common life, but is rather a diagnosis of competing desires and competing ends that cut across any existing structures. Rather than one city in which power is distributed among state, church, and civil society, Augustine writes of the two cities as two types of performance that cut across space and time.

In this chapter I would like to explore some possibilities in Augustine's thought for advancing what I discussed in the last chapter: *Caritas in Veritate*'s call for "dispersed political authority."[2] I would like to do this by exploring some convergences between Augustine's *City of God* and the work of secular political theorist Sheldon Wolin, one of the principal proponents of what is called "radical democracy." In doing so, let me be clear, I do not wish to claim that I have finally found the key to Augustine's political thought and identified him as a radical democrat, a claim that would be anachronistic and fatuous. My goal is rather simply to point to some of the resources in Augustine for Christians to negotiate the world in which we find ourselves today.

I will start with critique, examining what both Wolin and Augustine have to offer as diagnosis of our present condition. I will then explore the more positive ways both figures can contribute to a Christian practice of politics.

I. Superpower and the *Libido Dominandi*

Sheldon Wolin is a well-known political theorist who taught at Berkeley and Princeton. His early fame came from his massive 1960 book *Politics and Vision,* which was a plea for the importance of theory in a day when political science was increasingly trying to model itself on the hard sciences, with dubious results. Though a secular Jew, Wolin was remarkably sympathetic to the impact the Christian church had on the trajectory of Western political thought. When the Roman Empire

2. Benedict XVI, *Caritas in Veritate,* §41; http://w2.vatican.va/content/benedict-xvi/en/encyclicals/documents/hf_ben-xvi_enc_20090629_caritas-in-veritate.html; "*Political authority* also involves a *wide range of values,* which must not be overlooked in the process of constructing a new order of economic productivity, socially responsible and human in scale. As well as cultivating differentiated forms of business activity on the global plane, we must also promote a dispersed political authority, effective on different levels."

had concentrated power at the top and stifled citizen participation, "it fell to Christianity to revivify political thought."[3] It did so, according to Wolin, by putting "forward a new and powerful ideal of community which recalled men [sic] to a life of meaningful participation" (p. 87). Christians did not reflect directly on the political and were in some ways indifferent to it, but precisely by that indifference they opened up a space — the church — that transcended time and declared its own superiority to the political, thus both animating common life and preventing the political power from claiming a monopoly on authority. Christianity overcame the fatalistic classical view of cyclical time with a view of history that was both linear and vertical, that is, moving toward a consummated future while revealing elements of God's action that broke into time (pp. 111-15). This hopeful trajectory of a pilgrim people divided and refracted political authority, such that Wolin writes, "The only institution that ever rivaled the authority of the political order was the mediaeval Church" (p. 4). This healthy dispersal of political authority, however, ends as the church and state become bureaucratized and increasingly come to mirror one another. Wolin draws on the work of Henri de Lubac to show that, starting in the late medieval period, the mystical element of union that Christianity introduces migrates from the altar to the state, culminating in the creation of nationalism in the nineteenth century. The shriveling of the political importance of the church coincides with the drive toward unity — a kind of mystical union — of the liberal nation-state. Liberalism is the enemy of democracy, Wolin thinks, precisely insofar as it tries to make one from many, *e pluribus unum*.

Politics and Vision was republished in 2004 with another couple hundred pages added to its already significant heft. In the expanded edition, Wolin chronicles how the practice of participatory democracy has shriveled well beyond what he could foresee in 1960. The unifying drive to overcome particularity has been transmuted into what Wolin calls "Superpower," a new type of governability that seeks to extend its power while simultaneously rendering its citizens passive and impotent.

Superpower for Wolin is not so much the designation of an especially

3. Sheldon Wolin, *Politics and Vision: Continuity and Innovation in Western Political Thought,* expanded ed. (Princeton: Princeton University Press, 2004), p. 86. Page numbers to this work are placed in the following text.

powerful state — such as the United States or the Soviet Union — as it is a modality of power. Superpower, Wolin writes, "might be defined as an expansive system of power that accepts no limits other than those it chooses to impose on itself" (p. xvi). In a pinch, this could serve as a definition for Augustine's *libido dominandi,* or "lust for domination," as we will see. Aristotle thinks that every political form fails when its own distinctive virtue is pressed to excess by the ruling group. Wolin identifies the fatal "virtue" of Superpower as the furious drive for innovation and expansion, the attempt to find new opportunities, open new markets, and exploit new resources (pp. 594-95).[4]

The bounded nature of the modern state was already being superseded in the Cold War, which was a contest not so much between states as between ideological world powers. Now, however, the terms have shifted, both because stateless terrorism has replaced communism as the external enemy of American superpower, and because American power has sought ever greater mobility and flexibility (pp. 560-61). Corporate power and state power have largely merged, and both have sought to downsize and outsource whenever possible. The state privatizes its functions, giving them over to private contractors to manage, while the state simultaneously adopts business paradigms of management, efficiency, and treating the citizen as consumer. As Wolin writes, "traditional distinctions between the political and the 'social' or the 'economic' are superseded: the economic is joined to the political to form the hybrid denominator common to all domains" (p. 589). At the same time, access to politics depends on money, such that "State actors have become dependent more on corporate power than on their own citizens" (p. 589).

Erasing the boundaries between the state and the corporation and between the political and the economic is accompanied by the aspiration to transcend the borders of the nation-state. Increasingly, large corporations are not simply multinational but transnational. With stateless terrorism given as the enemy, the aspiration of Superpower is, as George W. Bush made clear, to oppose terrorism wherever it is. Wolin comments, "As a hybrid power and an empire, Superpower challenged the idea of a state whose identity was rooted in and restricted to a distinct territory" (p. 594). Superpower is not an empire in the traditional sense, however, in which territories are invaded and occupied, absorbed

---

4. Wolin places scare quotes around "virtue."

and administered. This would tie it down. Rather, Wolin writes, "Unlike a 'command regime' of domination (from the Latin *dominatio,* or mastery, irresponsible power, despotism) Superpower is better understood as *predominance,* as ascendancy, preponderance of power, terms that suggest a dynamic, changing character and, above all, an economy of power, a rational structure of allocation of resources. Superpower depends upon an ability to exploit pre-existing systems, to introduce or impose new ones only when necessary and, when opportune, to abandon and 'move on'" (pp. xviii-xix). Not only is violence and the threat of violence used to support corporate interests, but the "discipline of the market" is itself a form of control that replaces overt violence (p. xx).

Wolin is especially interested in what happens to democracy when the liberal constitutionalism that aspired to contain power within limits has been overrun by the new form of political economy. The totalizing effect of power is not traditional totalitarianism but what Wolin calls "inverted totalitarianism." It is an unfortunate choice of words, because it invites dismissal of Wolin as hysterical; we lack gulags and concentration camps and other markers of totalitarian societies. For Wolin, however, the phrase captures something more precise than any lazy comparison of American to Nazi power; rather than control through gathering — a binding together, as the term "fascism" captures — "inverted totalitarianism" controls by scattering, by demobilizing citizens and depoliticizing them. An active, engaged citizenry is antithetical to a system in which large conglomerates exercise power with radically unequal rewards. Capitalism works against the disinterested pursuit of common goods because it creates self-interested and competitive individuals who see each other, in Wolin's words, as "either a rival or a useful object" (p. 597). At the same time, however, patriotism is kept alive by fear of external enemies, especially terrorism; the constant stoking of fear after the September 11 attacks provided the occasion to rally around the flag while simultaneously justifying two more wars and the further erosion of citizens' power by multiple means, from loss of civil liberties to more tax cuts for the wealthy. People are simultaneously distrustful of government and fiercely loyal to the nation-state. True politics in the meantime has withered. "The citizen is shrunk to the voter: periodically courted, warned, and confused but otherwise kept at a distance from actual decision-making and allowed to emerge only ephemerally in a cameo appearance according to a script composed by the opinion takers/makers" (p. 565). The ideal citizen is apolitical but not alienated, patriotic and resigned or relieved to turn over her or his civic obligations to the experts who understand the economy and global power.

The kind of power that Wolin describes is recognizable, *mutatis mutandis,* from Augustine's description of the *civitas terrena,* the earthly city. Like Wolin, Augustine is not interested in theories of the state or an analysis of the ideal structures necessary for the proper governance of a political unit. Augustine instead tells the story of two different historical enactments of power, each described as the performance of a city. And like Wolin, Augustine tells the story of the negative type of power as embodied in a kind of empire. The earthly city, spread out over the earth, is held together "by a kind of fellowship based on a common nature, although each group pursued its own advantages and sought the gratification of its own desires,"[5] though no one can achieve satisfaction because they all have conflicting aims. So the earthly city is divided against itself, and the strong subdue the weak. "Now the society whose common aim is worldly advantage or the satisfaction of desire, the community which we call by the general name of 'the city of this world' has been divided into a great number of empires" (p. 762 [18.2]), of which Assyria and Rome have been the most prominent.

The restless lust for domination that Augustine locates at the root of the earthly empire is similar to Superpower's attempt to have no limits that are not self-imposed. In the preface to book 1, Augustine contrasts the security of the humble who receive grace from the hand of God with the arrogant spirit of the earthly city that has claimed security as its own, and is therefore insecure. "Therefore I cannot refrain from speaking about the city of this world, a city which aims at dominion, which holds nations in enslavement, but is itself dominated by that very lust of domination" (p. 5 [1.preface]). Rather than describe this as an excess of virtue, however, Augustine calls it a vice, one that is only held in check by other vices. Nasica and Scipio tried to ensure that the Romans had powerful enemies, so that "lust should be restrained by fear" (p. 42 [1.31]; see also p. 45 [1.33] and p. 68 [2.18]). The best the pagans were able to do was to restrain the lust of domination by the lust of glory. The love of praise, though a vice, could be considered a virtue because it restrains greater vices. Those who, motivated by love of praise and honor, risked their safety in war and restrained their

---

5. Augustine, *City of God,* trans. Henry Bettenson (Harmondsworth: Penguin, 1972), p. 762 (18.2). References to *City of God* have been placed in the text.

greed were "less depraved men" (p. 202 [5.13]), and they have received their earthly reward in full (pp. 204-5 [5.15]). Yet such earthly honors are fleeting, mere "smoke" (p. 206 [5.17]). The "extent and grandeur of empire" had "the fragile brilliance of glass, a joy outweighed by the fear that it may be shattered in a moment" (p. 138 [4.3]). The love of glory is much better than the lust for domination (pp. 212-14 [5.19]), but it remains a vice, a "contamination" that separates a person from God and from other people. By contrast, the apostles of Jesus achieved glory in their ministries. "And yet they did not rest on that glory, as if they had attained the goal of their own virtue. They ascribed it all to the glory of God, whose grace had made them what they were" (p. 203 [5.14]). For Augustine, it is the human self, not true glory, that is fragile. The human self is created *ex nihilo,* out of nothing; happiness can only be achieved by acknowledging our limits and receiving the offer of stability, eternal life, from the hand of God (pp. 471-72 [12.1]). Those who deny human limits and try to seize glory for themselves will perish, paradoxically dominated by their own lust for domination.

When Augustine describes the dynamics of pagan Roman society, he has in mind the elites, not the masses. Augustine would have assumed that, of course, the common people would generally be subjects and not citizens in the modern participatory sense. Yet the dynamic of scattering that Wolin describes is embedded in Augustine's description of the earthly city as "created by self-love reaching the point of contempt for God." "The earthly [city] lifts up its head in its own glory, the Heavenly City says to its God: 'My glory; you lift up my head.' In the former, the lust for domination lords it over its princes as over the nations it subjugates; in the other both those put in authority and those subject to them serve one another in love" (p. 593 [14.28]). The grasping at glory that Augustine describes is inherently competitive; earthly glory is only glory when one outshines one's peers. The earthly city is united by a kind of common love, but because it is a love of self, it is a very thin glue to hold common life together. The earthly peace is a mere cessation of active hostility (p. 866 [19.12]); the earthly city "limits the harmonious agreement of citizens concerning the giving and obeying of orders to the establishment of a kind of compromise between human wills about the things relevant to mortal life" (p. 877 [19.17]). As in Wolin's diagnosis, there is no true pursuit of common good, only necessary compromises among self-interested individuals. The city of God must make use of the earthly peace, but the common life of the earthly city falls far short of the life of the city of God gathered around the altar. The eucharistic sacrifice is such that we "cleave to God and seek the good of our neighbor for the same end" (p. 377 [10.5]). True sacrifice simply is being united to one's fellows in the act of being united to God; it is only communion in God that produces unity among people (pp. 379-80 [10.6]). For this reason, pagan Rome never was a true commonwealth, a *res publica,* because by Scipio's definition in Cicero's *De Republica,* there is no commonwealth — only a mob — where there is no justice, and justice means giving to each his due, says Augustine, and that includes giving God his due (pp. 881-83 [19.21]).

At this point it would seem that we have strayed from the realm of the "political" into the realm of the "religious," but Augustine's thought obeys no such boundaries. As Wolin correctly notes, for Augustine "the heavenly city was not the negation of the political society but a perfecting of it, a transmuting of its attributes to a glory that the former would never know . . . the *civitas dei* was more perfectly 'political' primarily because it was more perfectly 'social.'"[6] What Augustine is after is not a theory of how to organize that realm of human activity called "politics" or "government" or "the state"; he has rather identified two types of performances, two ways of handling the goods of this world, one that transcends the temporal by acknowledging its own limits and accepting eternity from the hand of God, and another that is tragically doomed because it tries to grasp eternity for itself rather than receive it. These are not the religious and the political, nor do they track the contrast between church and state, or between infinite goods and finite goods. Both cities use the same goods, but in very different ways. "Thus both kinds of men and both kinds of households alike make use of the things essential for this mortal life; but each has its own very different end in making use of them."[7]

II. Fugitive Democracy and the Two Cities

Sheldon Wolin's alternative to the hegemony of Superpower begins with expanding the "meaning of democracy so that it is not confined to political matters but applies as well to social, cultural, and economic

6. Wolin, *Politics and Vision,* p. 117.
7. Augustine, *City of God,* p. 877 (19.17).

relationships."[8] Wolin recognizes — like Augustine with the earthly city — that Superpower is not a political structure alone but penetrates and forms all kinds of human relationships and human approaches to the material world. This expansive definition of democracy at the same time helps Wolin to take talk of democracy beyond electoral politics and attempt to multiply the spaces in which true democracy can be practiced. This multiplicity is crucial to Wolin and other theorists who advocate radical democracy. The central vision is to remobilize citizens by opening up spaces for participation that outflank the hegemony of corporate-sponsored state elections. The passivity and resignation of the citizenry can be overcome by creating spaces where real deliberation and discernment can take place, where people meet each other face-to-face and cooperate on common projects.

> The power of a democratic politics lies in the multiplicity of modest sites dispersed among local governments and institutions under local control (schools, community health services, police and fire protection, recreation, cultural institutions, property taxes) and in the ingenuity of ordinary people in inventing temporary forms to meet their needs. Multiplicity is anti-totality politics: small politics, small projects, small business, much improvisation, and hence anathema to centralization, whether of the centralized state or of the huge corporation.[9]

True democracy for Wolin cannot be about the governance of a large and unwieldy bureaucratic institution. But his thought here is more radical than simply recommending that the government be scaled down, as in Republican Party calls for smaller government. For Wolin, democracy is not, as is so often assumed, a form of government in which the people govern. In the first place, Wolin does not think there is a "people" as a preexistent, continuous entity. The formation of one "people" is an imaginative project; there was no one "society" until the creation of the nation-state. In the second place, Wolin does not think that democracy is a form of government, because he does not think that governing is what people actually aspire to do. Wolin accepts Aristotle's critique of democracy: the *demos* has neither the time to govern, because they must work, nor the

8. Sheldon Wolin, *Democracy Incorporated* (Princeton: Princeton University Press, 2008), p. 212.
9. Wolin, *Politics and Vision*, p. 603.

means to hire proxies to govern for them. Before modernity, aristocrats had the time to devote to political affairs, and now the wealthy buy agents to do their bidding. But Wolin takes this to mean that democracy "is absolved of the requirement that in order to be a serious political alternative it must prove its capability to govern an entire society on a continuing basis."[10] Wolin wants to reconceive democracy as "an elemental politics about the needs and aspirations of the Many, not about a unitary polity that democrats must strive to control, and not about seeking 'a' permanent form."[11] The *pluribus* have always been excluded and controlled by those who run the *unum*. The solution is not to seek to control the *unum*, but to recognize that in reality there is not one unitary people or society or nation. Citizenship is invested not only in the nation, but more immediately and really in the neighborhood, locality, and region.[12]

Wolin sees the small scale of participatory democracy as being more than a tactical solution; as he says in closing the expanded edition of *Politics and Vision*, "being rooted in the ordinary, it affirms the value of limits."[13] There is a spiritual aspiration here that is very Augustinian. Unlike the Marxist aspiration to overturn hegemony by attacking it directly, Wolin sees that the only antidote to Superpower's ambition to exceed limits is to accept limits. Most people's spontaneous political hopes are not pinned on radical change, but on getting what they need to muddle through. The common people are the carriers of what Wolin calls "everyday cultural traditions." Since the seventeenth century, the elites have not been the carriers of continuity but the agents of discontinuity. The "permanent revolution" that capitalism and state power have together unleashed is overwhelmingly a revolution from above. That revolution bulldozes community and authority, replacing it with mere arbitrary power. The only possible response is not a different kind of revolution from above, but a slowing down of time and a limiting of space to allow ordinary people to reclaim some measure of control over the conditions that affect their everyday lives. True democracy also defends the value of a common good, which means that people will have to accept the way their individual interests will sometimes be limited by the good of the community.[14]

10. Wolin, *Politics and Vision*, p. 602.
11. Wolin, *Politics and Vision*, p. 603.
12. Wolin, *Politics and Vision*, p. 603.
13. Wolin, *Politics and Vision*, p. 606.
14. Wolin, *Politics and Vision*, pp. 604-5.

Despite the permanence of such local attachments, Wolin uses the term "fugitive democracy" to argue that true democracy is an "ephemeral phenomenon" with an "occasional character." Its fugitive character is directly related to Aristotle's observation: those who are not professional politicians must work for a living, not govern. But Wolin also seems to suggest a certain pessimism by the adjective "fugitive." He suggests that democratic politics is "doomed to succeed only temporarily,"[15] and says, in examining the new inverted totalitarianism, that the "pressing question is whether there are countervailing forces that, while not powerful enough to effect a transformation, may stake out a political place in which to develop a counter-paradigm."[16] Wolin at times seems to cede dominance to Superpower, and simply look for small spaces to run. Wolin's appreciation for the way that the medieval church dispersed authority and complexified political space is tempered by his refusal of political mysticism, which he sees as an unfortunate inheritance from Christian teleology. Wolin rejects grand narratives and pins his hopes on purely local and multiple forms of political knowing. Without Augustine's city of God, however, Wolin is clear on what we are running from, but not clear on what we are running to.[17]

Like Wolin, Augustine's heart is restless. Augustine writes that "we should escape from the city of this world" but adds "advancing by the steps of faith which 'becomes active in love,' to take refuge in the living God."[18] For Augustine, there can be no talk of happiness if there is no certainty that it can be eternal. The cyclical idea of history can only alternate between genuine misery and false bliss, because bliss can never escape the ravages of time.[19] Augustine recognizes the fragility of the creature in time, the necessity of accepting the limits imposed by the fact of being created.[20] But precisely because we are created by a good God, time is ultimately not tragic but comic. Much has been written about Augustine's supposed pessimism, but it is Augustine who

15. Sheldon Wolin, "Fugitive Democracy," in *Democracy and Difference,* ed. Seyla Benhabib (Princeton: Princeton University Press, 1996), pp. 42-43.

16. Wolin, *Politics and Vision,* p. 595.

17. I owe this way of putting the matter to C. C. Pecknold, "Migrations of the Host: Fugitive Democracy and the *Corpus Mysticum,*" *Political Theology* 11, no. 1 (January 2010): 98.

18. Augustine, *City of God,* p. 782 (18.18).

19. Augustine, *City of God,* p. 487 (12.14).

20. Augustine, *City of God,* pp. 440-42 (11.10).

reminds us that evil is not natural, but is rather a privation of good. The import of the Fall is precisely that there is an original good to fall away from, rather than seeing creation as flawed from the start. As Augustine says, "the choice of evil is impressive proof that the nature is good."[21] There is, therefore, an inherently revolutionary principle embedded in the biblical story right from the start: *the way things are is not the way things are supposed to be.* This state of affairs could elicit resignation, but Augustine goes further to explain that the way things are is not the way things *really* are. Evil is outflanked both ontologically — since evil is not what really is — and teleologically, since all history is moving toward the eschaton, in which the city of God will definitively triumph and the earthly city will pass away; it is the earthly city that is "doomed" in Augustine's language.[22] This is a type of comic reading of history to which Wolin does not seem to have access. Augustine assumes that history has a *telos*, union with God, toward which we are moving, despite the vicissitudes of the history that we can see with our eyes.

Rather than map the two cities across space, Augustine projects them forward in time. The city of God and the earthly city do not correspond to church and state, religious and secular, or spiritual activities versus mundane activities, nor is the city of God a merely otherworldly reality to contrast with life on planet earth. The city of God and the earthly city instead correspond with the *already* and the *not yet* of salvation history. The city of God lives in recognition that Christ has already definitively triumphed over sin and evil. And yet not all have accepted this reality, and so the earthly city continues to mingle with the heavenly city until the final consummation of history. Only after Augustine does the spiritual/temporal distinction name a division of labor within the one city, as it does in Pope Gelasius I's division of Christendom into priestly and princely spheres of competency.[23] Much later this division in the modern state will be transmuted into a spatial division between the religious and the secular — or the spiritual and the temporal — as dealing with two distinct sets of goods. For Augustine, the temporal indicates not a space but a time between the first and second comings of Christ in which coercive authority remains temporarily necessary. Coercive au-

21. Augustine, *City of God,* p. 448 (11.17).
22. Augustine, *City of God,* p. 595 (15.1).
23. Pope Gelasius I, "Letter to Emperor Anastasius," in *From Irenaeus to Grotius: A Sourcebook in Christian Political Thought,* ed. Oliver O'Donovan and Joan Lockwood O'Donovan (Grand Rapids: Eerdmans, 1999), p. 179.

thority belongs to the earthly condition of order made necessary by the Fall. For Augustine coercive government is not natural; God "did not intend that His rational creature, who was made in His image, should have dominion over anything but the irrational creation — not man over man, but man over the beasts." It is only sin "which brings man under the dominion of his fellow."[24] The city of God must make use of this order while on pilgrimage in this life, but it is alien to that city. The two cities deal not with two different sets of goods — one having to do with God and the other not — but rather with the same goods with different ends. It is the ends, the *teloi* — referred to their consummation in God or not so referred — that make the two cities.

This is precisely why Augustine is useful for a politics of multiplicity. Augustine does away with the idea that there is one city — the empire or the nation-state — that the church can seek to rule, flee, serve, advise, or transform. Like Wolin, Augustine can relieve us of the idea that there is one unitary society or people in which we can jockey for control. The church in Augustine is meant to perform what Wolin admires about Christianity and what Thomas Hobbes and Carl Schmitt found so problematic about it: what Schmitt called "the typical Judeo-Christian splitting" of the political order.[25] The action of Christ to gather together a community of people who see themselves as wayfarers through, rather than citizens of, this world is always going to divide the political order. The division is one that derives from the aftermath of the Fall. From Adam and Eve came two children: "the first to be born was a citizen of this world, and later appeared one who was a pilgrim and stranger in the world, belonging as he did to the City of God."[26] Abel the pilgrim founded no city; Cain did after murdering his brother, just as Rome was founded in the murder of Remus by his brother Romulus.

It would, of course, be too much to claim Augustine as a radical democrat; Augustine does not assume that it is up to us to decide the best form of government. At the end of book 5, he briefly acknowledges the possibility of "happy" Christian emperors who rule with justice and humility and love the heavenly kingdom more than their earthly ones.[27]

24. Augustine, *City of God*, p. 874 (19.15).

25. Carl Schmitt, *The Leviathan in the State Theory of Thomas Hobbes: Meaning and Failure of a Political Symbol*, trans. George Schwab and Erna Hilfstein (Westport, Conn.: Greenwood Press, 1996), p. 10.

26. Augustine, *City of God*, p. 596 (15.1).

27. Augustine, *City of God*, pp. 219-20 (5.24).

Augustine acknowledges the success and longevity of Constantine and Theodosius, while also recalling the untimely ends of other Christian emperors,[28] noting that "God dispenses freely to good and evil alike."[29] Other than these few pages, however, it is remarkable that, although Christians had been ruling the Roman Empire for a century when Augustine wrote the *City of God,* he says virtually nothing about the empire under Christian rule — no mention of its benefits. Empire as such is not a good; Augustine would prefer a situation in which "all kingdoms would have been small and would have rejoiced in concord with their neighbours. There would have been a multitude of kingdoms in the world, as there are multitudes of homes in our cities."[30] Furthermore, there is a sense in which Christians, like Wolin's democrats, are unsuited to rule. As Rowan Williams points out, for Augustine the Christian ruler faces an insoluble dilemma: "if he makes the state's earthly triumph or survival his over-riding goal, he betrays any real 'justice' in the *civitas* he seeks to defend."[31] Williams bases these comments on 22.6, where Augustine refutes Cicero's idea that one can go to war to defend the *fides* of the commonwealth. Augustine says that faith in the city of God is lost when one tries to possess it through war. The order of the commonwealth is worth preserving, but it can never be thought that one is thereby defending the city of God, and there is a point at which treating the earthly city as an absolute value to be defended undermines true justice. So the Christian ruler must know the point at which he must condemn his commonwealth to defeat.[32]

For a politics of multiplicity, it is important to see that not only does Augustine prefer a multitude of small kingdoms to empire, but each kingdom is itself internally divided into two cities, one of which is composed of those who are not citizens of this world but citizens of another world, on pilgrimage through this one. The image of "city" is an awkward one to express the kind of mobility that pilgrimage suggests; cities don't usually move. Augustine seems to have chosen this image because of its biblical associations with Jerusalem in both its earthly and eschatological versions, and more generally because of the deep associations of belonging that the city would have carried in the ancient

28. Augustine, *City of God,* p. 221 (5.25).
29. Augustine, *City of God,* p. 223 (5.26).
30. Augustine, *City of God,* p. 154 (4.15).
31. Williams, "Politics and the Soul," p. 66.
32. Augustine, *City of God,* pp. 1029-32 (22.6).

world. Outside of the family, the city was the primary locus of human sociability. Augustine clearly wanted to convey the sense that one's loyalty to the people that God had called together would be at least as strong as one's loyalty to the mundane city in which one lived. Nevertheless, the idea that two cities could be intermingled strains the literal sense of "city." The two cities, as we have seen, are poorly understood in merely spatial terms, though they do occupy spaces. As Augustine uses them, they represent the saved and the damned; in other words, two different kinds of relationship with God. As in Paul's distinction between walking according to the flesh and walking according to the spirit, the two cities represent not material life and spiritual life but two different ways of dealing with the same world. Paul is not antimaterial; the body (σῶμα) is, after all, the temple of the Holy Spirit (I Cor. 6:19). The Greek word σάρξ, translated as "flesh," is not the material world but a way of relating to the world that does not refer it to God. The two cities similarly are best understood as two ways of using the same things, two different performances, one tragic and the other comic, that take place on the same stage.[33]

Christian social ethics often confines itself to Ernst Troeltsch's church-sect dichotomy: the church type works within the world, the sect type rejects the world.[34] In both cases, there is a unitary world or

33. Elsewhere I illustrate this point with Richard Strauss's opera *Ariadne auf Naxos*. In the opera, the richest man in Vienna is throwing a huge party, in which the after-dinner entertainment consists of a tragic *opera seria* based on the Ariadne myth, followed by a light comedy featuring harlequins and buffoons. The director of the tragedy is enraged to discover that his masterwork will be followed by such frivolity, but the situation gets much worse for him when the master of the house — knowing that the fireworks will start promptly at nine o'clock — decides that the tragedy and the comedy will need to be performed together simultaneously and on the same stage. As the curtain rises on the second act of the tragedy, Ariadne is grieving her abandonment by her lover Theseus and awaiting Hermes to take her to the underworld, where death will mean an end to the suffering of this mortal life. At this point enters Zerbinetta and her troupe of comedians to alter the direction of the drama. Zerbinetta convinces Ariadne that what she wants is not death, but a new lover. In comes the dashing young god Bacchus, who woos Ariadne, convinces her to embrace life rather than death, and carries her off to the heavens amidst general good cheer. In my analogy, the church is the troupe of comedians, acting to divert the action on the one stage toward the good. See William T. Cavanaugh, *Migrations of the Holy* (Grand Rapids: Eerdmans, 2011), pp. 63-65.

34. Ernst Troeltsch, *The Social Teaching of the Christian Churches,* trans. Olive Wyon (New York: Harper and Row, 1960). Troeltsch's third type, "mysticism," is generally ignored.

society or state that is regarded as a given, with which the church must deal. The advantage of Augustine's vision of two performances moving through time is that the church is not resigned to contend for power within this one space or flee from it. The church is called to improvise each performance of space and time, trying to turn the action from a tragedy to a comedy. The church is neither a sect trying to keep itself apart from the world, nor is it simply required to play by the rules of some preestablished political order. By avoiding any theory of the state, Augustine permits a kind of flexible politics that allows for multiple unscripted performances of the city of God wherever the love of God and of one's fellows can be enacted.

III. Conclusion

The pilgrim politics that Augustine describes, then, has some features in common with the fugitive democracy of Sheldon Wolin. Both are, in the first place, a recognition of limits in the face of a power that tries to transcend all limits. Augustine juxtaposes the fragility of the creature in time with the lust for domination in much the same way that Wolin suggests a modest, local politics in the face of Superpower. For Wolin, only when we overcome the aspiration to transcend the local can true common goods be discovered, for only then can we meet each other in such a way that we do not see each other as rivals and threats. For Augustine too, the common life that the earthly city can attain is only a balance of competing interests, a tragic condition that is better than chaos but falls well short of the commonwealth that is the city of God, a people united by a sacrificial binding to the living God. The church that aspires to perform that city of God, as Wolin also recognizes in the early church, divides political authority, giving the Christian one foot in the temporal world and the other in eternity. The eternal city, however, is lived out already now in the course of this mundane life, which means that the now is itself divided. There is no one unitary polity to which we owe our earthly allegiance; Augustine's pilgrims, like Wolin's fugitives, resist being scripted into the overarching narrative of empire. The performance of the city of God opens spaces of resistance.

At the same time, Augustine and Wolin eventually part ways, because the pilgrim is not the fugitive. The pilgrim departs, but the pilgrim also arrives. For Wolin, there is no *telos* to fugitive democracy; democracy is what people make of it. For Augustine, on the other hand, the pilgrim city finds its end in God. For this reason, Augustine is more revolutionary than Wolin. Wolin is pessimistic that fugitive democracy can find anything more than temporary respites from the dominance of Superpower. Augustine, on the other hand, is confident that the pilgrim city will find its rest in God. The way things are is not the way things *really* are in God's eyes, and so the earthly city is passing away, giving way to the comic performance of the city of God, which begins in time but ends in eternity.

CHAPTER EIGHT

WHAT CONSTANTINE HAS TO TEACH US

I TEACH AN INTRODUCTORY undergraduate course entitled "Catholicism in World History: Jesus to 1500." Since we are on the quarter system, we have ten weeks for those 1,500 years, so we cannot linger too long on any topic. We do pause at Constantine, however, both because the theological stakes are so high and because the story is such a rollicking good one. As Peter Leithart, John Howard Yoder, and everyone in between agree, something momentous did indeed happen when the Roman emperor embraced Christianity. After reading excerpts from the *Apostolic Tradition* of Hippolytus, *The Martyrdom of Perpetua and Felicitas,* Eusebius's church history, and Athanasius's *Life of Antony,* I pose a simple question: Was the conversion of Constantine a net gain or loss for the church? The class tends to divide about evenly, and the conversation is wont to be the most animated of the quarter. I try to play devil's advocate. To those in favor I ask, "Don't you think it's odd that the sign of the man who died rather than fight is now being used by the Roman army to conquer others?" To those opposed I pick a student and say, "Okay, you're the pope in Constantine's time. Pope Britney, are you going to tell Constantine he can't become a Christian unless he finds a new job? Will you insist we get a new emperor who will continue the persecution?" I feel I have succeeded if everyone leaves the classroom less sure of their own position.

I am not trying to feign objectivity or neutrality; I am a theologian with a definite stake in the debate, and I generally don't mind if the students in a class end up thinking like me. However, teaching beginning students to think about the theological importance of church history is not, in the first place, getting them to endorse a particular theological position, but rather getting them to put themselves in the place of the figures from church history that we read. Sound theological judgments can only take place once we have gotten past the assumption that we are in a position to judge those who lived in circumstances that barely resemble our own. Entering into a tradition means first of all submitting to it.

I come to the debate over Constantine as a Catholic who has been attracted to the thought of John Howard Yoder, largely through Stanley Hauerwas, my dissertation director. As a Catholic, however, I have always been reluctant to accept at face value any Anabaptist-influenced reading of history that posits small groups of *cathari* who have maintained the true faith amidst the overwhelming apostasy of the church as a whole. For this reason I find Peter Leithart's book *Defending Constantine* and its challenge to the "fall" narrative of the church important and necessary. At the same time, however, I am deeply grateful to Yoder for the way in which he tirelessly insisted that the cross of Jesus Christ is the key to the theological interpretation of history.

In engaging with Leithart's book and his polemic against Yoder, I want first to talk about their ways of reading history, and acknowledge that Leithart's book provides some important correctives to Yoder, though I want to steer both away from moral readings of history that too quickly separate sheep from goats. Second, however, I will address the theology underlying Leithart's reading of history, and argue that only a theology of the cross can do justice to what it means to proclaim that Jesus is Lord. I will argue that Leithart is right to read church history pedagogically, as a movement toward greater maturity in Christ. Unfortunately, he is wrong to think that maturity means a greater ability to wield the sword.

I. The Long Pedagogy

Peter Leithart has written a book that needed to be written. We need to have a debate over the status of Constantine and Constantinianism, to get past lazy assumptions and slogans on both sides of a polarizing topic in political theology. Beyond praising Leithart for his timely provocation, we should commend him because he has done much well. He successfully debunks the Enlightenment prejudice that saw the Romans as tolerant rulers who were only forced into repression by the intolerance of Christian monotheism.[1] He clearly evokes the savagery of the persecution and thus the deep sense of relief and gratitude that Christians must surely have felt for Constantine for ending it (pp. 28-29). Leithart presents sufficient evidence to show that Constantine's policies favored Christianity but did not impose it on all subjects of the empire. In a brilliant polemic against Locke, Leithart argues that Constantine tolerated paganism in a way that was at least more honest than modern conceits of toleration that feign neutrality but in fact marginalize Christianity and other faiths while leaving public space to the domination of state and market (pp. 141-45). In so doing, Leithart refuses religion/politics and private/public distinctions that leave Christianity toothless in the face of injustice. Leithart makes a convincing case that Constantine did not rule the church autocratically but in matters of ecclesiastical controversy was rather easily talked into supporting the opinion of whomever he spoke to last (pp. 164-75). Leithart rightly takes Yoder and others to task for painting history with an overly broad brush. In the medieval period, for example, it is wildly inaccurate to say, as Yoder does, that "church government was in the hands of the civil government" (p. 178).[2] In fact, the relationship of ecclesiastical government to civil government was hotly contested and went through many different permutations in what is lumped together as "Christendom," including a long period following the investiture controversy in the eleventh century in which popes like Innocent III freely intervened in the affairs of civil government. Leithart easily dispatches Yoder's assimilation of Augustine to Constantine (pp. 85-86, 284-85). Most importantly, Leithart rejects the idea of a "fall" of the church from some pristine early purity to a state of wholesale unfaithfulness to the gospel by those who called themselves Christians (pp. 315-17).

There are a number of reasons why I think it is important to resist such fall narratives. First, they tend to be associated with anti-Catholic bias. The typical construction is that of Harnack, who posited an original Christianity that was subsequently tainted by Greek culture; the

1. Peter J. Leithart, *Defending Constantine: The Twilight of an Empire and the Dawn of Christendom* (Downers Grove, Ill.: InterVarsity, 2010), pp. 26-27. References to Leithart's book are in parentheses in the following text.
2. The quote is from John Howard Yoder, *Christian Attitudes to War, Peace, and Revolution,* ed. Theodore J. Koontz and Andy Alexis-Baker (Grand Rapids: Brazos, 2009), p. 60.

corrupted development of dogma was only corrected by the Reformation's return to a purer form of faith. Anabaptist histories place the fall later than do liberal Protestant histories — with Constantine — but the implication is also that the development of Catholicism in the centuries between the fourth and the sixteenth is, on the whole, a tale of corruption and decline. Second, fall narratives make it difficult to construct a coherent pneumatology. While it is true that the Holy Spirit blows where she will, and the church can never rest content with a guarantee of the Spirit's presence, the burden of proof is on any account of the Spirit's historical occultation. Third, fall narratives fail to deal with the simultaneous holiness and sinfulness of the church. Paul's recognition of the very body of Christ in the church at Corinth comes in the midst of his berating the church for its manifest sinfulness: jealousy, quarreling, sexual immorality, dragging each other before civil courts of law, ignoring the poor, and so on. The holiness and sinfulness in and of the church should not be neatly divided between visibility and invisibility, the pure and the apostate. As I have argued elsewhere, what we see when we look at the church is not the pure Christ but the Christ who "became sin" for our sakes (II Cor. 5:21).[3]

I wonder if we can take a theological approach to church history that does not immediately seek to judge every episode in terms of faithfulness or apostasy. I want to suggest that we can read the church's reaction to Constantine's conversion not as either the faithful recognition of God's long-awaited triumph over the Romans or the selling out of the church to power, but as the church muddling through a wholly unanticipated set of circumstances and learning some lessons in the process. Perhaps God's history of salvation is more full of surprises than either Leithart or Yoder allows; perhaps neither Davidic monarchy nor diaspora was as firmly established as the definitive social form of God's people as Leithart or Yoder would have us believe. I am not at all suggesting an atheological reading of history as pure contingency, one damn thing after another. I am rather suggesting that Constantine's conversion be read as part of the long pedagogy of God's people that did not end with the advent of Jesus Christ, even though Christ showed us the definitive shape of the story's end.

The pedagogical reading of salvation history has long been the way

3. William T. Cavanaugh, *Migrations of the Holy: God, State, and the Political Meaning of the Church* (Grand Rapids: Eerdmans, 2011), pp. 141-69.

that the church has dealt with difficult passages in the Old Testament, and is in fact the way that Yoder himself deals with the Old Testament narrative. In *The Politics of Jesus*, for example, Yoder considers the juxtaposition of Christian opposition to war with the wars in the Old Testament that reportedly issue from the will of God. Those who offer this objection, Yoder thinks, are adopting a legalistic attitude, and the way they put the question makes overgeneralizations. "This approach hides from us the realization that for the believing Israelite the Scriptures would not have been read with this kind of question in mind. Rather than reading with the modern question in mind, whether it confirms certain moral generalizations or not, the Israelite read it as his story, as the account of his own past. A story may include a moral implication, or presuppose moral judgments, but it does not necessarily begin at that point."[4] Yoder's approach here strikes me as a salutary way to begin the reading of church history. It is *our* story, like it or not. Constantine's church is not someone else's church, the church of the impure, the church of those who abandoned what *we* know is the true gospel. Our first reading of church history is furthermore not a moral reading, not the attempt to separate the faithful from the unfaithful, but rather the attempt to discern how God is acting in and through this body of saints and sinners.

According to Yoder, what would have struck the Israelite reading her or his story in the scriptures is not any generalization about the morality of war but rather the way that God acts in history, specifically the way that God saves God's people without their needing to act. "When we seek to test a modern moral statement, we are struck by the parts of the story that do not fit our modern pattern; but the Israelite reading the story was more likely struck by the other cases, where Israel was saved by the mighty deeds of God on her behalf."[5] Yoder then proceeds to narrate a number of the latter type of cases, where the victories of the Israelites in war were the result not of superior weaponry and military preparedness but of the miraculous intervention of God, overcoming the weakness of God's people. For Yoder, Jews in Jesus' time would have found it normal, or at least possible, to expect that the revolutionary messianic community that Jesus announced would not rely on military

---

4. John Howard Yoder, *The Politics of Jesus: Vicit Agnus Noster* (Grand Rapids: Eerdmans, 1972), p. 78.

5. Yoder, *The Politics of Jesus*, pp. 78-79.

technique and violence but on God's miraculous deliverance. "If, with the cultural empathy that is the elementary requisite for honestly understanding any ancient documents, we measure Jesus' meaning not by what *we* can possibly conceive of as happening but by what his listeners can have understood, then we are forbidden to filter his message through our modern sense of reality, of the uniformity of nature and the inconceivability of the extraordinary."[6]

Leithart points out that Yoder's preference for cases in which direct divine intervention saved the Israelites selectively ignores other cases in which weapons and preparations for war were decisive. The latter cases, says Leithart, are "part of our story, preserved 'for our instruction'" (p. 336). Yoder's deeper point, however, is that there is a way of reading the Old Testament in which moral questions are suspended in favor of a more profound theological message. Joshua, in other words, is neither to be read as giving license for Christian use of violence (as Leithart would use him) nor is he simply to be condemned as unfaithful for his treatment of the Canaanites. We are rather to read the Old Testament as the story of God's deliverance of God's people in spite of themselves, a story that will have its culmination in that of Jesus, who, in his renunciation of violence, in the Sermon on the Mount, and in his cross and resurrection, showed that the ultimate shape of Christian witness to God's salvation does not involve weapons and bloodshed. Joshua is to be read as a precursor, a representative of an incomplete stage in the long pedagogy of the people of God. My suggestion is that we read Constantine in roughly the same way.

Oliver O'Donovan's distinction between historical authority and moral authority is helpful here. The coming of Christ has historical authority because it confers a unique meaning on all historical events, both before and after the mission of Jesus on earth. This means that even apparently contradictory events can be drawn together into one narrative, and moral judgment superseded. "Historical authority can reconcile, where moral authority can only judge."[7] When reading about the conquest of Canaan and the ban, O'Donovan, like Yoder, wants to "suspend the moral question."

6. Yoder, *The Politics of Jesus*, p. 89.
7. Oliver O'Donovan, *Resurrection and Moral Order: An Outline for Evangelical Ethics* (Grand Rapids: Eerdmans, 1986), p. 157.

The moral question has pushed itself forward, either in indignant pro-test or (worse) in sophistic justification. Like the elder brother of the prodigal son, Christians reading the book of Joshua need to learn how to ask other questions before the moral ones: the history of divine reve-lation, like the waiting father in the parable, is not concerned only with justifying the good and condemning the bad. This Old Testament his-tory is concerned only to reveal the impact of the divine reality upon the human in election and judgment.[8]

Greater than the scandal of moral contradiction between the Old and New Testaments is the scandal of the very historicity of God's self-revelation, that God reveals Godself in history in such a way that such contradictions can be embraced.

> In God's self-disclosure something had to come *before* the vindication of the moral order: the transcendent fire of election and judgment had to be shown in all its nakedness, in all its possible hostility to the world, if we were to learn what it meant that in Christ the Word of God became flesh and took the cause of the world as his own cause.... Before we could learn of God as vindicator of the moral order we had to learn something even more basic.[9]

This "had to," O'Donovan makes clear, is not because God is bound by any necessity, but because of human weakness in understanding the full import of what O'Donovan calls "moral order."

This pedagogical approach is much like what we find in Irenaeus. Against his Gnostic opponents, Irenaeus argues that the differences be-tween the Old and New Testaments are not due to the existence of two separate gods, but are due to the patience of the one God with human development. Just as a mother gives milk and not "strong meat" to her baby, so God has nourished us through our infancy until we were ready to receive the full revelation of God in Christ. Even at Christ's advent, Irenaeus describes humans as still in their infancy.

> And for this cause our Lord in these last times, when He had summed up all things into Himself, came to us, not as He might have come, but

8. O'Donovan, *Resurrection and Moral Order,* p. 158.
9. O'Donovan, *Resurrection and Moral Order,* p. 158.

as we were capable of beholding Him. He might easily have come to us in His immortal glory, but in that case we could never have endured the greatness of the glory; and therefore it was that He, who was the perfect bread of the Father, offered Himself to us as milk, [because we were] as infants. He did this when He appeared as a man, that we, being nourished, as it were, from the breast of His flesh, and having, by such a course of milk nourishment, become accustomed to eat and drink the Word of God, may be able also to contain in ourselves the Bread of immortality, which is the Spirit of the Father.[10]

The Old Testament is not the climax of the story, but neither is it discontinuous with the New. According to Irenaeus, even the sins of the Israelites were committed to writing so "that we might derive instruction thereby, and not be filled with pride."[11] As this indicates, in reading the Old Testament theologically, moral questions are temporarily suspended but not forgotten. As O'Donovan says, "We are not mistaken to think that Joshua was morally unworthy of Gethsemane, any more than the elder brother was mistaken to think that the prodigal was unworthy of his father's compassion."[12] Christ is a moral challenge to all ages, but Christ's historical authority means that faith in Christ is able to take up the "fragmentary utterances of God's voice" in warlike conquests and ritual purity laws and put them into a coherent story culminating in the gospel.[13]

Given that Yoder is already committed to reading the Old Testament story in this way, could we not read church history in an analogous way? Granted that church history is not Scripture — there is no one canonical text from which to read — as a Catholic I am inclined to see Scripture and church history as telling one continuous story of God's people, in many different subplots and with many highlights and lowlights. There is not an absolute divide between Scripture and the continuation of the story in church tradition; as the Vatican II document *Dei Verbum* attests, "there exists a close connection and communication between sacred tradition and Sacred Scripture. For both of them, flowing from the same divine wellspring, in a certain way merge into a unity and tend toward

10. Irenaeus, *Against Heresies* 4.38, trans. at http://www.newadvent.org/fathers/0103438.htm.

11. Irenaeus, *Against Heresies* 4.27.

12. O'Donovan, *Resurrection and Moral Order*, p. 158.

13. O'Donovan, *Resurrection and Moral Order*, p. 159.

the same end."[14] "Tradition" in this sense is of course a narrower term than the history of the church; tradition is the teaching that has been handed down from the apostles and the growth in understanding of that teaching as the church moves through history.[15] But the essential idea is that "God, who spoke of old, uninterruptedly converses with the bride of His beloved Son";[16] the story that God begins telling in the scriptural narrative of the people of God does not end when the canon is closed but continues to be told in the story of the body of Christ as it moves through history. We ought not to have two completely different hermeneutics for reading the Old Testament and church history, "cultural empathy" in the former case, suspicion and the resulting narratives of corruption and decline in the latter. In both cases sin permeates in abundance and variety; how could it be otherwise when telling a history that is human? In both cases, however, it makes a difference if we do not give priority to the moral reading, but rather see the story as telling how God is acting now to lead humanity to salvation from itself.

Although the story comes to an unsurpassable climax in the events of Jesus' life, death, and resurrection, it might take a while for humanity to come to grips with those events. If the Irenaean reading of history is correct, there is no reason to expect the early church always to "get it" in ways that the later church would not. Proximity to Jesus is no guarantee of faithfulness, as those fleeing from or watching the crucifixion ought to make plain. Indeed, we might expect just the opposite to be the case; sometimes it takes a lot of maturity through hard experience for the church to get it right. Arriving at the doctrine of the Trinity took several centuries of argument. The ban on slavery and the embrace of religious liberty took far longer. The Christian critique of war that has gathered so much momentum and authority since the second half of the twentieth century might not be — as some politically conservative commentators fear — the selling out of the church's "just war" tradition to a woolly liberalism but rather a new stage in the fruition of the gospel. Whatever the case, the pedagogical model need not be strictly linear and progressive, as every parent and teacher knows. The Christian un-

14. *Dogmatic Constitution on Divine Revelation (Dei Verbum)*, §9; available at http://www.vatican.va/archive/hist_councils/ii_vatican_council/documents/vat-ii_const_19651118_dei-verbum_en.html.

15. See *Dei Verbum*, §8.

16. *Dei Verbum*, §8.

derstanding is subject to reversals and detours, though in the long run we hope that something is learned in the process.

Is it possible, then, to read the "Constantinian shift" as something that "had to" happen, in O'Donovan's sense of "had to," in order for the church to learn something it otherwise would not have learned? In this case, the learning would not simply be the way one learns from a mistake; there is something positive to be learned as well. Perhaps what was learned is that God does not want the church to be a persecuted minority. The minority status of the early church is *not* normative; it is *not* the way that God wants it to be. God wants the whole world to be evangelized. Leithart presents a fairly convincing and "culturally empathetic" reading of the relief and joy of Christians in Constantine's time who saw being fulfilled what they always expected: that God's control of history would be made manifest in God's deliverance of the church from torture and in the evangelization of the known world. In that respect the Christians in Constantine's wake were little different from the Israelites who, Yoder says, read the Old Testament similarly struck by God's providential deliverance of the people of God from their foes. Nevertheless, the church was suddenly confronted by a new set of circumstances that they could not have foreseen and to which preexisting models did not neatly conform. Neither Davidic monarchy nor synagogue-based diaspora models fit the new reality of a dual authority: the bishops on the one hand, and a Christian emperor on the other who claimed an ambiguous type of oversight[17] with regard to the church. The church tried to muddle through this new situation as best it could. Throughout the Middle Ages the relationship of ecclesiastical to civil authority constantly changed. In the end I would argue that the church learned that God does not want the church to evangelize the world through the coercive apparatus of civil authority, for to do so is to try to wrest control of history from God's hands. Here I come down on Yoder's side. But if this reading of the overall sweep of church history is correct, then Leithart is right to reject the idea of a "Constantinian shift"; it is more like a "Constantinian moment," one more episode in the long pedagogy of God's people.

17. The Greek ἐπίσκοπος, literally "overseer," is also of course the early Christian term for "bishop." Eusebius refers to Constantine as a "universal bishop"; see Eusebius, *Life of Constantine,* trans. Averil Cameron and Stuart G. Hall (Oxford: Oxford University Press, 1999), 1.44, p. 87.

II. What the Church Has Learned

If the pedagogical reading of history is right, the key question then becomes what the church has learned. Leithart concentrates much of his efforts on the question of violence as perhaps the key difference between his own account and Yoder's. The lesson that Leithart takes from the Old Testament is that the people of God are entrusted with greater access to the means of war as they mature. Constantine is then not a departure from Christian nonviolence but the fulfillment of what God has already been doing in history: preparing the followers of Christ for the assumption of the means of violence so that they may defend the church from its enemies, spread the gospel, and protect the vulnerable from injustice.

Leithart's portrayal of Constantine is not without discussion — brief though it is — of Constantine's occasional brutality (pp. 161, 228-30). What strikes Leithart most about Constantine, however, is his recognition that he is not a god, but stands in the service of the one true God. Leithart accepts Eusebius's contention that Constantine accepted the sacral trappings that surrounded the person of the emperor but "treated them lightly" (p. 49). Crucial to Leithart's defense of Constantine is his portrayal of the emperor as a sincerely pious Christian believer. Most of the positive evidence of Constantine's character comes from Eusebius's *Church History* and Constantine's own writings. According to Leithart, the Constantine we find there "expresses a soldierly faith in the powerful God of Christians, in the cross of Jesus as a victory over evil, and in the church as the unifier of the human race" (p. 95). So great is Constantine's piety that he prays to the Christian God before battle and says of the Donatists, "Those same persons who now stir up the people in a such a war as to bring it about that the supreme God is not worshipped with the veneration that is His due, I shall destroy and dash in pieces" (p. 84). After military victory over his rival Licinius, Constantine installed a portrait of himself over the entrance to his palace that portrayed him, Christlike, trampling a serpent with a cross overhead. Leithart comments, "Constantine thought too highly of himself, but in thinking he could join Christ in crushing Satan, he was simply thinking like a Christian" (p. 94).

There is certainly New Testament precedent for Christ's victory over Satan, but the identification of this victory with the Roman emperor's military victories is something quite new. In what way is the "powerful God of Christians" powerful? What theology of the cross underlies Constantine's idea of the cross as "victory"? Granted that Constantine saw himself not as a god but as dependent on the one God, it remains to be answered whether or not this God is really the God of Jesus Christ. These theological issues will need to be addressed theologically; it is unlikely that they will be answered by comparing the empirical church before and after Constantine. Leithart provides some evidence that the church was not as united on these questions before Constantine as any simple fall narrative will allow. But although Leithart provides some evidence of Christians serving in the military before Constantine (pp. 261-67), he does not provide evidence of Christian justification for serving in the military before Constantine. Indeed, most of the evidence of Christian participation in the military before Constantine comes from condemnation of the practice by Tertullian and others. Leithart contends that all he need do to refute any fall narrative is show that there is diversity among Christians pre-Constantine on the question of violence. But Leithart clearly wants to do more than this; he wants to claim that those Christians who accepted the use of violence were more faithful readers of the tradition. What they had learned from both the Old Testament and the New Testament — and what the church as a whole would learn after Constantine — is that God had prepared his people to accept the reins of history, using the means of violence when necessary.

Leithart's pedagogical reading takes Galatians 4 as its jumping-off point, where Paul describes the actions of Jesus and the Holy Spirit in history as rescuing both Jews and Gentiles from a "childhood" in which they were enslaved to the "elementary things of this world." Just as Jews were in bondage to dietary, sacrificial, and purity regulations of Torah, so the Gentiles occupied a world that revolved around animal sacrifice and the avoidance of contagion from unclean people and things (pp. 324-25). Roman society was held together by sacrifice; the gods were appeased by sacrifice, the entertainments of the Colosseum offered release for the bloodlust of the populace, and homage was paid through sacrifice to the emperor, who was acknowledged as Lord and Savior. Constantine swept all this out of Rome, and replaced it with a bloodless sacrifice, a eucharistic community that worships the one true God. Here sacrifice is, as Augustine claims, the compassion and mercy that unite Christians to God and to one another. The church did not fall under Constantine, but was recognized and honored as the true city that offers the true sacrifice (pp. 329-31).

Leithart's comments on sacrifice are to my mind one of the most compelling parts of his argument; Christ comes to replace bloody sacrifice with a bloodless sacrifice centered on the eucharistic memorial of his death and resurrection. It would not be difficult here to link Leithart's comments on sacrifice with the work of René Girard, who likewise sees the sacrificial system of pagan Rome as maintaining social stability by deflecting intramural rivalry and conflict onto scapegoated victims. Jesus Christ, for Girard, is the undoing of violence precisely because he is the identification of God with the victims of sacrifice, and thus the revelation of the injustice of societal violence. According to Girard, the Old Testament anticipates Christ in its identification of God with the victims of violence. Girard contrasts, for example, the Oedipus story with that of Joseph, to argue that the Old Testament begins to undo the scapegoating mechanism of pagan myth by revealing the innocence, not the guilt, of the victim.[18]

It is precisely here that Leithart moves in the opposite direction from Girard, and from Yoder; according to Leithart, "the Bible is from beginning to end a story of war" (p. 333). Yahweh himself is a "man of war." "From the beginning, this Creator made men to participate in and prosecute his wars. His goal in history is to train hands to fight" (p. 333). Furthermore, the modalities of that fight are not different from those of the world: "Eye for eye, tooth for tooth: so goes the pattern of biblical justice" (p. 334). Given that humans under the old covenant were still in their childhood, however, God was reluctant to allow them full access to the means of violence. "Swords are sharp, and fire burns, and so long as human beings were in their minority, the Lord restricted access to dangerous implements" (p. 334). Even so, God did give authority to some righteous men and women — Moses, Phinehas, Joshua, David, et al. — to carry out deadly acts of justice. But the fullness of our maturity would await the coming of Jesus Christ, the "warrior-savior" depicted in Revelation. Leithart acknowledges that the weapons of the Spirit that Jesus brings are "righteousness, truth, faith, salvation, the Word of God and the gospel of peace" (p. 335). Nevertheless, Leithart thinks a pacifist reading of the Bible is necessarily Marcionite (pp. 335-36). Leithart takes Yoder's point about Israel's reliance on Yahweh to fight for it in the Old Testament as support for his own position that our increasing

18. See René Girard, *I See Satan Fall Like Lightning,* trans. James G. Williams (Maryknoll, N.Y.: Orbis, 2001); on Joseph and Oedipus, see pp. 103-20.

maturity means increasing participation in the activity of God in ruling history. "When we were children, Yahweh our Father intervened to save us from bullies. Now that we have reached maturity in Jesus, we share more fully in those wars" (p. 336). Leithart does not think this contradicts his earlier statement about the spiritual weapons that Christ gives to us. "Finally, we might make an argument from greater to lesser: if the Lord lets Christians wield the most powerful of spiritual weapons, does he not expect us to be able to handle lesser weapons? If he has handed us a broadsword, does he not assume we know how to use a penknife?" (p. 336).

It strikes me as a severe abuse of analogy when "righteousness, truth, faith, salvation, the Word of God and the gospel of peace" are represented by "broadsword," while stealth bombers, drones, tanks, cruise missiles, white phosphorous, and nuclear warheads appear as "penknife." Leithart is attempting to place on a continuum of greater to lesser what are in fact two entirely different senses of "powerful" that do not belong on the same continuum at all. Yoder's work is marked by his emphasis on the way that the cross *redefines* power. Jesus oddly triumphs over the powers and principalities and makes a spectacle of them by dying rather than resisting with violence. Jesus does have a politics, but it is not politics defined in the same way that politics is usually defined. Leithart agrees with Yoder on the centrality of Jesus to politics: "If there is going to be a Christian politics, it is going to have to be an evangelical Christian politics, one that places Jesus, his cross and his resurrection at the center. It will not do to dismiss the Sermon on the Mount with a wave of the hand ('that's for personal life, not political life')" (p. 332). Unfortunately, Leithart gives nothing like a politics that places Jesus at the center. He acknowledges that "it seems I have left a blank at the center of the panorama: What of Jesus?" (p. 336). He asks, "Does he not go to the cross, like a lamb to slaughter, and just in this way win his great victory?" (p. 337), and other similar questions, but he does not really answer them. Leithart spends just two pages (pp. 338-39) outlining a "politics of Jesus," but does not attempt to give anything like a theology of the cross.

In these two pages, Leithart does address the Sermon on the Mount in putting together a Christian ethic for rulers. He suggests that if rulers were instructed not to look at a woman lustfully, there would be fewer wars. He proposes that the church insist that rulers tell the truth, and not give alms or pray or fast for public show. He recommends that rulers love their enemies, even when using military force against them. He advises the church to urge rulers not to lose sleep over budget short-falls, but rather to store up treasures in heaven. All these recommen-dations, if followed, would indeed alter the face of the nation's politics. But Leithart is evasive when dealing with the passages in the Sermon on the Mount that have to do with violence. According to Leithart, "turn the other cheek" (Matt. 5:38-42) is about honor and shame, not self-defense. He thinks that removing honor, insult, and retaliation from politics would reduce the instance of war, but he does not give any convincing reason why the reader should accept his assertion that this saying of Jesus is irrelevant to the question of self-defense. If it is irrelevant, why does Jesus pair it with "eye for eye and tooth for tooth"? Why does Jesus say, "Do not resist an evildoer" (5:39)?

We need to look at the six antitheses (or, more accurately, hyper-theses) in the Sermon on the Mount (Matt. 5:21-48) to see what Jesus is saying about the maturity of which Paul writes in Galatians. In each of these, Jesus takes an aspect of the Mosaic law ("You have heard it said . . .") and extends it ("But I say to you . . ."). Now that the Messiah has come, we are capable of more than merely refraining from mur-der; we are now directed to remove anger from our hearts. Now that the Messiah has come, we are capable of more than merely abstaining from sleeping with another's spouse; we are now directed to overcome lust as well. The fifth and sixth antitheses (5:38-48) have directly to do with nonretaliation against enemies. Now that the Messiah has come, we are capable of more than merely limiting revenge to an eye for an eye or merely loving our neighbors; we are now instructed to renounce revenge entirely, and to love even our worst enemies and our perse-cutors. *Pace* Leithart, history does not seem to be moving in the di-rection of greater human access to the means of violence; quite to the contrary. The fulfillment, rather than abolition, of the law includes the movement toward the renunciation of violence. Thus we can reconcile what Jesus says about the law in the Sermon on the Mount — "Do not think that I have come to abolish the law or the prophets; I have come not to abolish but to fulfill" (Matt. 5:17) — with what Paul says about the law in Galatians — "Therefore the law was our disciplinarian until Christ came, so that we might be justified by faith. But now that faith has come, we are no longer subject to a disciplinarian" (Gal. 3:24-25). The maturity of which Paul writes is not the mere abolition of sacrificial and dietary laws; it is also the completion of the moral law, such that the Decalogue is not ignored but extended. It is not that prohibitions on adultery and murder no longer apply in the adulthood of our faith. It is rather that now in our maturity we no longer need to be reminded to refrain from murder, just as we do not need to tell our friends not to steal anything when we invite them to our house. We have moved beyond the basics of the Ten Commandments. Now that the Messiah has come, we are capable of so much more, including renouncing revenge, loving our enemies, and putting up no violent resistance to evil.

Some such account seems necessary if the abolition of sacrifice is to accord with the movement of history that the Messiah brings to its decisive phase. In Leithart's account, increased access to the means of violence works at cross-purposes to the abolition of sacrifice; it would be odd for followers of Christ to mark the Messiah's reign by a decrease in the shedding of animal blood and an increase in the shedding of human blood. Most significantly, Leithart never deals directly with the crucifixion of Jesus. The renunciation of revenge and the love of enemies that mark the fulfillment of the law are nothing less than what Jesus practices in his death on the cross. As Leithart himself acknowledges, "This is surely the most powerful pacifist line of argument" (p. 337), and he never even attempts to refute it directly. This lack of a coherent theology of the cross leaves Leithart with an inadequate theology of martyrdom. According to Leithart, the martyrs shared Constantine's conviction that God would bless the friends of the church and frustrate its enemies, through military conquest when necessary. "It was an essential part of the theology of the martyr church, one of the bases for their utter confidence that someday their blood would be avenged" (p. 83). Leithart makes clear his conviction that the martyrs expected this vengeance not only in heaven or on the last day but also "on earth and in time" (p. 309). But a theology of martyrdom that is based on vengeance rather than the renunciation of vengeance does not do justice to the fact that the martyrs chose to receive death rather than to deal it out. They did so as an act of *imitatio Christi,* not in the hope that more blood would eventually be shed, but in the conviction that the triumph of Christ through his death and resurrection meant that the cycle of violence had been broken. Because of Christ's triumph, their deaths were robbed of their sting. Leithart's theology of martyrdom, on the other hand, is in danger of conforming to Nietzsche's caricature of Christianity as a resentful slave religion in which fantasies of revenge compensate for weakness.

Leithart is right to see the culmination of the pedagogy of the people of God in the abolition of blood sacrifice, but I am unconvinced that that abolition can be separated from the renunciation of the shedding of human blood that Christ's cross represents. At the end of his book, Leithart too acknowledges that animal sacrifice and human sacrifice are not easily separated. Despite his earlier contention that Constantine did away with sacrifice and "[t]o this extent, Constantine's polity has remained in place until the present" (p. 328), Leithart sees that the modern state, in refusing to welcome the church as model city, "reasserts its status as the restored sacrificial state. This means that there must be blood" (p. 340). In medieval Christendom life could be brutish, "But believing that the Eucharistic blood of Jesus founded the true city provided a brake on bloodshed" (p. 340). In modernity, Leithart rightly sees, the state has been released from being disciplined by the church and has been re-sacralized. With no god to recognize, the state becomes god. Sacrifice has been reintroduced in the form of the "ultimate sacrifice" by soldiers on behalf of the state, the mortal god. Animal sacrifice is eliminated, "Yet there is blood, more blood than ever, more blood than any ancient tyranny would have thought possible, and *all of it human*" (p. 341).

This critique of the modern nation-state is exactly right, as is Leithart's intuition that the eucharistic blood of Jesus founds a city that is essentially counter to violence. But Leithart's solution is not the Christian renunciation of violence; Leithart believes that violence is best held in check when Christians wield it. The problem, according to Leithart, is that "modern nations are post-Christian; they benefit from the new covenant privilege of handling the sword and the fire but refuse to listen to Jesus when he tells them how to avoid cutting or burning themselves" (p. 341). But perhaps they don't listen because Jesus never tells them any such thing. Leithart provides no scriptural evidence of Jesus' instructions on how to use the sword and the fire because of course there is none. When one of his followers uses a sword, Jesus tells him to knock it off: "Put your sword back into its place; for all who take the sword will perish by the sword" (Matt. 26:52; parallels at Luke 22:51 and John 18:11). This is hardly the drill sergeant Jesus that Leithart is looking for.

Leithart is right, I think, to present the medieval period sympathetically. It was not an era of wholesale apostasy, but fostered a series of often-serious attempts to apply the gospel — the good news of Jesus' sacrifice and the embodiment of that sacrifice in the Eucharist — to the restraint of bloodshed. What we have learned from that experience is what is at issue. If the trajectory of the story of the people of God is toward the peaceable kingdom of which Christ's cross is not the frustration but the firstfruits, then we have learned that the church should not try to enforce the gospel through coercive power. To kill for Jesus is to move away from the new covenant; the same is true a fortiori of killing for the state. If on the other hand, as Leithart contends, the new covenant brings with it a privilege of handling the sword and the fire, then we must return to some version of Christendom, what he calls "Christianizing the state" (p. 342). What we have learned is that the golden age has passed, and we must return. The long pedagogy of God's people has hit a dead end. The demise of Christendom has nothing to teach us except that, barring "the revival of a *purified* Constantinianism," "we are facing nothing short of apocalypse" (p. 342). Leithart says little about what this restored Constantinianism would look like. Should Christians support political candidates who will promise to shape a Christian social order? Should Christians attempt to Christianize the armed forces of the United States and other countries? It is hard to see what sword and fire Christians could wield except that of the nation-state. And if that is the case, the danger of blood sacrifice to the wrong god seems greater than ever.

III. Conclusion

Leithart's critique of the modern nation-state is devastating, though I fear that many readers will miss the seriousness of his emphasis on the transformation of the current order, and see his book as nothing more than an endorsement of the Republican Party's confusion of Christianity and patriotism. Leithart's rejection of a fall narrative for the church is a bracing challenge for Christians of a more radical stripe as well, primarily for the seriousness with which it takes our Christian forebears. Leithart will not allow us to cast stones from our postmodern enclaves without taking seriously the efforts of those Christians who were suddenly given the world and had to figure out how to act as though God really were King of it. Where Leithart's account fails to convince, in my judgment, is in its conviction that the use of the sword was a central and permanent fixture of the new covenant. As we move into the final part of this book — on violence — I think it is necessary to restate what the church continues to learn: that the King it serves still wears his crown of thorns.

III

FURTHER EXPLORATIONS IN RELIGION AND VIOLENCE

CHAPTER NINE

RELIGIOUS VIOLENCE AS MODERN MYTH

THE IDEA THAT religion has a peculiar tendency to promote violence has achieved the status of truism. "It is somewhat trite, but nevertheless sadly true," according to Charles Kimball, "to say that more wars have been waged, more people killed, and these days more evil perpetrated in the name of religion than by any other institutional force in human history."[1] The title of my book *The Myth of Religious Violence* is enough to make people dismiss it out of hand, as if I were denying that the world is round. The book has, nevertheless, stirred up a fair amount of comment, and in this chapter — and this section of the book more generally — I want to continue the conversation, especially given the continued prevalence of charges that religion is inherently dangerous. In this chapter, I must necessarily give a brief overview of the argument of my book, in which I challenge the conventional wisdom, for the sake of those who have not read the book. This step is necessary but dangerous, since such a drastically abbreviated account will inevitably leave out much of the detail that I think makes the argument convincing. My main purpose in this chapter, however, is not simply to rehearse the book's argument but to take the discussion forward. I will begin, then, with a brief summary of the book's argument, and then spend most of the chapter responding to objections that have been raised by other scholars. The responses will, I hope, make the argument clearer.

Let me be clear from the outset that my argument, if properly under-

---

1. Charles Kimball, *When Religion Becomes Evil* (San Francisco: Harper, 2002), p. 1.

stood, cannot be used to excuse Christianity or Islam or any other faith system from careful analysis. Given certain conditions, they can and do contribute to violence. My argument is not a defense of "religion" or Christianity or Islam or anything else from the charge of promoting violence. What is implied in the conventional wisdom is that Christianity, Islam, and other faiths are inherently *more* inclined toward violence than ideologies and institutions that are identified as "secular." It is this story that I attempt to refute. Put in simple terms, there is no reason to suppose that people are more likely to kill for a god than for a flag, the universal spread of freedom, oil, the workers' revolution, or a whole other host of "secular" ideologies and practices that behave in the way that "religions" do.

For the indictment of religion to hold, religion must be contrasted with something else that is inherently *less* prone to violence: the secular. I argue that there is no good reason for thinking that so-called religious ideologies and institutions are more inherently prone to violence than so-called secular ideologies and institutions, and that this is so because there is no *essential* difference between religious and secular to begin with. These are invented categories, not simply the way things are. I look at the political reasons why these categories were invented in the modern West. I then show that the idea that something called religion is essentially prone to violence is an ideological justification that can be used to justify the violence of so-called secular orders. The myth of religious violence promotes a dichotomy between *us* in the secular West who are rational and peacemaking, and *them,* the hordes of violent religious fanatics in the Muslim world. *Their* violence is religious, and therefore irrational and divisive. *Our* violence, on the other hand, is secular, rational, and peacemaking. And so we find ourselves regrettably forced to bomb them into the higher rationality.

I. The Argument

The idea that religion has a peculiar tendency to promote violence depends on the ability to distinguish religion from what is not religion — the secular, in other words. In the first chapter of *The Myth of Religious Violence,* I examine nine different examples of the argument that religion promotes violence. The arguments are arranged in three different types: religion promotes violence because it tends to be (1) absolutist, (2) divisive, and (3) not rational. The argument types overlap somewhat. Their exact taxonomy does not interest me, since I do not try to refute them by arguing that religion is not absolutist, divisive, and nonrational. What interests me is the way that religion is treated in all the arguments as a transhistorical and transcultural phenomenon that is essentially distinct from secular phenomena. That is, religion is thought to exist in all times and places, and it is essentially absolutist, divisive, and nonrational in ways that secular phenomena are not.

As I examine the religion-and-violence arguments in the first chapter, however, it becomes apparent that the authors themselves cannot maintain a coherent distinction between religious and secular. Martin Marty indicts religion for its divisiveness, but he gives seventeen different definitions of religion, then begs off giving his own definition, since "scholars will never agree on the definition of religion,"[2] then — in lieu of a "definition" — gives five "features" of religion, then shows how politics displays all five of the same features. Mark Juergensmeyer charges religion with a peculiar tendency to exacerbate violence, but the distinction between religious and secular violence is hopelessly confused by his statements like "the secular is a sort of advanced form of religion"[3] and "secular nationalism is 'a religion.'"[4] Christopher Hitchens excoriates religion for all manner of evils, but when confronted with the violence of atheist regimes like those of Stalin and Kim Jong-Il, he simply declares that such atheist regimes are religious too, since totalitarianism is an essentially religious impulse.[5] The distinction between secular and religious is nothing more than the distinction between things Hitchens likes and things Hitchens does not like. Richard Wentz's book *Why People Do Bad Things in the Name of Religion* attempts to avoid such problems with the definition of religion by openly expanding the category to include consumerism, secular humanism, faith in technology, football fanaticism, and a host of other

2. Martin E. Marty with Jonathan Moore, *Politics, Religion, and the Common Good* (San Francisco: Jossey-Bass, 2000), p. 10.

3. Mark Juergensmeyer, *Global Rebellion: Religious Challenges to the Secular State from Christian Militias to al Qaeda* (Berkeley: University of California Press, 2008), p. 23.

4. Mark Juergensmeyer, *The New Cold War? Religious Nationalism Confronts the Secular State* (Berkeley: University of California Press, 1993), p. 15.

5. Christopher Hitchens, *God Is Not Great: How Religion Poisons Everything* (New York: Twelve, 2007), pp. 232-48.

ideologies and practices that others consider "secular."[6] Religion ends up meaning anything people take seriously, which makes the idea that people do violence for religion a tautology.

Everyone appears to agree that religion promotes violence, but there is nothing like a coherent distinction between what counts as religion and what does not. The whole argument depends on the religious/secular distinction, but no one provides a coherent argument for supposing that so-called secular ideologies such as nationalism, patriotism, capitalism, Marxism, and liberalism are any less prone to be absolutist, divisive, and irrational than belief in, for example, the biblical God. In fact, all the authors undercut this argument. Empirical evidence does as well. American Christians, for example, are far more willing to kill for their country than for Jesus.

Such empirical evidence accounts for why many scholars reject substantivist definitions of religion that try to restrict religion to a few "world religions" on the basis of belief in God or gods or some sort of transcendence. To include Theravada Buddhism — with no belief in God or gods — in the list of religions, the category must be expanded beyond gods to include "transcendence" or some such. But "transcendence" is a Judeo-Christian category dependent on the distinction between creation and a creator God. To apply the term to Buddhism, which has no such distinction, one needs to make the category vague, but doing so makes it impossible to exclude such experiences of transcendence as nationalism or consumerism from the category of religion. So some scholars, following Durkheim, employ a functionalist definition of religion, as Wentz does. What matters is not what people claim to believe but how an ideology or practice functions in a person's life. If a person claims to believe in God but never darkens the door of a church and spends most of every day shopping on the Internet, then the notion that consumerism is that person's religion is empirically accurate and useful. If it walks like a duck and quacks like a duck, it's a duck. So when Carolyn Marvin says "nationalism is the most powerful religion in the United States,"[7] she is not speaking metaphorically.

Such functionalist approaches are useful, but they still try to locate

6. Richard E. Wentz, *Why People Do Bad Things in the Name of Religion* (Macon, Ga.: Mercer University Press, 1993), pp. 13-14, 37.

7. Carolyn Marvin and David W. Ingle, "Blood Sacrifice and the Nation: Revisiting Civil Religion," *Journal of the American Academy of Religion* 64, no. 4 (Winter 1996): 768.

an essence of religion and decide once and for all what counts as a religion and what does not. I think a more satisfactory approach is neither substantivist nor functionalist but constructivist. That is, there is no once-and-for-all definition of religion or the secular. The religious/ secular distinction is a modern Western construction that arose as an adjunct to the rise of the modern state and the triumph of civil over ecclesiastical authorities in early modern Europe.

Chapter 2 of *The Myth of Religious Violence* is a genealogy of this distinction. As Wilfred Cantwell Smith showed over fifty years ago, the concept of religion and the religious/secular distinction as we understand it were simply absent from premodern Europe and non-European cultures.[8] The word "religion" comes from the Latin *religio,* but the way the Romans used the term undermines rather than supports the idea that our conception of religion is transhistorical and transcultural. For the Romans, *religio* referred to any binding social obligation (*re + ligare* = to rebind); to say *religio mihi est* indicated that some relationship or duty was nonoptional for me. Such duties included cultic observances, but also included civic and familial obligations. As Augustine writes in the *City of God,*

> in Latin usage (and by that I do not mean in the speech of the illiterate, but even in the language of the highly educated) "religion" [*religio*] is something which is displayed in human relationships, in the family (in the narrower and the wider sense) and between friends; and so the use of the word does not avoid ambiguity when the worship of God is in question. We have no right to affirm with confidence that "religion" [*religio*] is confined to the worship of God, since it seems that this word has been detached from its normal meaning, in which it refers to an attitude of respect in relations between a man and his neighbor.[9]

Religio included obligations that modern Westerners would consider "secular"; there simply was no useful distinction to be made between cultic obligations and other obligations that maintained the fabric of the Roman social order. The religious/political distinction was similarly

8. Wilfred Cantwell Smith, *The Meaning and End of Religion* (New York: Macmillan, 1962), pp. 18-19.
9. Augustine, *City of God,* trans. Henry Bettenson (Harmondsworth: Penguin Books, 1972), p. 373 (10.1).

absent; what sense could be made of such a distinction when Caesar was worshiped as a god?

According to John Bossy, the ancient meaning of *religio* as reverence or worship or piety "disappeared" in the medieval period. "With very few exceptions, the word was only used to describe different sorts of monastic or similar rule, and the way of life pursued under them."[10] This meaning held when the word passed into English around 1200; the earliest meaning of "religion" cited in the *Oxford English Dictionary* is "a state of life bound by monastic vows." In time, the term came to include the condition of members of other nonmonastic orders, such that the religious/secular distinction was the distinction between two types of clergy, those who belonged to orders and those who belonged to dioceses. It is still common Roman Catholic usage to speak of entering an order as entering the religious life. *Religio* does appear in Thomas Aquinas's *Summa Theologiae* as one of the nine subvirtues attached to the cardinal virtue of justice; here Aquinas uses it in a way approximating the ancient meaning of "piety" or "worship." But for Aquinas and the Middle Ages more generally, *religio* was not contrasted with "politics" or "the secular" or any such other realm of human activity. As a virtue, *religio* was essential to good governance, because acts of good governance were meant to direct people to their ultimate end in God, which is the same end toward which proper *religio* was directed.

It is only with the birth of the sovereign modern state that the concept of religion as it is now generally understood was born. Over the course of the fifteenth through seventeenth centuries, religion came to be an essentially interior impulse, demarcated by sets of beliefs or propositions about reality, and essentially distinct from "secular" pursuits such as politics, economics, and the like. The transition took place in thinkers like Nicholas of Cusa, Marsilio Ficino, Guillaume Postel, and Herbert of Cherbury; in these thinkers, religion became a universal human impulse, the genus of which the various "religions" were species.

It was not a coincidence that the birth of the concept of religion and the birth of the sovereign state occurred in the same period. The birth of the state is realized in the consolidation of sovereign power over the institutions of medieval society that served to disperse the power of the king: clans, guilds, towns, and most especially the church. The religion/

10. John Bossy, "Some Elementary Forms of Durkheim," *Past and Present* 95 (May 1982): 4.

politics distinction becomes a tool in the subordination of ecclesiastical power to civil power, and their eventual separation. The political importance of the new concept of religion is most apparent in the influential writings of John Locke, whose project was to separate the outward force of the magistrate from the essentially interior life of religion. "All the life and power of true religion consist in the inward and full persuasion of the mind."[11] The religion/politics, religious/secular, private/public distinctions for Locke are vital to determining the proper boundaries of ecclesiastical and civil authorities.

Locke assumes that this business of distinction is the proper separation of two things — religion and government — that had somehow gotten mixed up together. But to tell the story that way is to assume that religion is a transhistorical and transcultural human impulse waiting to be separated from the secular by modernity like a precious metal from its ore. It is more accurate to see that the new concept of "religion" as a separate pursuit from "secular" life was born as a product of the long medieval struggle for predominance between ecclesiastical and civil authorities in Europe. The religious/secular distinction should be seen as reflecting a contingent and local set of political arrangements.

Precisely the opposite happened in the course of the European colonization of much of the rest of the world that followed the creation of the sovereign state in Europe. The concept of religion and its remainder concept of the secular came to be seen not as a peculiar product of European history, but as a basic fact about the world in all places and at all times. All cultures were declared by European colonists and academics to have religions that could be separated out from secular pursuits. And the imposition of this way of dividing up the world just happened to have significant advantages for the colonizers.

In their initial encounters with the native peoples of the rest of the world, European explorers reported back home with remarkable consistency that the natives had no religion at all. According to David Chidester, this denial was a way of asserting the superiority of European culture over that of the natives, who seemed to lack one of the basic building blocks of a civilized culture.[12] Once the native people

11. John Locke, *A Letter concerning Toleration* (Indianapolis: Bobbs-Merrill, 1955), p. 18.
12. David Chidester, "Colonialism," in *Guide to the Study of Religion,* ed. Willi Braun and Russell T. McCutcheon (London and New York: Cassell, 2000), pp. 427-28.

were colonized, however, the term "religion" came to be seen as a useful way of categorizing different aspects of the local culture. According to Wilfred Cantwell Smith, in precolonial India there was not "any term enabling an Indian to discriminate conceptually between the religious and the other aspects of his society's life."[13] Nevertheless, the categorization of Hinduism as a religion was useful to British colonists; it meant that Indian culture could be seen as essentially private, while British culture could occupy the public realm.

Over the course of the nineteenth century, a European "science of religion" *(Religionswissenschaft)* would compile lists of "world religions" into which the newly discovered religions of colonized lands would be fitted. In some cases, the categorization of aspects of native cultures as "religions" met with resistance from native elites. Hindus in India, Shintos in Japan, and Confucianists in China refused the label "religion" while Western scholars insisted on it. A whole wave of scholarship — ignored by the religion-and-violence types — has been telling this story for decades now. The very titles of the books — Tomoko Masuzawa's *The Invention of World Religions,* Daniel Dubuisson's *The Western Construction of Religion,* Derek Peterson and Darren Walhof's *The Invention of Religion*[14] — indicate that the religious/secular distinction is not transhistorical and transcultural, but an artifact of European power.

In chapter 3 of *The Myth of Religious Violence,* I apply this genealogy to the so-called Wars of Religion in Europe in the sixteenth and seventeenth centuries, which are commonly used to justify the necessity of the Western secular state. Protestants and Catholics were killing each other over religious difference, so the story goes, so religion had to be relegated to the private realm by the peacemaking secular state. I begin to question this story by addressing the obvious fact that Catholics and Protestants often fought on the same side in the so-called religious wars; Catholics killed Catholics and Protestants killed Protestants. To cite only one of the forty-some examples I cite in the book, Cardinal Richelieu brought Catholic France into the Thirty Years' War on the

13. Smith, *Meaning and End,* pp. 55-56, 64-65; quote at p. 56.

14. Tomoko Masuzawa, *The Invention of World Religions: Or, How European Universalism Was Preserved in the Language of Pluralism* (Chicago: University of Chicago Press, 2005); Daniel Dubuisson, *The Western Construction of Religion: Myths, Knowledge, and Ideology,* trans. William Sayers (Baltimore: Johns Hopkins University Press, 2003); Derek R. Peterson and Darren R. Walhof, eds., *The Invention of Religion: Rethinking Belief in Politics and History* (New Brunswick, N.J.: Rutgers University Press, 2002).

side of the Lutheran Swedes, and the last half of the war was largely a battle between the two great Catholic dynasties of Europe. Something more than doctrinal zealotry was clearly going on, but I do not argue that the wars were really political or economic and not religious. The very distinction between religious and political or religious and economic was what was at stake in the wars; those distinctions were being invented as a consequence of the so-called Wars of Religion, which José Casanova says are more accurately called "the wars of early modern European state formation."[15] In chapter 3 I marshal three hundred footnotes' worth of evidence that the rise of the state was a primary cause of — not solution to — the so-called Wars of Religion.

If the myth of religious violence and religious war is so incoherent and inaccurate, why is it so prevalent? Because it is useful for the promotion of certain interests; this is my argument in the fourth and final chapter. In general, the myth of religious violence promotes the idea that our Western way of marginalizing "religion" from public power is necessary to save us from mayhem. In domestic life, I examine the Supreme Court's use of the myth of religious violence since the 1940s to ban practices like school prayer, subsidies for parochial school teachers, remedial public education on parochial school grounds, etc. Until the 1940s the Supreme Court cited religion as a unifying force in American society; since the 1940s, religion has been seen by the Court as a divisive and dangerous force, at the precise time of American history when tensions between denominations are at their lowest levels. The myth of religious violence is not a response to empirical reality but a just-so tale told to justify secularizing arrangements.

In foreign policy, the myth is used similarly to draw a sharp line between our benevolent and peaceful social order and the social orders of the religious fanatics over there — Muslims especially — who have not learned to tame the passions of religion in public. I examine various arguments that use the myth of religious violence to justify secular violence. We must spread the benefits of liberal social orders, by force if necessary. And force will often be necessary, precisely because of the irrationality of people who still think that religion has a place in the public sphere. So the story goes.

15. José Casanova, "Eurocentric Secularism and the Challenge of Globalization," *Innsbrucker Diskussionspapiere zu Weltordnung, Religion und Gewalt;* http://www.uibk.ac.at/plattform-wrg/idwrg/idwrg_25.pdf.

If there is a simple way to sum up the thesis of the book, it is this: people kill for all sorts of things that they treat as gods, including supposedly "secular" things like "freedom." This insight is no more startling than the biblical critique of idolatry — human beings are spontaneously worshiping creatures whose allegiances fall on all sorts of mundane things. The point is not at all to deny that Christians and Muslims, for example, sometimes use their faith as justification for violence; the point is to level the playing field, so that we examine not just violence on behalf of *jihad* or Jesus, but violence on behalf of free markets and free elections.

II. Responses to Critiques

I would like now to carry the conversation beyond my book and respond to some of the commentary that has appeared on my work on religion and violence. Two years before the book appeared in print, I published a précis of the argument in the *Harvard Divinity Bulletin*. Mark Juergensmeyer responded in a letter to the editor, writing that "it strikes me as odd that William Cavanaugh, in recent pages of the *Harvard Divinity Bulletin*, would describe as 'the conventional wisdom' something that few thoughtful persons would allege — that 'religion causes violence.' Odder still that his target would include me." According to Juergensmeyer, his own work on what he calls "the undeniable rise of religious violence in our times" argues not that religion is the problem, but that it is problematic. That is, religion is often not the cause of conflict, but exacerbates already-existing conflicts. "The grand narratives of religious scenarios and the absolutism of authoritarian claims buttressed by the religious images of cosmic war are — if not the problem — problematic."[16]

In the opening paragraph of my article I identify the "conventional wisdom" not as the idea that religion causes violence but as the idea that "religion has a dangerous tendency to promote violence."[17] Juer-

<hr/>

16. Mark Juergensmeyer, "Thinking about Religion and Violence," online at www.juergensmeyer.com/files/HDS%20bulletin.doc.

17. William T. Cavanaugh, "Does Religion Cause Violence? Behind the Common Question Lies a Morass of Unclear Thinking," *Harvard Divinity Bulletin* 35, no. 2 & 3 (Spring/Summer 2007); online at http://bulletin.hds.harvard.edu/articles/springsummer2007/does-religion-cause-violence.

gensmeyer's protestations that his voluminous work on "religious violence" shows that religion is not "the problem" but "problematic" make no difference to my argument. Whether "religion" is said to originate or to exacerbate conflicts, there remains a mystifying category of "religion" that is said to have a peculiar tendency to encourage violence. As I show at length in my book, Juergensmeyer undermines the religious/secular distinction while continuing to use "religion" as a peculiar, *sui generis* contributor to violence. The distinction between problem and problematic does not rescue his work on "religious violence" from my critique.

The problem is with the category of religion, or more specifically the religious/secular divide. At least two reviewers have taken my critique of the category of religion to be a functionalist one,[18] despite my disavowals of such a position in my book.[19] Functionalists and substantivists both assume there is something out there called "religion" that is a constant in all human societies across time. What I try to stress is that the religious/secular divide is a modern Western construction, not embedded in the nature of things, but subject to being constructed in different ways for different purposes in different times and places. It would have helped if I had identified my position in the book as "constructivist." Substantivists and functionalists are labeled in my book; I should have labeled my own position to make it clearer.

Constructivism does not mean that there is "no such thing" as religion. Hector Avalos has taken my argument in this way: "If there is no such thing as religion, then it follows that there is no such thing as religious violence."[20] Avalos then mounts several critiques. It is an etymological fallacy, he writes, to think that a word's original usage determines

---

18. Cyril O'Regan, "What Comes after Essentialist Religion?" *Pro Ecclesia* 20, no. 4 (Fall 2011): 342-48; and R. Scott Appleby, "Fire and Sword," *Commonweal* 137, no. 7 (April 9, 2010): 12.

19. William T. Cavanaugh, *The Myth of Religious Violence: Secular Ideology and the Roots of Modern Conflict* (New York: Oxford University Press, 2009), pp. 118-19: "Ultimately, however, functionalist approaches to the question of religion and violence are also unsatisfactory. . . . Functionalist approaches — like substantivist approaches — tend to assume that there really is something out there called religion that is a constant feature in all human societies across time; functionalists just argue for a more expansive definition of what religion really is."

20. Hector Avalos, "Explaining Religious Violence: Retrospects and Prospects," in *The Blackwell Companion to Religion and Violence,* ed. Andrew R. Murphy (Malden, Mass., and Oxford: Wiley-Blackwell, 2011), p. 143.

the way it is used today. He also appeals to a distinction between emic (insider) and etic (outsider) anthropological descriptions of people's behaviors. A descriptive term is not necessarily invalid just because it is not one that the practitioners themselves would use.[21] Religion exists even if premodern or non-Western people did not or do not use the term.

But Avalos has misunderstood my argument. In the text I explicitly disavow the idea that there is "no such thing" as religion.[22] Religion exists, but as a constructed category. The point of my extensive genealogy is not that words cannot change meaning or that outsider descriptions are invalid. The point is that when words do change meaning and when outside observers describe insiders' behavior, there are often acts of power involved that need attention. Modern Westerners have created the religious/secular distinction as an accompaniment to certain shifts in power between ecclesiastical and civil authorities, among other shifts. To impose this lens on other societies — distant in time and/or space — that do not arrange society as we do is not necessarily an innocent act of objective description. The burden of proof lies on anyone who would insist that the modern Western way of distinguishing religious from secular is normative for all times and places, and that the same essence of "religion" underlies all the diverse practices and beliefs of ancient, medieval, and modern peoples the world over.

Avalos goes on to criticize my argument for claiming that there is no difference between "religious violence" and "secular violence" because they have the same results. There is a difference, says Avalos, between murder and accidents, even though both result in death. Avalos contends there is a big difference between the rationales and referents of killing for God and killing for a nation. Nations are empirically verifiable entities with boundaries, but Allah is not verifiable to both religious and nonreligious people.

I do not think, however, that the distinction between verifiable and unverifiable is as neat as Avalos makes it. National borders are empirically verifiable in the same way that churches are; one can see border stations and armed guards in the same way that one can see cathedrals and priests. Nations, however, are no more or less verifiable than God. Nations cannot be seen; nations are contingent products of the collective imagination of citizens, not simply part of nature. But even if,

21. Avalos, "Explaining Religious Violence," p. 144.
22. Cavanaugh, *Myth of Religious Violence*, pp. 59 and 119.

despite long odds, one could construct a religious/secular distinction that followed exactly the unverifiable/verifiable distinction, it would not affect my thesis, which is *not* that there is no difference whatsoever between belief in God and belief in other things, but that people are just as likely to kill for the latter as for the former. Of course, there are differences between Presbyterianism and American nationalism, but the question of whose beliefs are more verifiable is utterly irrelevant to the question of which is more violent.

I gave a talk recently for the political science doctoral students at a prestigious state university. The students and some of the faculty were delighted that religion was finally getting attention there after decades of neglect. I told them they should try to avoid the term "religion," as it just sows confusion, but I realized shortly thereafter that I was wrong to say that. They had worked so hard to get people to take religion seriously, and I come along and say, "Don't talk about it"! We do need to talk about religion, but as a lens, not an object. The categories of religious and secular are a way of seeing the world. I am looking at this cup through my glasses; the religious/secular divide is not the cup, it's the glasses. The only problem with that analogy is that my glasses almost always let me see better, whereas the religious/secular divide is often distorting. The way to talk about religion and the secular is to talk about the work these categories do. A good example is Elizabeth Hurd's book *The Politics of Secularism in International Relations,* which shows how the religious/secular divide often distorts work in her field.[23] I should add that the categories might not always work negatively; departments of religious studies, as incoherent as they are, allow for theology to go on covertly at state universities, which I consider a good.

Several critics have noted the lack of an examination of the term "violence" in the book; I simply state in the introduction that — for the purposes of this book — I assume that "violence" means whatever the "religion-and-violence" theorists take it to mean. But for some this is not sufficient, because if I want to level the playing field, then I seem to be saying that violence itself is the problem. But what counts as violence? Is there never any justified use of "violence" or "force"? Must anyone who accepts my argument be committed to pacifism?[24]

23. Elizabeth Shakman Hurd, *The Politics of Secularism in International Relations* (Princeton: Princeton University Press, 2008).

24. John D. Carlson, "Religion and Violence: Coming to Terms with Terms," in *The*

I avoided addressing these normative questions in this book because they would require another book and because I wished to address a secularist audience that would not share my theological convictions, without which I could not address the normative questions. There certainly remains plenty of need for moral discernment about when, if ever, war, for example, is justifiable. The book's contribution to this discernment is simply to clear away one distorting myth that makes lucid thinking about violence difficult or impossible.

I wrote the book without any overt theology in it to appeal to a secularist audience, but it has not escaped the attention of some that I am in fact a theologian, a fact that is noted on the book's cover and has probably led many to assume that the book is not worth reading. I think that secularist arguments about religion and violence fail on their own terms, and one need have no theological commitments to find my argument convincing. Nevertheless, there is a theological theme running through the book, albeit covertly. The theme is idolatry. I will discuss this theme at greater length in chapter 11. Put briefly for now, the argument of *The Myth of Religious Violence* is that people kill for all sorts of things, things like money and flags and oil and freedom that function as gods in people's lives. This is a basic biblical theme — people are spontaneously idolatrous, which is why the first commandment is what it is. Some commentators have seen the biblical obsession with idolatry as evidence that religion promotes violence; the ban on idolatry is one more symptom of monotheistic intolerance. I think it works exactly the opposite way: the biblical critique of idolatry exposes the notion that so-called religion is more prone to violence than secular ideologies as a myth. People treat all kinds of things as their gods, even their own bellies, as Paul tells the Philippians (3:19). In the very next verse Paul tells them that their citizenship is in heaven, which means it does not belong to any mundane political power.

I have attempted in my book to loosen such mundane loyalties insofar as they promote violence. Of course, loyalties to God or gods can also promote division and violence. A theology of peace needs to be articulated, which I and others attempt elsewhere, in which God requires reconciliation, not blood. In the Christian context, something like what René Girard has attempted will be necessary. But the modest contri-

---

Blackwell Companion to Religion and Violence, pp. 12-14; and A. Alexander Stummvoll, "Demythologising Religious Violence," *European Political Science* 9 (2010): 515-23.

bution of this book is simply to say that so-called religious ideologies and practices are not *essentially* different from supposedly secular ones when it comes to questions of violence and peace.

The most extensive critical engagement with my book that I have seen comes from a theologian, Ephraim Radner, in his 2012 book *A Brutal Unity*. I have great esteem for Radner's work in general, and *A Brutal Unity* contains much of value. Unfortunately, he begins the book by making my work the foil for his own argument that the church's historical failures lead us to the conclusion that "Religion — and I will use the Christian Church and churches as the instance in this chapter — does in fact *need* the liberal state."[25] According to Radner, my argument "encourages religious groups like Christian churches to face away from their own responsibility for violence."[26] It does so, Radner thinks, by shifting the blame for violence away from religion and onto something else. Radner appears to think that my argument is a defense of religion from the charge of violence. Given my deconstruction of the term "religion," I hardly see how I can be seen as either attacking or defending religion as such.

Radner lays out my argument in two mutually contradictory ways, both of which are misreadings of the text. In the first way, he thinks that I argue that so-called religious wars are not really religious but political: "It is erroneous, Cavanaugh argues, to call these conflicts 're-ligious wars' because their impulse was more fundamentally political, driven by territorial interests of various ruling individuals and groups." To make this argument, Radner continues, I "must reduce 'religious' conviction to a sideshow in some other performance. The result is that, in history's most horrendous moments and corridors . . . the world is ironically depicted by Cavanaugh as being at its most disenchanted, the product of political powers and self-interest without reference to faith, because fundamentally unattached to faith's potential perversions."[27]

I have no idea how Radner, alone among reviewers of the book, could have come to this conclusion about my argument. As I state in the introduction to my chapter on the Wars of Religion, "I do not argue that these wars were not really about religion, but were really about pol-

---

25. Ephraim Radner, *A Brutal Unity: The Spiritual Politics of the Christian Church* (Waco: Baylor University Press, 2012), p. 22.

26. Radner, *A Brutal Unity*, p. 22.

27. Radner, *A Brutal Unity*, p. 23.

itics or economics or culture. . . . To make such arguments is to assume that one can readily sort out what is 'religion' from what is 'politics' and so on in Reformation Europe. But these wars were themselves part of the process of creating those very distinctions."[28] As I sum up later in the same chapter, "I think we must conclude that any attempt to assign the cause of the wars in question to 'religion' — as opposed to politics or other 'secular' causes — will get bogged down in hopeless anachronism. The same, of course, is true of attempts to pin the blame on political and economic causes as opposed to religion."[29] The idea, furthermore, that I see the wars in question as political and therefore "disenchanted" is quite simply the opposite of my actual argument. I appeal to John Bossy's depiction of the migration of the holy from the church to the state and argue that "The state was increasingly *sacralized* in the sixteenth and seventeenth centuries."[30] This conclusion follows my argument in the first two chapters of my book about the malleability of the term "religion": "if it is true, as we have seen in chapters one and two, that nationalism exhibits many of the characteristics of 'religion' — including, most importantly for our purposes, the ability to organize killing energies — then what we have in fact is not a separation of religion from politics but rather the substitution of the religion of the state for the religion of the church."[31] The entire burden of my argument is to show that the enchantment that produces violence is just as likely to appear in so-called secular form — such as the putatively secular nation-state — as it is in the so-called religions such as Christianity.

Radner notices my constructivist reading of the term "religion," and so puts forth a second characterization of my argument, one that contradicts the first but is equally mistaken. In this second telling, I do not simply downplay religious factors in favor of political factors leading to violence but claim instead that "if there was, in early modernity, no such thing as 'religion' outside of a culturally integrated social existence in which faith is bound up but not capable of distillation, then there was no such thing as 'religious violence' from which the state could have somehow saved us."[32]

This second way of characterizing my argument is again a misun-

28. Cavanaugh, *Myth of Religious Violence*, p. 124.
29. Cavanaugh, *Myth of Religious Violence*, p. 160.
30. Cavanaugh, *Myth of Religious Violence*, p. 174.
31. Cavanaugh, *Myth of Religious Violence*, p. 177.
32. Radner, *A Brutal Unity*, p. 24.

derstanding that I explicitly disavow in the actual text. As I state in the introduction to chapter 2, "The point of this exercise is *not* to dissolve the problem of religion and violence by saying that religion is a fuzzy concept, so there is no such thing as religion and therefore no such problem of religion and violence."[33] Again: "So, do we conclude that there is no such thing as religion, no coherent concept of religion, and therefore we need not bother with the question of religion and violence? No. The point is not that there is 'no such thing' as religion. The concepts that we use do not simply refer to things out there in a one-to-one correspondence of words with things. In certain cultures, religion *does* exist, but as a product of human construction."[34]

If my goal is not simply to excuse religion of violence by dissolving the category of religion, what is my purpose in showing that the category is a modern Western construction and not simply embedded in the nature of things? With regard to the early modern period, the point is that to blame religion as opposed to politics is anachronistic, because there was not yet any such distinction. The point is not that Christianity was not involved; of course it was. The point is that one cannot finger a transhistorical, transcultural human impulse "religion" that — as opposed to more "secular" and mundane pursuits — was the main cause of the conflicts. The European wars of the early modern period were fought by Christians, and Radner is right that this outburst of brutality marks a signal failure of the church to be an instantiation of Christ's peace. This is beyond dispute. As I state in the chapter on the Wars of Religion,

> The point of this again is *not* that these wars were really about politics and not about religion, or that the state is to blame and the church is innocent of the violence. If the transfer of power from church to state contributed to the upheavals of the sixteenth and seventeenth centuries, that transfer generally took the form of the absorption of the church into the apparatus of the state. The church was of course deeply implicated in the violence of the sixteenth and seventeenth centuries. The point is that the rise of the modern state was not the solution to the violence of "religion."[35]

33. Cavanaugh, *Myth of Religious Violence*, p. 59.
34. Cavanaugh, *Myth of Religious Violence*, p. 119.
35. Cavanaugh, *Myth of Religious Violence*, p. 166.

Radner thinks that eliminating religion as an independent cause of early modern war leaves me unable to account for the "motivating conceptual structures of meaning to legitimize it."[36] He cites renowned historian Brad Gregory's work as arguing "against historians who would dampen the specifically religious meaning given to both the active murdering and passive victimization involved."[37] Gregory's acclaimed book *Salvation at Stake* does indeed argue against those who would reduce the violence of early modern Europe to political or economic or social causes as opposed to religious ones.[38] But in Gregory's review of *The Myth of Religious Violence*, he calls the book a *"tour de force"* and writes, "The book should become a classic." I mention this not merely to brag but to show that Gregory understands, as Radner does not, that my argument and Gregory's own do not contradict one another. Gregory writes that "[Cavanaugh] correctly notes the inseparability of religion from politics and society in the sixteenth and seventeenth centuries. Hence, one cannot, for example, say that a Catholic Eucharistic procession was religious *rather than* political or social — unless one applies, anachronistically, a conception of religion that itself arose only as a rejection of the human realities it sought to refashion."[39] Radner seems to think that I reject any analysis of early modern violence from a theological perspective,[40] but I don't at all deny that there was a particular kind of violence bound up with, to stick with Gregory's example, theological loci such as the Eucharist. What I deny is that such kinds of violence belong in a wholly different category — "religious violence" — than violence done in the name of the state, the nation, capitalism, and other supposedly "secular" causes. This is precisely because such causes are not "disenchanted" at all, but are rather prone to idolatry, the worship of false gods.

With regard to not only the early modern period but also the pres-

36. Radner, *A Brutal Unity*, p. 41.

37. Radner, *A Brutal Unity*, p. 42.

38. Brad S. Gregory, *Salvation at Stake: Christian Martyrdom in Early Modern Europe* (Cambridge: Harvard University Press, 1999).

39. Brad S. Gregory, "Pacifying Violence," *First Things*, May 2010; http://www.firstthings.com/article/2010/05/pacifying-violence.

40. For example, Radner, *A Brutal Unity*, p. 45: "If invoking the name of God in the physical 'extirpation of heretics' cannot be analyzed from a specifically *theological* perspective, both in terms of the object and in terms of the judgments one makes about the object, we have simply imprisoned theological discourse itself."

ent day, Radner feels he "must respond pointedly," against me, "that *there is such a thing as religious violence:* when people abuse, imprison, drive out, attack, maim, and kill others in the name of God."[41] Radner argues that my approach renders me unable to deal with the church's complicity in violence in Rwanda. But I have never denied that people kill in the name of God or gods, nor am I so oblivious or mendacious to deny that "Christians act violently; many do so, claiming to do so *as* Christians, for the sake of their belief in God."[42] What I deny is that violence in the name of God or a god is of an essentially different and inherently more troublesome nature than violence in the name of supposedly more mundane realities like kings or nations or flags or freedom or oil. I do not buy Radner's contention that, "when Christians turn violent, their violence is of another order than the violence of the nations."[43] I make exhaustive arguments in the first two chapters of the book as to why attempts to claim that religious and secular violence are of fundamentally different orders fail, arguments that Radner does not so much refute as ignore. He occasionally throws scare quotes around the word "religion," but continues to use it as if it marked a self-evident category of which Christianity is a prime example, as if my extensively annotated genealogy of the concept has had no effect whatsoever.

With regard to the present day, the point of showing that the religious/secular divide is a constructed one, and not simply part of the way things are, is to put both "secular" and "religious" motivations for abusing, imprisoning, driving out, attacking, maiming, and killing others in the same analytical framework. As I write in the conclusion of the book, the point is "to level the playing field so that violence of all kinds is subject to the same scrutiny."[44] The myth of religious violence has drawn our attention to certain kinds of violence — labeled religious — and away from others — labeled secular. But the reality is that "People kill for all kinds of reasons. An adequate approach to the problem must begin with empirical investigations into the conditions under which beliefs and practices such as jihad, the invisible hand of the market, the sacrificial atonement of Christ, and the role of the United States as worldwide liberator turn violent."[45]

41. Radner, *A Brutal Unity,* p. 22.
42. Radner, *A Brutal Unity,* p. 48.
43. Radner, *A Brutal Unity,* p. 29.
44. Cavanaugh, *Myth of Religious Violence,* p. 230.
45. Cavanaugh, *Myth of Religious Violence,* p. 56.

Radner thinks my attempt to redirect our attention is an attempt to ignore Christian complicity with violence. He writes, "What Cavanaugh and contemporary antiliberal revisionists do not address, then, is the fact that the notion of religious tolerance over and against religious violence was later overthrown by the ongoing and spectacular failures of *Christians* especially in the midst of and in the face of violence in which they participated."[46] But my attempt to draw attention to the violence of the nation-state — especially, in the fourth chapter of my book, the United States — is an attempt to draw attention to what Christians actually kill for. The nation-state is not *them;* it is *us,* us Christians. The 80 percent of Americans who self-identify as Christians is mirrored in the almost 80 percent of U.S. military personnel who self-identify as Christians. Any critique of the violence of the American military would have to take this obvious fact into consideration. As I write in chapter 1, "For most American Christians, even public evangelization is considered to be in poor taste, and yet most would take for granted the necessity of being willing to kill for one's country, should circumstances dictate."[47] I simply do not see how my argument can be construed as an attempt to ignore or excuse Christian complicity with violence. I am trying to call attention to what Christians today, here and now, actually kill for. It is telling that the examples of Christian violence to which Radner appeals — the European wars of the sixteenth and seventeenth centuries and the 1994 genocide in Rwanda — are remote in either time or space to the actual audience of his book and their context in North American liberal states. This is so necessarily because Christians in the North American context today don't kill for *anything but* the liberal nation-state, with very few exceptions. It is of course reprehensible that Christians in early modern Europe or contemporary Rwanda should kill each other, and especially troublesome for the church when they should invoke theological reasons in so doing. But I am interested in what Christians are tempted to kill for *here* and *now.* Some Christians in the United States use theological justifications for supporting war. More commonly, Christians support war for the same secularist reason that Americans as a whole support war: for "freedom," a freedom that was born out of revulsion to the so-called religious wars. As I write in the introduction to my book, "In the West, revulsion to killing and dying

46. Radner, *A Brutal Unity,* p. 55.
47. Cavanaugh, *Myth of Religious Violence,* p. 56.

in the name of one's 'religion' is one of the principal means by which we become convinced that killing and dying in the name of the nation-state is laudable and proper."[48]

This is where the real disagreement between Radner and me lies. We do not disagree about the complicity of Christians and Christianity in violence. We disagree on the extent to which Christians need to throw our grateful support behind the nation-states in which we find ourselves. For Radner, "it is appropriate to see the rise of the 'state' in a modern sense as but the particular definition of a more general peace-building political sovereignty whose origins and quite robust analogues are deeply rooted in Christian experience."[49] The "right answer" to "preventing or resisting violence," according to Radner, is "that churches must reorient their practice more fully, not less so, to the needs of a stable and accountable liberal democracy."[50] Radner fears that my "concerns over the liberal state's attitudes to religion and Christianity in particular will join with an outright rejection of the liberal state's intrinsic value."[51] Christians must face the hard task of full participation in pluralistic democracy, which is "the necessary means by which, as it were, churches will save their souls in the face of their own violent complicities. And any call away from the facing of this task is a dangerous distraction."[52]

Here we are getting close to some real disagreements between Radner and me, but it must first be said that Radner overstates the case I make in *The Myth of Religious Violence*. The argument is certainly a call for Christians to take a more skeptical view of their own participation in, and support for, the military adventures of secular nation-states, especially the United States. The argument is not, however, a wholesale dismissal of liberalism or democracy. As I write at the end of chapter 3,

> To say that the foundational myth of the wars of religion is false is not to say that liberal principles are therefore false; the separation of church and state is, to my mind, important to uphold for several reasons, some of them theological. It is to say, however, that the triumphalist narrative that sees the liberal state as the solution to the violence of religion needs

48. Cavanaugh, *Myth of Religious Violence*, pp. 4-5.
49. Radner, *A Brutal Unity*, p. 54.
50. Radner, *A Brutal Unity*, p. 55.
51. Radner, *A Brutal Unity*, p. 22.
52. Radner, *A Brutal Unity*, p. 56.

to be abandoned. . . . The shift from church power to state power is not the victory of peaceable reason over irrational religious violence. The more we tell ourselves it is, the more we are capable of ignoring the violence we do in the name of reason and freedom.[53]

The negative task of loosening our lethal allegiance to the nation-state and its enormous military and security apparatus is the sole direct aim of my book.

Were I to give a more positive and theological account of the church's political engagement, as I have done elsewhere, I would begin by differentiating among terms like "state," "liberalism," and "democracy," terms that tend to be conflated in Radner's critique. To be fair, I have not always differentiated between them carefully in my own writings. What I have tried to articulate, however, is a type of political presence of the church that is, like Radner, grateful that the church has been separated — often against its misguided will — from coercive power, but deeply dissatisfied with the power that now claims a God-like monopoly on violence. I have written in favor of pluralistic democracy,[54] but the problem with the contemporary nation-state is that it is neither sufficiently democratic nor pluralistic. The mythos of the nation and the reach of the state have created a unitary and homogenized space that is not truly pluralistic, and democracy has been reduced to a caricature. In Sheldon Wolin's words, "The citizen is shrunk to the voter: periodically courted, warned, and confused but otherwise kept at a distance from actual decision-making and allowed to emerge only ephemerally in a cameo appearance according to a script composed by the opinion takers/makers."[55] My vision of the church's participation in politics would look more like Wolin's "fugitive democracy" — which I discussed in chapter 7 — or Alasdair MacIntyre's vision of communities of discernment than the patriotic embrace of the American nation-state with its bloated war machine, enhanced interrogation techniques, NSA surveillance, and the rest.

I suspect that there is much here on which Ephraim Radner and I could have a serious conversation, agreeing and disagreeing on many

53. Cavanaugh, *Myth of Religious Violence*, p. 179.

54. William T. Cavanaugh, *Migrations of the Holy: God, State, and the Political Meaning of the Church* (Grand Rapids: Eerdmans, 2011), chaps. 2 and 9.

55. Sheldon Wolin, *Politics and Vision: Continuity and Innovation in Western Political Thought,* expanded ed. (Princeton: Princeton University Press, 2004), p. 565.

different aspects of the church's role as witness. Radner comments, "Cavanaugh's overriding worries are proving well founded, as the liberal state itself betrays its founding principles for the sake of a self-consciously 'godless' ideology that increasingly itself engages the rhetoric of violence."[56] For my part, I am deeply appreciative of Radner's emphasis on the need for the church to repent. Indeed, I have drawn on Radner's work elsewhere to argue that the basis of the church's aversion to violence of all kinds is not a sense that we are pure, but rather that we are simply not good enough to use violence rightly.[57] I take up this theme again in the final chapter of the present book.

With regard to the notion that I encourage churches to face away from responsibility for violence, I think Radner has simply misread my argument. Our true disagreement, and the place for a more interesting dialogue, is over Radner's contention that the church "does in fact *need* the liberal state."[58] I think I am willing to agree that the marginalization of the church from public power is a potentially restorative punishment for the church's unfaithfulness. I tend, however, to see the liberal nation-state in which I live as just another form of empire that the church must creatively engage, rather than a peace-building fruit of the gospel.

In the next chapter, I consider another defense of liberal polity based on the myth of religious violence.

56. Radner, *A Brutal Unity*, p. 55.

57. See Cavanaugh, *Migrations of the Holy*, pp. 141-69. At the end of this chapter, I appeal to Radner's book *The End of the Church: A Pneumatology of Christian Division in the West* (Grand Rapids: Eerdmans, 1998).

58. Radner, *A Brutal Unity*, p. 22.

CHAPTER TEN

POLITICAL THEOLOGY AS THREAT

I SOMETIMES DESCRIBE MY field of specialization as "political theology." In the eyes of some, this marks me as a dangerous man. Political theology is itself considered a threat in some circles, a bane to human civilization. Especially since prominent terror attacks in Western countries signaled the beginning of the twenty-first century, political theology has often been held in contempt. For many observers, the rise of fundamentalism is especially worrisome because of the volatile mixture of politics with theology. Anytime the merely mundane questions of how to organize a society politically get sidetracked by supramundane questions of the will and law of God — so the story goes — the irrationality and transcendence-seeking passions of religion can only lead to confrontation and chaos. Combining politics with theology is like dropping bullets into the cup of the raving lunatic on the street corner.

Letters to the editor and op-ed pieces commonly treat some version of this story as obvious. They are encouraged by polemics from the "new atheists," Christopher Hitchens, Sam Harris, Richard Dawkins, and the like. Rather than address the idea of political theology as a threat in its crude form, however, I would like to take it in its most sophisticated form, and examine the much-discussed argument of Mark Lilla in his book *The Stillborn God: Religion, Politics, and the Modern West*. Lilla is professor of humanities at Columbia University, a learned and thoughtful scholar. His book has won acclaim in part because it straddles academic and lay audiences. It is entertaining, lucid, and organized around a central metaphor — the "Great Separation" — that provides easy access to the central claim of the book. What is being separated in the Great Separation is precisely "politics" and "theology." And Lilla thinks that separation is a good and necessary thing.

In the first two sections of this chapter, I unpack Lilla's argument, paying particular attention to his use of the term "religion" and its relationship with politics. In the next two sections, I critique his argument and show that the Great Separation is both a historical myth and theoretically incoherent. There is no reason to suppose that "religious" politics are any more inherently dangerous than "secular" politics, because — as I argued in the last chapter — there is no *essential* difference between the two. The religious/secular distinction is not simply a universal fact about human life, but is itself an ideological tool that can be used to privilege certain kinds of politics and anathematize others.

I. The Great Separation

Lilla begins his book by speaking in the name of "we." We had thought that the battles over revelation and dogmatic purity were relics of the past, but we now find ourselves confronted by enemies who take this sort of thing with deadly seriousness. "We are disturbed and confused. We find it incomprehensible that theological ideas still inflame the minds of men, stirring up messianic passions that leave societies in ruin. We assumed that this was no longer possible, that human beings had learned to separate religious questions from political ones, that fanaticism was dead. We were wrong" (p. 3).[1] Exactly who this "we" is, is unspecified, other than the occasional "we in the West." The assumption seems to be, however, that all of "us" are equally puzzled by the persistence of political theology, which puts me and many readers of the present book in the peculiar place of not recognizing ourselves as part of the "we." "Political theology is a primordial form of human thought" (pp. 3-4), Lilla tells us, and "we in the West find it difficult to understand the enduring attraction of political theology" (p. 4). We are separated from political theology by four centuries of political thought that has had no need of reference to the divine. "We live, so to speak, on the other shore. When we observe civilizations on the opposite bank, we are puzzled, since we have only a distant memory of what it was like to think as they do" (p. 4).

1. Mark Lilla, *The Stillborn God: Religion, Politics, and the Modern West* (New York: Knopf, 2007). References to this book have been placed in the text.

The book appears to open, then, with a rather stark separation between Lilla and his friends in Manhattan, reading the *New York Times* over an espresso macchiato, and me and my friends, who are still drawing pictures of bison on cave walls. But Lilla claims to be more nuanced than this. He casts his argument as a corrective to Western triumphalism, chiding those who complacently assume that secularization is simply the fate of all humanity, discovered first in the West but a historical inevitability as sure as the eventual triumph of science over obscurantism of all kinds. Lilla sets himself against such quasi-eschatological accounts of modernity (pp. 5, 305-6). "[I]t is we who are different, not they" (p. 5), says Lilla. Most of the world throughout most of history has seen politics and theology as inseparable. We are the odd ones who have undertaken this fragile experiment in separating the two. And there is nothing historically inevitable about it; the Great Separation is the result of some thoroughly contingent responses to problems that uniquely plagued Christian Europe. Lilla has in fact taken heat from sympathetic critics like Christopher Hitchens[2] and Rebecca Goldstein, who think he has conceded too much on this point. As Goldstein puts it, "Lilla offers a cogent explanation for why Christian Europe got to the Enlightenment first. It doesn't follow that the Enlightenment's solution to the political problems religion universally poses is not a thing to be universally recommended."[3]

Lilla claims in his introduction that his "book contains no revelations about the hidden course of history, identifies no dragons to be slain, has nothing to celebrate or promote, and offers no plan of action" (pp. 12-13). Despite his attempts to appear evenhanded and nonnormative, however, it is hard to read the book as anything but a sophisticated endorsement of the idea of the Great Separation. Lilla has more to promote than the normative conclusion that we must recognize the contingency of the Great Separation. As Goldstein comments, "One can read Lilla's story and draw precisely the opposite normative conclusions from the ones he asks us to draw: that the West's experimental testing and retesting of political theology, trying to see if there is any safe way

2. Christopher Hitchens, "God's Still Dead: Lilla Doesn't Give Us Enough Credit for Shaking Off the Divine," *Slate*, August 20, 2007; http://www.slate.com/articles/news _and_politics/fighting_words/2007/08/gods_still_dead.html.

3. Rebecca Newberger Goldstein, "The Political and the Divine," *New York Times*, September 16, 2007; http://www.nytimes.com/2007/09/16/books/review/Goldstein -t.html?pagewanted=all.

of mixing politics and religion, has delivered an answer from which all may learn."[4] Indeed, it seems fairly obvious that this is the lesson that Lilla wants the reader to draw. Lilla's very attempt to present us as different — ours as a fragile experiment — exudes a definite Western exceptionalism that any reasonably alert reader would find hard to miss, and it is a short step from such exceptionalism to recommending our path as the ideal for all.

Lilla tries hard not to say that all other civilizations must follow our path. The choice, he says, is not between "the West and the rest," quoting Samuel Huntington's contentious phrase. The choice is rather between "two ways of envisaging the human condition. We must be clear about those alternatives, choose between them, and live with the consequences of our choice. That *is* the human condition" (p. 13). There are only two choices, and there are "real dangers in trying to forge a third way between them" (p. 307). Regardless of what is wise for other civilizations, Lilla makes clear what "we in the West" have chosen: "We have chosen to keep our politics unilluminated by the light of revelation" (p. 309). This choice to reject political theology apparently encompasses all of "us" in the West, and it is total and irrevocable. Lilla has written a scathing dismissal of historian Brad Gregory's book *The Unintended Reformation* for its argument that the secularization of the West and the withering of Christianity as a public reality were not inevitable, that a world where theology mingles with politics and economics and science was not and is not impossible in the West.[5] For Lilla there can be no compromise and no plurality of types of politics; we have made our choice against political theology, and it is the only road open to us now.

The first chapter of Lilla's book presents Christian political theology as a worthy but inherently unstable way of approaching political life. Since time immemorial people have engaged in political theology, and the kind of politics it rendered depended on the kind of God that was worshiped. The immanent God of pantheism, the absent God of Gnosticism, and the transcendent God of theism each produced a certain stable kind of political order. The Christian God, however, destabilized

---

4. Goldstein, "The Political and the Divine."

5. Mark Lilla, "Blame It on the Reformation," *New Republic,* September 14, 2012; http://www.newrepublic.com/article/books-and-arts/magazine/107211/wittenberg-wal-mart?page=0,0; Brad S. Gregory, *The Unintended Reformation: How a Religious Revolution Secularized Society* (Cambridge: Harvard University Press, 2012).

political order, because the transcendent Hebrew God became immanent in Jesus, and then, after his ascension, reigned *in absentia* like the
Gnostic God. Different Christian schools of political thought stressed
one or another of these attributes of God, leading to irreconcilable and
conflicting political theologies (pp. 24-35). Unlike Islam, Christianity
was never directly political, and so Christian political thinking in the
Middle Ages was a confused grab bag of metaphors and images.

> Withdrawal into monasticism, ruling the earthly city with the two
> swords of church and state, building the messianic New Jerusalem —
> which is the true model of Christian politics? For over a millennium
> Christians themselves could not decide, and this tension was the source
> of almost unremitting struggle and conflict, much of it doctrinal, pit-
> ting believer against believer over the very meaning of Christian rev-
> elation. . . . All politics involves conflict, but what set Christian politics
> apart was the theological self-consciousness and intensity of the con-
> flicts it generated — conflicts rooted in the deepest ambiguities of Chris-
> tian revelation. (pp. 51-52)

Lilla goes on to say that these conflicts "reached a crisis in the Protestant Reformation and the bloody religious wars that followed" (p. 52),
but he has inflated the usual tale of liberalism born in the sixteenth- and
seventeenth-century Wars of Religion by tracing this crisis back to the
nature of Christian political theology itself. But this is not enough; the
Wars of Religion become a verdict, not only on Christian political theology, but also on the combination of religion and politics — political
theology — as such: "Hanging in the balance was the very legitimacy of
the primordial form of argument that has existed since the beginnings
of civilization, and that we have called political theology. The crisis in
Christian politics was the trigger of a much larger intellectual crisis with
implications extending far beyond a few European kingdoms" (p. 53).

Despite his claims to his argument's contingency and modesty, then,
Lilla raises the stakes well beyond contingent events in European history to a general argument about the possibility of any politics that takes
theology seriously; hence the stark choice he offers us. The brevity and
sketchiness of his one chapter on Christian political theology leave the
reader with the distinct impression that he was never really very interested in — or knowledgeable about — the details of Christian theology.
Lilla never attempts any historical account of the "unremitting struggle

and conflict" over doctrine that supposedly characterizes the whole of the medieval period, nor does he explain how such conflicts resulted in violence. How and where exactly did arguments over Christology and the Trinity lead to war? How and where exactly did the "withdrawal into monasticism" spark conflict with other models of Christian politics? There was unquestionably a great deal of conflict and violence in medieval Christendom, and there was undoubtedly a diversity of political theologies, but Lilla provides no evidence that the latter was the cause of the former. At this point of the argument, innuendo suffices to establish the "greatest lesson" of Christian history: "that entering into the logic of political theology in any form inevitably leads into a dead end" (p. 54). The six subsequent chapters of the book, which — unlike the first — are quite detailed and lie within Lilla's area of expertise, map the attempts of modern political philosophers to escape political theology once and for all.

II. Religion and Politics

Significantly, when Lilla turns to discussing the philosophers who pioneered the Great Separation, he talks about "religion." The Bible, Lilla points out, is silent about religion. There is no attempt in the Bible to explain why "man" is religious, what the varieties of religious experience are, and so on. The Bible has no conception of religion as a characteristic of human beings in general. The other "religions" of the world are explained in terms of idolatry; there is the worship of the true God, and there is the worship of false gods, but they do not together fit under the general rubric of human religious behavior (pp. 66-69). Thomas Hobbes and other early modern thinkers, however, began to examine religion as a universal human phenomenon. This, for Lilla, is a decisive breakthrough. Early modern Stoics were not merely interested in Christian theological-political struggles. According to Lilla, they wanted to answer "the deeper question: what is it about religion that allows it to be distorted and misused in this way?" Hobbes similarly began with questioning the nature of religion as such, but he thought that the Stoics' ideas about religion were too optimistic. The relationship between religion and violence was not accidental, according to Hobbes, but embedded in the very nature of religion.

Lilla's Hobbes is an unambiguously anti-Christian thinker intent on destroying the Christian conception of humans as made in God's image.[6] The subject of theology is not God but man. Religion is born of human desire and ignorance. Humans have desires they do not know how to satisfy, so they turn in fear to gods for solace. But solace soon turns into fear of God. Because of their ignorance, they turn to prophets and priests to discern God's will, but the prophets and priests, also being ignorant, disagree. "A bidding war for souls gets under way, frenzy takes hold among believers intoxicated by bizarre superstitions and fanatical, intolerant claims" (p. 84). The resulting violence is so difficult to contain because the stakes are so high: eternal life or eternal damnation. As Lilla puts it, "men fight to get into heaven" (p. 85). Hobbes's solution was to establish the complete authority of one political sovereign, "the earthly God," who would swallow Christianity into a civil religion to serve the good order of the state.

For Lilla, Hobbes's system is not a political theology, despite the overtly theological terms in which Hobbes writes of his ideal sovereign. According to Lilla, we need not accept the absolutist implications of Hobbes's politics nor Hobbes's extremely negative view of religion to appreciate Hobbes's accomplishment in "successfully changing the subject of Western political discourse." Hobbes has pointed the way out of the "labyrinth" of political theology. From now on, we can "discuss religion and the common good without making reference to the nexus between God, man, and world. The very fact that we think and speak in terms of 'religion,' rather than of the true faith, the law, or the revealed way, is owing in large measure to Hobbes" (p. 88).

"Religion," and its relationship to politics, is the subject of the rest of Lilla's book. Lilla works his way through some other canonical figures of Western philosophy and shows that, although subsequent figures had a more sanguine view of religion, Hobbes had successfully changed the subject from God to religion as a human phenomenon. "By the nineteenth century continental Europe would be awash in nostalgia for its religious past and in dreams of a new, improved religious future. Not

6. This reading of Hobbes is contentious, to say the least. I think a more plausible reading shows Hobbes to be a sincere, if grumpy and idiosyncratic, Calvinist Christian. Such a reading would, among other gains, help explain why Hobbes devotes over half of *Leviathan* to close scriptural exegesis. For a Christian Hobbes, see A. P. Martinich, *The Two Gods of* Leviathan: *Thomas Hobbes on Religion and Politics* (Cambridge: Cambridge University Press, 1992), and Matthew Rose, "Hobbes as Political Theologian," *Political Theology* 14, no. 1 (February 2013).

because Europeans had shifted their orientation back again, to the God of Abraham and his Messiah, but because so many had come to feel that the modern Epicureans had not given religion its due as a human phenomenon" (p. 108). Here "Europeans" seems not to mean the 90-some percent of Europeans who considered themselves Christians in the nineteenth century, but rather the philosophers from that era that Lilla likes to read. Rousseau and Kant, for example, pointed in different ways to a post-Christian moral religion that was based not on revelation but on the workings of the human mind. Unlike Hobbes, who hoped that religion would fade to political irrelevance, Rousseau and Kant thought that religion was a universal human impulse that must be harnessed for the sake of a well-functioning social order (p. 159). Hegel similarly located religion in the human mind, but went further in advocating a grand mythology of shared spirit that would serve as the basis of service to the state. This latter line of thinking was born of the Great Separation that Hobbes made possible, but for the "children of Rousseau," as Lilla calls them, religion itself was not the problem. Christian political theology needed to be abandoned in favor of a religion purified by reason that would serve as a foundation for the political order (pp. 218-20).

Though Lilla is sympathetic with these attempts to treat religion as something more than just the combination of ignorance and fear, ultimately he thinks that they undermined the Great Separation. They are based on "the fantasy that politics could still be connected to the grand themes of biblical faith . . . without jeopardizing the principles of the Great Separation" (pp. 299-300). The children of Rousseau may have been right that religion can sustain hope and build community. "But as that lesson was learned, another was lost — that religion can also express darker fears and desires, that it can destroy community by dividing its members, that it can inflame the mind with destructive apocalyptic fantasies of immediate redemption" (p. 260). The children of Rousseau opened the door for the recrudescence of political theology in the nineteenth and twentieth centuries, first in the form of German liberal theology, and then in the form of Karl Barth's and Franz Rosenzweig's reactions against liberal theology. Liberal theology tried to unite orthodox biblical theology with the romantic glorification of community, resulting in a thoroughly accommodationist nationalism; "in the end this liberal theology did what all political theologies eventually do: it sanctified the present, putting God's seal of approval on the modern

European state" (p. 300). Barth and Rosenzweig reacted against liberal theology's idolatry and emphasized the transcendence of God, the eschatological breaking in of God in history, and the necessity of human decision to follow God's commands. Lilla acknowledges that Barth and Rosenzweig did not think of redemption in political terms, and he recognizes Barth's role in forming the Confessing Church to resist the Nazi regime. Nevertheless, Lilla thinks that the theological discourse of "shock," "crisis," "decision," and so forth that Barth and Rosenzweig created was easily appropriated by the false messianism of Nazism.

> The generation that Karl Barth's *Romans* helped to form had no taste for compromise with the culture that their liberal teachers celebrated and that committed suicide in the Great War. They wanted to confront the unknown God, the "wholly other," the *deus absconditus*. They wanted to live in the paradox, feel the eschatological tension embedded in creation. They longed to inhabit a chiaroscuro world of "either-or," not "yes, but." They wanted to experience the moment of absolute decision and to have that decision determine the whole of their existence. Well! They did experience it. (p. 285)

And it is here that Lilla chooses to end his story; Hitler is the face of political theology reborn. The last two figures Lilla introduces in the book are Friedrich Gogarten and Ernst Bloch. The former is a friend of Barth who turned propagandist for the Nazis, the latter an atheist who used biblical rhetoric to support Stalinism. The successors to Barth and Rosenzweig, according to Lilla, "fueled by messianic expectation and cultural despair, brought the modern Western argument over religion and politics to an inglorious close, by returning it to where it began" (p. 278). Where it began, of course, is in the violence and despotism of religion that Hobbes had sought to escape by making the Great Separation between religion and politics.

III. What Is Political Theology?

So a book that "identifies no dragons to be slain" ends by playing the Hitler card. This strikes me as both disingenuous and grossly unfair. To insinuate that Karl Barth, one of the most significant Christian critics of Nazism, is somehow implicated in the rise of Nazism indicates a prejudgment that one simply cannot distinguish false gods from the true one, a judgment Barth himself would have considered both blasphemous and stupid. To end the story of political theology in the 1930s is also to ignore the tremendous postwar proliferation of political theologies. To think that "the modern Western argument over religion and politics" ended in World War II is to ignore Dietrich Bonhoeffer, Dorothee Sölle, Johannes Baptist Metz, Gustavo Gutiérrez, Jon Sobrino, Rosemary Radford Ruether, John Howard Yoder, Stanley Hauerwas, and the host of other political theologians who do anything but what Lilla says "all political theologies eventually do": sanctify the present. A book about political theology that claims to be relevant to the present but doesn't cite any political theology written in the last eighty years is not to be taken as the final word on the subject, to put it mildly.

The problem with Lilla's book on political theology goes deeper than his ignorance of political theology; the deeper problem is in identifying what counts as political theology and what does not. Political theology is identified with appealing to God when answering political questions (p. 3), or it appeals "at some point to divine revelation" (p. 307). Throughout much of the book, however, political theology is the bringing together of politics with religion, even when religion is seen as an entirely immanent human phenomenon. And sometimes the net is cast wider, such that not only political theology but "political messianism" or "cosmology" or "larger historical drama" comes under scrutiny. "Only with effort and a great deal of argument can people be trained to separate the basic questions of politics from questions of theology and cosmology. . . . As we have seen throughout this book, the temptation to break the self-imposed limits of the Great Separation and absorb political life into some larger theological or historical drama has been strong in the modern West" (p. 307). Political theology is not just reflection on politics in light of Christian revelation, but also includes Rousseau's and Hegel's slippery-slope constructions of religion without appeals to revelation, Adolf Hitler's political messianism, and the atheist Ernst Bloch's justification of the atheist Stalin's totalitarian regime.

It would help if Lilla would identify what does *not* count as political theology, but — despite Lilla's assurances that "we" are separated by four centuries and a body of water from civilizations on the "other shore" — the only figures in the book that have gotten the Great Separation right are Hobbes, Hume, and Locke. All subsequent history — everything after the eighteenth century — Lilla tells as a story of backsliding into political theology. Besides a few references to "liberal democracy," Lilla gives no real indication of what a purely mundane politics looks like on this side of the Great Separation, as we scratch our heads and marvel at the primitives on the other shore. Lilla even acknowledges that American political language is messianic, but somehow we remain free of the taint of political theology: "Political rhetoric in the United States, for example, is still shot through with messianic language, and it is only thanks to a strong constitutional structure and various lucky breaks that political theology has never managed to dominate the American political mind" (p. 307).

For the Great Separation to be something more than the gap between Politics That Mark Lilla Likes and Politics That Mark Lilla Does Not Like, Lilla must show that a pure politics shorn of dangerous religious passions is a historical reality. He relies on the common legend of the European Wars of Religion of the sixteenth and seventeenth centuries as the moment at which Europeans finally realized that religion needed to be removed from politics for the sake of peace. According to Lilla, this historical moment is when Europeans asked, "Why should disagreements over the Incarnation — or divine grace, or predestination, or heresy, or the sacraments, or the existence of purgatory, or the correct translation of a Greek noun — why should such disagreements threaten the peace and stability of a decent political order?" (p. 58). The problems with this tall tale begin with the fact that no Great Separation resulted from the Wars of Religion. In fact, the 1648 Treaty of Westphalia that brought the wars to a close recognized a Europe dominated by confessional states in which the state presided over established churches. Separation of church and state would not come for another century and a half, and then only on the other side of the Atlantic. Furthermore, the idea that "religion" was to blame for the wars ignores the obvious fact that Catholics and Protestants often collaborated against their own coreligionists. The Thirty Years' War that brought the era to a close was, for its latter and bloodier half, a war between the two great Catholic dynasties of Europe, with Catholic France and Protestant Sweden allied against the Holy Roman Empire. To narrate these wars as a product of quibbling over Greek nouns and not as a result of the state-building process — as "religious" and not "political" — is distorting, if not preposterous.[7]

7. I analyze the myth of the Wars of Religion at length in chapter 3 of my book *The*

In response to critiques of his historical narrative, Lilla has stated that he intended to write only an analytical history of ideas, not a history of actual political transformations.[8] Setting aside the dubious desirability of a history of ideas that floats free of actual political and social and economic history, it is clear that Lilla does in fact make ample claims about how ideas and actual history intersect: Hobbes responds to the Wars of Religion, Barth paves the way for Hitler, and the way "we" are — our contemporary politics — is all about the ideological choice we have made that put us on the opposite shore. Lilla must be able to show that the analytical separation of religion and politics is at least a coherent possibility in history, especially since he claims not only that "we" have made that separation, but that the separation is so decisive that we can scarcely think otherwise.

Lilla's narrative is driven by the idea that "we" have tamed the "messianic passions" that "inflame the minds of men" and "leave societies in ruin" by learning "to separate religious questions from political ones" (p. 3). The notion that religion has a peculiar tendency to promote irrationality and violence is a common liberal trope. As Lilla rightly points out, the first thinkers to examine religion as a universal human phenomenon were early moderns like Hobbes. According to Lilla, such thinkers were thus able to understand religion's peculiar pathologies and isolate religion from politics. But what Lilla does not grasp is that early modern figures like Hobbes did not so much *discover* the religion/politics distinction as *invent* it. Lilla regards the lack of analysis of religion in the Bible and in medieval Christendom as a peculiar form of blindness to one of the most salient and universal aspects of human life. But as I have indicated in chapter 9, the idea that something called "religion" can be separated out from the rest of life — politics, art, economics, social life — is a modern Western invention, not a universal truth about human life. In 1962, Wilfred Cantwell Smith went looking for an equivalent concept to religion in ancient, medieval, and non-Western cultures, and found none: there is in fact no "closely equivalent concept in any culture that has not been influenced by the modern West."[9] In Smith's wake, a host

---

Myth of Religious Violence: Secular Ideology and the Roots of Modern Conflict (New York: Oxford University Press, 2009).

8. See Lilla's response to José Casanova on the Immanent Frame blog, http://blogs .ssrc.org/tif/2007/12/07/the-great-separation/.

9. Wilfred Cantwell Smith, *The Meaning and End of Religion* (New York: Macmillan, 1962), pp. 18-19.

of other scholars have done detailed genealogies of the creation of the concept of religion in Europe and in lands colonized by Europe. Tomoko Masuzawa's book *The Invention of World Religions* concludes: "This concept of religion as a general, transcultural phenomenon, yet also as a distinct sphere in its own right . . . is patently groundless; it came from nowhere, and there is no credible way of demonstrating its factual and empirical substantiality."[10]

Although Lilla acknowledges the historical contingency of the Great Separation, he nevertheless treats religion and politics as two universal phenomena to which there are only two approaches: either combine them or separate them. Lilla sees figures like Hobbes and Locke as the founders of modern Western politics because they are the first to try the latter approach. In reality, however, it was not the problem of religion that produced modern Western politics, but the other way around. Religion as a universal, essentially interior and nonpolitical human impulse was a creation of figures like Hobbes and Locke. By creating religion as an essentially apolitical impulse that springs from the inner psychology of the human individual, the theorists of the Great Separation could claim that church authorities should stick to the care of souls and stay out of the business of government and commercial enterprise. As Brent Nongbri argues in his 2012 book *Before Religion: A History of a Modern Concept,* the new concept of religion was a product of a political move, "*isolating* beliefs about god in a private sphere and *elevating* loyalty to the legal codes of developing nation-states to loyalties to god."[11]

As Nongbri goes on to point out, "These provincial debates among European Christians took on a global aspect since they coincided with European exploration and colonial activities in the Americas, Africa, and elsewhere."[12] Even though local cultures had no separation of "religion" from "politics," the classification of the local culture as a religion served the interests of the colonists well. If "Hinduism," for example, could be seen not as the whole of Indian life, but as a religion, then what it meant to be Indian could be privatized and marginalized from the public business of government and commerce, which was administered by the Brit-

10. Tomoko Masuzawa, *The Invention of World Religions: Or, How European Universalism Was Preserved in the Language of Pluralism* (Chicago: University of Chicago Press, 2005), p. 319.

11. Brent Nongbri, *Before Religion: A History of a Modern Concept* (New Haven: Yale University Press, 2012), p. 6.

12. Nongbri, *Before Religion,* p. 6.

ish colonial authorities. For this and similar reasons, some native scholars in India, China, and Japan objected to the use of the term "religion" to classify the native cultures.[13] This remains the case today. As Richard Cohen points out, contemporary advocates of Hindu nationalism *(Hindutva)* reject the confinement of Hinduism to "religion." "The proponents of Hindutva refuse to call Hinduism a religion precisely because they want to emphasize that Hinduism is more than mere internalized beliefs. It is social, political, economic, and familial in nature."[14]

The point of all this is that the choice with which Lilla presents us — either combine religion and politics or keep them separate — is already rigged in favor of the latter because religion and politics are presented as two essentially separate universal human activities that only subsequently get mixed up together. Lilla acknowledges that most people throughout most of history have assumed that their worship life is inseparable from how society is organized, but he persists in assuming that religion and politics are identifiably distinct universal human phenomena. Lilla presents separating politics from religion as a difficult achievement, something like separating gold from its ore. The consequences are serious. In the West, for example, we speak of the "politicization" of Islam, as if Islam were a religion that was subsequently — and dangerously — mixed with politics. As John Esposito writes, to describe Islam as a religion already marks out Islam as an "abnormal" religion, precisely because it does not conform to the Western standard of religion as essentially apolitical.

> However, the modern notions of religion as a system of belief for personal life and of separation of church and state have become so accepted and internalized that they have obscured past beliefs and practice and have come to represent for many a self-evident and timeless truth. As a result, from a modern secular perspective (a form of "secular fundamentalism"), the mixing of religion and politics is regarded as necessarily abnormal, (departing from the norm), irrational, dangerous, and extremist.[15]

13. See chapter 2 of my book *The Myth of Religious Violence,* and Nongbri, *Before Religion,* chap. 6.

14. Richard S. Cohen, "Why Study Indian Buddhism?" in *The Invention of Religion: Rethinking Belief in Politics and History,* ed. Derek R. Peterson and Darren R. Walhof (New Brunswick, N.J.: Rutgers University Press, 2002), p. 27.

15. John L. Esposito, *The Islamic Threat: Myth or Reality?* 3rd ed. (New York: Oxford University Press, 1999), p. 258.

IV. Religious and Secular

The claim that religion is a modern Western invention seems odd because religion in the West has been presented as having to do with the worship of God or gods, and such worship has been present in many cultures ancient and modern, Western and non-Western. This fact is undeniable. As Nongbri writes, however, "What is modern about the ideas of 'religions' and 'being religious' is the isolation and naming of some things as 'religious' and others as 'not religious.'"[16] To say that religion is a modern invention is to point out that the identification of a "religious" sphere of life separate from "nonreligious" or "secular" activities like politics and economics and sports and so on is not simply an analytical description of different transcultural and transhistorical human activities but marks a normative choice about the correct way of organizing society.

Lilla assumes that there is a type of politics that is not religious — as opposed to political theology — and that the West has definitively embraced this form of politics over the past four hundred years. He believes, furthermore, that the West is less prone to violence now that we have rejected combining messianic religious passions with "secular" politics. There are a number of significant problems with this tale. As José Casanova points out, the separation of church and state that first took root in the United States was not a separation of religion and politics. Separating church and state in early America owed a great deal to dissenting Christian sects who wanted the government off their backs, but did not at all accept the terms of the Great Separation. Indeed, from abolition to temperance to women's suffrage to civil rights, some American social and political movements have been deeply intertwined with biblical faith.[17] The Enlightenment provides one important strand of American politics, but not the only one.[18]

More crucial, however, is the question of whether liberalism has in fact produced a separation of religion from politics and a diminishment of violence. Is the abandonment of Christian theological politics in the West an abandonment of theological politics, or merely, in John Bossy's

16. Nongbri, *Before Religion*, p. 4.

17. José Casanova, "The Great Separation," Immanent Frame blog, December 7, 2007, http://blogs.ssrc.org/tif/2007/12/07/the-great-separation/.

18. William T. Cavanaugh, "Messianic Nation: A Christian Theological Critique of American Exceptionalism," in *Migrations of the Holy: God, State, and the Political Meaning of the Church* (Grand Rapids: Eerdmans, 2011), pp. 88-108.

phrase, the migration of the holy from one location to another? The question is particularly fraught because the boundary between religious and secular is fluid. In Lilla's own analysis, the divide between the two sides of the Great Separation shifts, depending on what Lilla wants to condemn and what he wants to commend. One side of the Great Separation is occupied by "religious" politics, which Lilla usually identifies with politics that make reference to God or revelation. But when it suits his purposes, atheist ideologies such as Stalinism and Nietzscheanism or ideologies of the *Übermensch* such as Nazism appear on the opposite shore from the mundane and rational politics Lilla finds so congenial.

So, can atheist ideologies count as "religious" too? If Lilla were to make this move, he would have plenty of company. Faced with the obvious fact that atheist ideologies caused tens of millions of deaths in the twentieth century, for example, Christopher Hitchens simply declares that totalitarianism is a type of religion too, thus adding atheists like Stalin and Kim Jong Il to his indictment of the violence of religion.[19] Lilla does not directly claim that totalitarianism is religious, perhaps because he recognizes that such a move would scramble the line between religious and nonreligious politics upon which the Great Separation depends. Lilla instead uses Christian theological terms like "messianic" and "eschatological" to describe totalitarianism, and associates Nietzscheanism and Nazism and Stalinism with figures like Gogarten and Bloch who supported those causes by drawing on biblical themes (even though Bloch himself was also an atheist) (pp. 251-95). Lilla is trying to have it both ways: he wants the Great Separation between religious and nonreligious politics to remain intact, but he also wants all the kinds of politics he doesn't like to end up on the opposite shore. Thus does Karl Barth the Nazi fighter, who is clearly on the religious side of the Great Separation, find — undoubtedly to his great surprise — that he has dragged the Nazis with him to his side of the river. As Casanova points out, one could surely draw a much more direct and plausible line from Hobbes's Leviathan to totalitarianism; Carl Schmitt, who was for a time the Nazis' favored legal theoretician, was a dedicated disciple of Hobbes.[20] To do so, however, would challenge the neat tale of separation that Lilla has constructed.

19. Christopher Hitchens, *God Is Not Great: How Religion Poisons Everything* (New York: Twelve, 2007), pp. 231-47.
20. Casanova, "The Great Separation."

The idea of Stalinism and Nazism as religions is not implausible. There is a significant body of scholarship on various forms of Marxism and fascism as religions, and there is an English-language journal dedicated to the study of "political religions."[21] Such scholarship abides by a "functionalist" view of religion that defines religion not in terms of the substance of beliefs in gods or transcendence but rather in terms of how it functions in people's lives. The large body of scholarship on nationalism as a religion, for example, considers it irrelevant that people do not actually claim that nations are gods; the real question is to what they give their devotion. Pledging allegiance to the flag, ritualized singing of hymns to the nation, and especially giving one's life for one's country are all markers of religion for functionalists. One must take a functionalist approach in order to include atheistic ideologies on the religious side of the Great Separation. The problem for Lilla is that, if one applies functionalism consistently, the separation between religion and nonreligion upon which the Great Separation depends breaks down very quickly.

What do "we" do when we discover that we have "an elaborate and well-institutionalized civil religion in America" that, in sociologist Robert Bellah's words, "has its own seriousness and integrity and requires the same care in understanding that any other religion does"?[22] If, as even Lilla admits, American politics is "shot through with messianic language," then perhaps political theology is not such a distant memory to us. Lilla might want to blame political theology in the West on the residue of Christian influence, but liberal democracy is perfectly capable of generating its own political messianism. As political scientist Colin Dueck writes, the United States goes to war "either for liberal reasons, or not at all."[23] At least since Woodrow Wilson, American military interventions have been launched under the missionary banner of spreading "freedom" — meaning open elections and open markets — to the world. The United States' National Security Strategy issued in the wake of the 9/11 attacks makes the political messianism of liberalism

21. See the summary of this literature in Cavanaugh, *Myth of Religious Violence*, pp. 109-13.
22. Robert N. Bellah, "Civil Religion in America," in *American Civil Religion*, ed. Donald E. Jones and Russell E. Richey (San Francisco: Mellen Research University Press, 1990), p. 21.
23. Colin Dueck, *Reluctant Crusaders: Power, Culture, and Change in American Grand Strategy* (Princeton: Princeton University Press, 2006), p. 26.

explicit: "These values of freedom are right and true for every person, in every society — and the duty of protecting these values against their enemies is the common calling of freedom-loving people across the globe and across the ages." The document goes on to say that "our best defense is a good offense."[24] The Great Separation between fanatical, violent religion and modest, peaceful liberalism begins to look dubious when such evangelical zeal and the world's largest military apparatus are deployed on behalf of liberal democracy.

The great Hobbesian Carl Schmitt saw clearly that political theology was never rejected by the West; theology rather migrated from the church to the state. Thus Schmitt's famous lines from his 1922 book *Political Theology: Four Chapters on the Concept of Sovereignty:* "All significant concepts of the modern theory of the state are secularized theological concepts not only because of their historical development — in which they were transferred from theology to the theory of the state, whereby, for example, the omnipotent God became the omnipotent lawgiver — but also because of their systematic structure, the recognition of which is necessary for a sociological consideration of these concepts."[25] Paul Kahn's 2011 book *Political Theology: Four New Chapters on the Concept of Sovereignty* — which I discussed in chapter 5 — updates Schmitt's basic insight for the contemporary United States. As Kahn shows, ritualized nationalism, the invocation of states of emergency, the threat of nuclear destruction, the language of "sacrifice," the way that the president embodies the people as in the body of Christ — all can only be understood if our politics is understood theologically. The Great Separation that Lilla describes simply never happened; as Kahn writes, "the state is not the secular arrangement that it purports to be. A political life is not a life stripped of faith and the experience of the sacred, regardless of what we may believe about the legal separation of church and state."[26]

Despite this demolition of Lilla's historical tale, however, Kahn regards the sacred as entirely of human making, and he stridently differentiates the kind of political theology done by people who believe God's

24. Introduction to "The National Security Strategy of the United States of America," September 2002; http://www.state.gov/documents/organization/63562.pdf.

25. Carl Schmitt, *Political Theology: Four Chapters on the Concept of Sovereignty*, trans. George Schwab (Cambridge: MIT Press, 1985), p. 36.

26. Paul W. Kahn, *Political Theology: Four New Chapters on the Concept of Sovereignty* (New York: Columbia University Press, 2011), p. 18.

will is relevant for political life from the kind of theological analysis of politics that he does. "The latter is an entirely secular field of inquiry, while the former expresses a sectarian endeavor that is no longer possible in the West."[27] For Kahn, political theology is a secular analysis of the sacred structures people — including liberal democrats — continue to invent for themselves. Kahn, then, does not go far enough, because — like Lilla — he continues to regard the religious/secular boundary as simply part of the way things are. To say that American nationalism is a religion is to leave the religious/secular boundary intact. The real point goes deeper: the religious/secular distinction is a thoroughly contingent construction of Western societies undertaken for certain political purposes.[28] There is no reason that we should accept as fact the fanciful idea that Christianity occupies a religious realm of fantasy and fanaticism while secular ideologies describe a mundane and sober "real world." Secular politics continues to try to fill a God-shaped hole that modernity has left. The most rational explanation for this persistent longing for God might just be the existence of God.

That Christians generally view the separation of church and state as a positive gain does not mean that the separation of theology and politics need follow. There are indeed noxious forms of Christian political theology, just as there are destructive forms of secular political theology. People kill for all sorts of things: gods, flags, oil, freedom, the invisible hand of the market, and so on. The fact that people spontaneously worship all sorts of false gods does not necessarily mean that true worship is impossible. This is the basic biblical approach to idolatry, which I will discuss in the next chapter. What needs to be separated is good political theology from bad political theology. The idea that we can and must make a Great Separation between theological politics and sensible politics is itself a piece of bad political theology.

27. Kahn, *Political Theology*, p. 124.
28. See Talal Asad, *Formations of the Secular: Christianity, Islam, and Modernity* (Stanford: Stanford University Press, 2003), pp. 187-94.

CHAPTER ELEVEN

SECULARIZATION, VIOLENCE, AND IDOLATRY

I N THIS CHAPTER I want to expand on the sketchy comments I made about idolatry at the end of the last chapter. My argument about religion and violence is really an argument about idolatry, but in the opposite way that religion, violence, and idolatry are usually brought together. It is often argued that religion — which is assumed to imply belief in a God or gods or some equivalent — demands a kind of absolute loyalty that increases the stakes in any dispute until violence is licensed or required. The biblical obsession with idolatry is seen as one symptom of this relentless religious demand for absolute and uncompromising loyalty to God and intolerance of other beliefs and practices. People can see, the argument goes, that other kinds of loyalty, to one's family or one's country or one's oil company, are mundane matters, but there is nothing greater than God, who by definition transcends and exceeds all earthly realities. Loyalty to God must therefore take precedence over all other loyalties, with violence often as the result. It is not that people don't commit violence in the service of secular ideologies and institutions; it is rather that religion, because of its absolutism, has a greater tendency to rule out compromise solutions short of violence, and a greater tendency to make that violence intractable once it begins.

In my work on religion and violence, summarized in chapter 9, I have argued that the essential distinction between religion and the secular upon which the religion-and-violence notion depends is a false distinction. There is no transhistorical and transcultural "religion." The religious/secular distinction is a modern, Western invention, created to serve very particular political purposes in the history of the modern state. There is no reason to think that religion has a greater tendency to promote violence than secular ideologies and institutions because there is no essential distinction between religious and secular. The fact is that people kill for all sorts of things, including Jesus and jihad, but also freedom, the fatherland, oil, the invisible hand of the market, the workers' revolution, and the American flag.

It is precisely here that the biblical critique of idolatry serves not to bolster but to undermine the argument that religion promotes violence. For if the religion-and-violence notion depends on the religious/secular distinction, the biblical critique of idolatry makes clear that the distinction does not hold. In the biblical view, people are spontaneously worshiping creatures who treat all sorts of things as gods: golden calves, mute statues, Mammon, even, as Paul says, their own bellies (Phil. 3:19). The Bible recognizes only one true absolute, the God of Abraham, Isaac, and Jacob, but understands that people have a tendency to treat all sorts of created things as absolutes. There is no neat distinction between the world of worship, of treating God as absolute, and the world of mundane, purely secular, pursuits. The fact is that worship, albeit false worship, pervades the so-called secular world. There simply is no way to carve up the world into the essentially religious and the essentially secular if in actual empirical fact people treat all sorts of things as their "religions." The biblical critique of idolatry makes clear that the religious/secular distinction is an ideological, rather than purely descriptive, distinction. It does not articulate facts about the world but rather serves to draw our attention toward certain kinds of absolutism and violence and away from other kinds.

In this chapter I want to suggest some avenues into the theological critique of idolatry that shed light on the current debate over religion, violence, and secularization. I will discuss the biblical material in the light of functionalist and constructionist views of religion, highlight some themes in postbiblical Christian critiques of idolatry, and suggest some ways idolatry critique can be useful in addressing the issue of violence today.

I. Biblical Critiques of Idolatry

Biblical critiques of idolatry have certain affinities with functionalist approaches to religion. As discussed in chapter 9, functionalism expands the definition of religion so that it may potentially include Marxism, nationalism, consumerism, and a host of other ideologies and practices that are considered secular by the substantivist approach. Functionalists define religion not based on what people claim to believe but on how certain ideas and practices function in their lives, that is, the social, psychological, and political work that such ideas and practices do to produce the sort of overarching meaning and coherence that Christianity, Confucianism, et al. do. As Peter Clarke and Peter Byrne put it, "Functionalists prefer to define 'religion' not in terms of *what* is believed by the religious but in terms of *how* they believe it (that is in terms of the role belief plays in people's lives). Certain individual or social needs are specified and religion is identified as any system whose beliefs, practices or symbols serve to meet those needs."[1] Functionalism is, in effect, a return to the ancient Roman definition of *religio* as any binding obligation or devotion that helps to structure one's social relations.

One advantage of functionalism over substantivism is that it is more empirical, and therefore more adequate to reality. Functionalism is based on observation of people's actual behavior, and not on supposed knowledge of one's interior mental state. Not only is it more difficult to peer into the interiority of a person's beliefs, but also, what people claim to believe often has less impact on their lives than their implicit beliefs. If a man claims to believe in the Christian God but has not been in a church since his wedding and spends most of his waking hours trading stocks and obsessing about the market, then the colloquial idea that capitalism is his religion conforms more closely to reality. This has important implications for the idea that religion promotes violence. A functionalist might agree that religion has a tendency to promote violence, but in this case "religion" would mean anything to which people are devoted, which includes all sorts of practices like nationalism and sports fanaticism that a substantivist would consider "secular." The argument that religion promotes violence therefore loses its bite, because "religion" is contrasted not with "secular" ideologies and institutions like liberalism and nationalism and capitalism and Marxism, but with "things that are not taken so seriously," or something of the sort. But to say that people are more inclined to do violence for things they take

1. Peter B. Clarke and Peter Byrne, *Religion Defined and Explained* (New York: St. Martin's Press, 1993), p. 7.

seriously than for things they don't is a truism with which no sane person would disagree.

The godfather of functionalist approaches to religion is Émile Durkheim. According to Durkheim, "a religion is a unified system of beliefs and practices relative to sacred things, that is to say, things set apart and surrounded by prohibitions."[2] What is sacred and what is not, however, is not defined by content. For Durkheim, anything can be regarded by a society as sacred. Totems and flags and so on are made of readily available earthly materials like wood and stone and gourds and cloth. Such can be used as representations of gods and other forces. Durkheim is interested not so much in the wood and cloth or even in the gods or other forces being symbolized as in the function that such separation of the sacred from the profane serves in any given society. Durkheim thought that the sacred was society's way of representing itself to itself. The social order is reinforced or contested by the symbolization of communal solidarity among the members of society. There is no essential difference between the rituals and taboos surrounding the flag and those having to do with God or gods; both represent a society's symbolization of itself to itself. For Durkheim, all religion, insofar as it does not make explicit the reference to the society itself, is a kind of misrepresentation. Durkheim thought the origin of this misrepresentation lay in the complexity of society itself. People experience the constraints of social forces beyond the individual's control, but since these forces are too complex to understand, they give rise to mythological accounts and ritual practices that pay homage to these forces under the guise of mystery.[3]

What Durkheim and his functionalist followers are articulating is little different from the basic biblical theme that people are inclined to turn their worship toward all kinds of earthly realities. There are two problems with a Durkheimian approach, however. First, as I pointed out in chapter 9, functionalism is unhelpful and misleading insofar as it assumes that religion is a transcultural and transhistorical phenomenon. Second, Durkheim was a reductionist, reducing God to an epiphenomenon of collective human consciousness. What separates the biblical

2. Émile Durkheim, *The Elementary Forms of Religious Life,* trans. Carol Cosman (Oxford: Oxford University Press, 2001), p. 46.

3. See Timothy Jenkins, "Why Do Things Move People? A Sociological Account of Idolatry," in *Idolatry: False Worship in the Bible, Early Judaism, and Christianity,* ed. Stephen C. Barton (Edinburgh: T. & T. Clark, 2007), p. 294.

critique of idolatry from Durkheim's approach to religion is that the former relies on the recognition that, although people worship many things, there is in reality only one true God. Durkheim's implication that the sacred/profane distinction always rests on a misrepresentation need not be accepted. The Bible holds that there is one true God that can be distinguished from among the false ones.

What is most important for our purposes is that the biblical critique of idolatry calls into question the whole modern narrative of secularization. It is common these days to declare that the "secularization thesis" developed over the course of the twentieth century has been proven wrong. Peter Berger has repented of the idea that he and other sociologists popularized in the 1960s that religion was on the wane in the face of the rationalization of modernity. In the light of evidence such as the emergence of liberation theology and militant Islam in the 1970s, the rapid growth of Christianity in Africa, and the continuing high levels of church practice in the United States, the secularization thesis has been largely abandoned. Religion, we are told increasingly, has made a comeback. If the biblical critique of idolatry is correct about the spontaneous human proclivity to worship, however, then neither the secularization thesis nor the comeback-of-religion thesis is correct. Worship of the sacred has not made a comeback, because it never went away. The holy merely migrated in the modern era from the church to the state and the market.

This should not be the least bit surprising to anyone who regards the Bible as scripture. The Tanakh is filled with denunciations of idolatry in the form of the worship of images of other gods and in the form of improper representations of the true God. My main concern here is with the former, because it more directly addresses the problem of worship directed at things other than God. The term "idol" comes from the Greek *eidolon,* which indicates something that lacks substance, or is vacuous.[4] The Old Testament sometimes mocks those who worship idols as worshiping what is merely material. "Our God is in heaven, he creates whatever he chooses. They have idols of silver and gold, made by human hands. These have mouths but say nothing, have eyes but see nothing, have ears but hear nothing, have noses but smell nothing" (Ps. 115:3-6 NJB). Second Isaiah is incredulous that a man can use half of a

4. Robert Hayward, "Observations on Idols in Septuagint Pentateuch," in *Idolatry,* ed. Barton, pp. 42-43.

piece of wood for fire to cook his dinner and the other half to craft an idol to worship, never asking, "Am I right to bow down before a block of wood?" (Isa. 44:19 NJB). As Moshe Halbertal and Avishai Margalit have argued in their analysis of idolatry in Jewish literature, however, the Hebrew Bible does not regard idolatry primarily as an error, as the mistaken belief that mere statues are in fact gods. The main problem is betrayal, not stupidity.[5] The biblical text generally assumes that the worship of other gods is a mere parody of the worship of the God of Abraham, Isaac, and Jacob, that the other gods are not-gods, lacking in substance and power.[6] But the ban on idolatry does not necessarily deny the existence of other gods; it only forbids worshiping them.[7] Idolatry is not primarily considered a metaphysical error, a question of ontology. The key question is not what people believe but how they behave. What constitutes idolatry is usually not the mistaken attribution of certain qualities to material objects, but the attitude of loyalty that people adopt toward created realities. Here the biblical approach is closer to the functionalist than to the substantivist, for what is decisive is function, not content. Idolatry is primarily a way of life, not a metaphysical worldview.[8] This is not to say that idolatry cannot be metaphysical, that people cannot attribute false being to gods that do not exist. It is only to say that the Bible appears to consider allegiance most commonly to be the decisive factor in separating idolatry from true worship. For this reason, the primary biblical metaphors for idolatry are adultery and political disloyalty.

The metaphor of adultery is exemplified by the story of Hosea, who is told to marry a whore to symbolize the dalliances of Israel with other gods, "for the country itself has become nothing but a whore by abandoning Yahweh" (Hos. 1:2 NJB). Halbertal and Margalit point out that the avoidance of anthropomorphism is not what distinguishes idolatry from true worship, since the rejection of idolatry in the Bible depends on comparing human relationships with God to other human relationships like marriage. The rejection of idolatry ironically depends on drawing similarities between God and humans. So a personal, somewhat anthropomorphized God is required to speak of idolatry, because

5. Moshe Halbertal and Avishai Margalit, *Idolatry* (Cambridge: Harvard University Press, 1998), pp. 108-9.

6. Hayward, "Observations on Idols," p. 44.

7. Halbertal and Margalit, *Idolatry*, p. 22.

8. Halbertal and Margalit, *Idolatry*, p. 24.

God must be a person in order to speak of betrayal. Loyalty must have been created within a history of specific relations, which is salvation history. The ban on idolatry is not universalistic in this sense, but depends on the concrete covenantal relations of a people to the God of Abraham, Isaac, and Jacob.[9] What is at stake is not so much metaphysical propositions about God or gods as the devotion or lack thereof to the one true God.

The Israelites are also warned against exchanging the kingship of YHWH for that of human kings. As YHWH says to Samuel when the people ask for a king, to be like other nations, "It is not you they have rejected but me, not wishing me to reign over them anymore. They are now doing to you exactly what they have done to me since the day I brought them out of Egypt until now, deserting me and serving other gods" (I Sam. 8:7-8 NJB). In comparison to the marital metaphor, however, the political metaphor for idolatry is somewhat less exclusive; one cannot have a stand-in for one's spouse, but human kings can be seen as God's agents, provided they make clear that they depend on God. In contrast to the kings of other nations, who set themselves up as gods, the monarchy is not to be seen as part of the cosmic order but only as a result of a stubborn people's request.[10] God's favor can rest upon the king, but only if the king learns to fear YHWH, and does not accumulate horses and wives and wealth (Deut. 17:16-20). As Isaiah makes plain, pride is the root sin. Kings are not to trust their own power or that of human allies. "Woe to those going down to Egypt for help, who put their trust in horses, who rely on the quantity of chariots, and on great strength of cavalrymen, but do not look to the Holy One of Israel" (Isa. 31:1 NJB). Isaiah continues on to link this turning away from God with the idolatrous reliance on what is created instead of the Creator: "The Egyptian is human, not divine, his horses are flesh, not spirit" (Isa. 31:3 NJB). Here idolatry is not fundamentally a matter of mistaking material things for God, nor of consciously assigning God's attributes — immortality, omnipresence, omnipotence, etc. — to an earthly king. The key question is one of trust. Kings are guilty of idolatry and self-deification when they rely upon their own power and neglect the source of true power. Their subjects are guilty of idolatry when they transfer unconditional obedience from God to the king.

9. Halbertal and Margalit, *Idolatry*, pp. 10-11, 21-22.
10. Halbertal and Margalit, *Idolatry*, pp. 216-21.

Two important conclusions result from the political metaphor of idolatry, the notion of God as king. First, idolatry is not necessarily a black-and white issue. It is rare that someone makes a golden calf and declares, "Here is your God who brought you here from Egypt!" (Exod. 32:4 NJB). Most forms of idolatry, like trust, are on a continuum of more or less. Israel is suffered to have kings, but only with a great deal of ambivalence. Sometimes they are instruments of God's purposes; sometimes they threaten to usurp the place of God among the people. Second, if idolatry does not depend on the deliberate attribution of divine qualities to human kings, then it may be that political idolatry did not die with the ancient Egyptian and Mesopotamian and Roman civilizations. The divine right of kings, the transfer of sovereignty to the modern state, the glorification of the nation, the reliance on military might, the threat to destroy the world through nuclear weapons to ensure one's own survival — all these and more make putting one's trust in horses look positively meek.

In Walter Brueggemann's reading of Israelite praise, liturgy is a constitutive enterprise in the sense that the world we inhabit is narrated by the liturgies we perform. Israelite liturgy is a political act in which God's triumph over idols is not only commemorated but also made effective.[11] Official royal liturgy was, nevertheless, sometimes co-opted by the powerful, in the service of the status quo, which was often corrupt. According to Brueggemann, royal liturgy then becomes a type of idolatry, if idolatry is defined, as we have seen, as worshiping a god that does nothing. Royal doxology shows a god who does not act in any concrete or specific way; nothing changes, and nothing can be critiqued.[12] Bruggemann reads Jeremiah's attacks on temple worship, for example, as extending the critique of idolatry beyond intentionally bowing down to other gods, but also including neglecting the widows and orphans (Jer. 7:6) and crying "Peace, peace!" when there is no peace (Jer. 8:11). Brueggemann writes of Jeremiah, "The idolatry he had to meet was the self-deceiving worship of an indifferent god who provided cover, security, and rationalization for covenant breakers."[13] Brueggemann applies this critique of idolatry to the contemporary United States as

---

11. Walter Brueggemann, *Israel's Praise: Doxology against Idolatry and Ideology* (Philadelphia: Fortress, 1988), pp. 8-11, 34-35.

12. Brueggemann, *Israel's Praise*, pp. 105, 113.

13. Brueggemann, *Israel's Praise*, pp. 124-25.

well, where he says that all too often we worship an established, im-
mobile god and are incapable of critiquing a self-confident militarism
and consumerism.[14]

Along with circumcision, kosher laws, and Sabbath observance,
anti-idolatry was one of the prime markers of Jewish identity in the
Greco-Roman period. Although Christians departed from Jews on the
first three markers, there is substantial continuity on the critique of
idolatry. And once again the critique of idolatry is not restricted to the
explicit and intentional worship of gods with other names, but rather
pertains to the disproportionate devotion shown to all manner of created things. Though explicit mention of idolatry is rare in the Gospels,
Jesus' admonition about God and Mammon in the Sermon on the
Mount (Matt. 6:24) makes clear that people are prone to serve money
as a god, and that one must choose between the true God and the false
one. The Greek word for "serve" here (δουλεύειν) is most commonly
used for the master-slave relationship and allegiance to transcendent
beings, and the term "Mammon" is left untranslated so that it sounds
like a proper name, a personified god.[15] Jesus' warning is given in the
context of other sayings (Matt. 6:19-21 and 6:25-34) on trust in God over
worries about material goods. The saying against storing up treasures
on earth is concluded with "For wherever your treasure is, there will
your heart be too" (Matt. 6:21 NJB). Idolatry again is not so much a
matter of conceptual error as of devotion; one can be perfectly clear
conceptually that coins made of earthly metals are not actually divine
beings, and yet one can be an idolater if one's heart is set on such objects, or one trusts in them to provide security. Function, not merely
belief, is the most common marker of idolatry.

This is especially clear in the Pauline letters, where idolatry takes
a more prominent place than in the Gospels. Colossians follows the
general idea from the Tanakh that idolatry is devotion to what is earthly
as opposed to what is heavenly: "That is why you must kill everything
in you that is earthly: sexual vice, impurity, uncontrolled passion, evil
desires and especially greed, which is the same thing as worshipping
a false god" (Col. 3:5 NJB). In Paul's letter to the Philippians, he be-

14. Brueggemann, *Israel's Praise*, pp. 127-29.
15. Joel Marcus, "Idolatry in the New Testament," in *The Word Leaps the Gap: Essays on Scripture and Theology in Honor of Richard B. Hays*, ed. J. Ross Wagner, C. Kavin Rowe, and A. Katherine Grieb (Grand Rapids: Eerdmans, 2008), p. 115.

moans those who are "destined to be lost; their god is the stomach; they glory in what they should think shameful, since their minds are set on earthly things" (Phil. 3:19). In Romans, Paul takes a slightly different approach, in which sexual vices, injustice, greed, murder, and a host of other sins are not so much idolatry itself as the effects of idolatry. "While they claimed to be wise, in fact they were growing so stupid that they exchanged the glory of the immortal God for an imitation, for the image of a mortal human being, or of birds, or animals, or crawling things" (Rom. 1:22-23 NJB). As a result, Paul says, God abandoned them to "filthy practices" (Rom. 1:24 NJB), "unacceptable thoughts and indecent behaviour" (Rom. 1:28 NJB). Here it is difficult to draw the line between idolatry and its consequences; as G. K. Beale argues, this passage is simply a continuation of the idea found in the Hebrew scriptures that we become like what we worship (see Ps. 135:18, where it says of idols, "Their makers will end up like them" [NJB]). Corrupt and stupid behavior is simply a mirror of making corruptible and stupid images of gods.[16]

II. Idolatry Critique in Christian History

Later Christian thinkers have contended that the root of idolatry is the worship of creation; the explicit worship of other gods is a problem insofar as merely created realities are mistaken for divine beings. So, for example, in Augustine's withering treatment of the Roman multiplication of gods in book 4 of *The City of God,* the creation of gods is a product of a city that claims to be self-legitimating. The gods do not precede the founding of the *civitas,* but are the creations of the Romans meant to ensure their dominance over nature and over other peoples. Augustine's critique of Roman violence in book 3 shows that it stems from the same *libido dominandi.* The Romans created gods and goddesses to celebrate and protect their military victories and dominance over others.[17] As Gregory Lee points out, "On Augustine's account, then, violence and idolatry are both symptoms of the same impulse: an in-

16. G. K. Beale, *We Become What We Worship: A Biblical Theology of Idolatry* (Downers Grove, Ill.: IVP Academic, 2008), pp. 202-3.

17. Augustine, *City of God,* trans. Henry Bettenson (Harmondsworth: Penguin, 1972), pp. 153-54 (4.14-15).

ordinate desire for earthly goods coupled with a refusal to seek them from God."[18] Augustine thus turns the common idea that monotheism is inherently more violent and intolerant than polytheism on its head. Violence comes from the refusal to see that all creation depends on the Creator for its true being. Violence is the attempt to seize and grasp at creation, turning away from recognition of our status as created and dependent. This inordinate attachment to created things is the root of idolatry as well. In the forgetting of the source of being, we attach ourselves to created things and thereby slip back into the nothingness from which creation was summoned by God.[19] Idolatry is not the same as violence, in Augustine's view, but violence can result from idolatry.

One of the potential dangers of Augustine's view, and arguably of the biblical view that precedes him, is that the charge of idolatry will be leveled at any and all types of worship that do not conform to one's own. When all other gods are dismissed as false gods, all other faiths fall under suspicion of idolatry. Certainly this was a standard Western approach to Hindu worship before the nineteenth century. In this sense, the taxonomies of religions that were formulated in the nineteenth century were an advance over simply dismissing Hindus and others as idolaters. The possibility of engaging in "interreligious dialogue" that became a reality in the twentieth century was facilitated by the movement of Hindu forms of worship from the category of "idolatry" to that of "religion." Without abandoning belief in the existence of one God, the Second Vatican Council of the Catholic Church, for example, extends the circle of God's activity far beyond the church: "Nor is God remote from those who in shadows and images seek the unknown God, since he gives to all men [*sic*] life and breath and all things (cf. Acts 17:25-28)."[20] In this passage from Acts, Paul begins in Athens "revolted at the sight of a city given over to idolatry" (Acts 17:16 NJB). Paul then, however, calls the citizens of Athens δεισιδαιμονεστέρους, literally

---

18. Gregory W. Lee, "Republics and Their Loves: Rereading *City of God* 19," *Modern Theology* 27, no. 4 (October 2011): 560.

19. For Augustine, evil creeps into a good creation "when, in consequence of an immoderate urge towards those things at the bottom end of the scale of good, we abandon the higher and supreme goods, that is you, Lord God, and your truth and your law"; Augustine, *Confessions,* trans. Henry Chadwick (Oxford: Oxford University Press, 1991), p. 30 (2.5.10). Evil is nothingness, the privation of good, as Augustine makes clear in book 7.

20. *Lumen Gentium,* §16.

"demon-fearing," which can be translated either as "too superstitious" (KJV) or as "extremely religious" (NRSV). Paul is both critical of the Athenians' idolatry and, more decisively, sees in their worship a groping for the "unknown God" (Acts 17:23) who, as Vatican II highlights, made everything and gives breath to everyone. "And he did this so that they might seek the deity and, by feeling their way towards him, succeed in finding him; and indeed he is not far from any of us, since it is in him that we live, and move, and exist, as indeed some of your own writers have said: 'We are all his children'" (Acts 17:27-28 NJB).[21] Augustine too, in his *De Vera Religione*, recognizes that there are *vestigia* of God in all of creation, and the impulse to worship is found in all human beings as an inchoate longing for their Creator. False worship arises when we pay homage to creation, to the neglect of the Creator. What presents itself even in Augustine, then, is the possibility that the naming of other gods is not idolatry per se, but may be an inchoate reaching toward the Creator, and not the worship of creation.

I cannot attempt to develop an adequate model of interfaith dialogue here. I merely want to signal that the critique of idolatry need not be extended to the intolerance of all forms of worship that depart from the biblical emphasis on the oneness of God. If Halbertal and Margalit are right to say that the biblical ban on idolatry is not universalistic but depends on the specific history of covenantal relations between the people of God and their God, then the critique of idolatry need not be readily extended to others. If, as we have seen, the biblical critique of idolatry is not primarily concerned with metaphysical claims but rather is concerned with actions that manifest one's loyalties to the God of Abraham, Isaac, and Jacob, then it is possible to construct models of interfaith dialogue that honor other faiths without automatically casting them as idolatrous. I would argue as well, given the problems with the term "religion" that I pointed out above, that such dialogue need not be limited to dialogue among the usual parties designated as "religions." I do not think, for example, that Christian-Marxist dialogue need necessarily proceed in a way *essentially* distinct from Christian-Hindu dialogue.[22] There can, of course, be idolatrous elements to criti-

21. The internal quote is from the Greek philosopher Aratus. On this passage in Acts, see Marcus, "Idolatry in the New Testament," p. 124.

22. It might be fruitful, for example, to treat Marxism as an alternative type of soteriology, a Christian heresy that, like many heresies, has gotten hold of some truths.

cize in all such traditions — including Christianity, needless to say — but there can also be things to honor in such traditions, as elements of grace that can point, whether it is recognized or not, to God the Creator. The critique of the religious/secular distinction I have been developing, in other words, requires a much more open and flexible concept of dialogue with other traditions than is found in the standard conception of "interreligious dialogue," which is focused on a rather exclusive group of "religions."

In part because of the well-founded sensitivity to other faiths since the early twentieth century, contemporary Western critiques of idolatry have tended to focus on self-critique, primarily with regard to the nation-state and economic systems as primary loci of idolatrous devotion. Jacques Ellul, for example, thought that modern Westerners put their trust in the state and in money out of their inability to accept that they have an invisible God. Idolatry is the attempt to make God visible.[23] More recent critiques of the idolatry of money, on the other hand, have tended to focus on the *immateriality* of late capitalism. Graham Ward, for example, thinks that the power of money is precisely in its power to vanish. In a late capitalist economy, materiality is always deferred; there is no way to get underneath exchange value to the pure use-value of objects. Idolatry takes place in the mystification of commodities and the triumph of the virtual.[24] Another way of getting at this critique of idolatry is Bernd Wannenwetsch's tracing of the history of advertising in the twentieth century from an emphasis on the product to the absence of the product in marketing campaigns. The operation of the brand in the mind, not the product itself, is what is desirable. Desire for desire itself has become the heart of idolatry in a consumer culture.[25] In consumer society, idolatry manifests itself not so much in attachment to material goods as in detachment from the material, the constant search for novelty, the restless desire that moves from one object to the next. Regardless of whether idolatry is an attempt to make God visible or an attempt to render material reality invisible and mystical, the key characteristic of idolatry remains devotion to creation rather than the Creator. Functionalist analyses of religion, as in Emilio Gen-

23. Andrew Goddard, "Jacques Ellul on Idolatry," in *Idolatry*, ed. Barton, pp. 233-35.
24. Graham Ward, "The Commodification of Religion or the Consummation of Capitalism," in *Idolatry*, ed. Barton, pp. 302-14.
25. Bernd Wannenwetsch, "The Desire for Desire: Commandment and Idolatry in Late Capitalist Societies," in *Idolatry*, ed. Barton, pp. 317-25.

tile's book *Politics as Religion*[26] or Robert H. Nelson's book *Economics as Religion*,[27] only underscore what has been a basic theological theme from the Bible to today.

III. Conclusion

None of the preceding analysis in any way absolves Christians or Jews or Muslims or anyone else from the charge of promoting violence. The mere claim that one believes in God does not prove that what one believes in is really God. Christians are highly susceptible to idolatry, and it is not at all clear that our first trust is in God and not in the nation's military might or our retirement accounts. Indeed, Nicholas Lash has made a case that the Catholic Church's very sacramental nature makes it susceptible to mistaking sign for reality, church for kingdom.[28] The critique of idolatry should always be self-critique, first and foremost. It is clear that Christians and Jews are susceptible to idolatry, and that this idolatry can and does result in violence. Putting our trust in horses and chariots and the great strength of cavalrymen — military might, in other words — is a way of life in which Christians often participate enthusiastically along with their "secular" neighbors. This is not necessarily to say that all uses of violence are inherently idolatrous; the question of the justifiable use of violence is a famously difficult one, and I cannot begin to address it here. The point is simply that when people kill, they do so for all sorts of things they hold dear. Christians kill, but when they do, attributing their violence to their belief in God or their "religion" is often misleading. The real question is, "What god are they actually worshiping?" or "What is their true religion?" If we find that the answer to these questions is, for example, nationalism, this does not let Christianity and Judaism off the hook, as it were. We then are only at the beginning of our idolatry critique. We then need to determine what it is about various expressions of Christianity and

26. Emilio Gentile, *Politics as Religion,* trans. George Staunton (Princeton: Princeton University Press, 2006).

27. Robert H. Nelson, *Economics as Religion: From Samuelson to Chicago and Beyond* (University Park: Pennsylvania State University Press, 2001).

28. See Paul D. Murray, "Theology 'Under the Lash': Theology as Idolatry-Critique in the Work of Nicholas Lash," in *Idolatry,* ed. Barton, p. 256.

Judaism that make them susceptible to replacing loyalty to the one true God with loyalty to the nation.

But the same critique applies to "secular" actors as well. What the critique of idolatry depends upon is the recognition that all human beings are spontaneously worshiping creatures whose devotion falls upon all sorts of objects and ideologies and institutions. If this is the case, then religion is not one discrete aspect of human experience that can be cordoned off the way substantivists would desire. And if this is the case, then the common idea that religion promotes violence can only be true if the term "religion" is extended to all those other devotions to which people sacrifice money and time and lives, including many things commonly thought of as nonreligious or "secular": nationalism, science, capitalism, Marxism, liberalism, and so on. If the term "religion" is extended in this way, then the argument that religion promotes violence cannot do what its proponents want it to do, which is to establish the inherent superiority of "nonreligion" to "religion" or "secular" social orders to ones in which "religion" takes an active role. Indeed, if the critique of idolatry is taken seriously, we may have to revisit the entire tale of secularization that is commonly told about the modern era. We live in a secularized society if by that is meant that the church has largely been removed from public coercive power. We can accept this as a good. But we do not live in a secularized society if by that is meant that we do not worship gods. Rather than speak of secularization, it may be more accurate to speak of a landscape in which worship is nearly ubiquitous.

In the next chapter, I will examine more implications of the contemporary use of the term "religion," and how it affects Christian loyalties.

CHAPTER TWELVE

ARE WE FREE NOT TO BE A RELIGION?

THE AMBIVALENCE OF RELIGIOUS FREEDOM

I N JANUARY 2012, the Department of Health and Human Services (HHS) issued a mandate under the Affordable Care Act that required all employer health plans to provide coverage for contraception, sterilization, and abortion-inducing drugs. In response to objections, the rule was subsequently changed so that insurance providers, not employers, could directly pay for such coverage. The U.S. Conference of Catholic Bishops and others — under the banner of religious freedom — continued to object that all employers were still being obliged to provide such coverage, despite moral objections.

The ensuing debate over religious freedom has generally assumed that the primary contest is over defining freedom, not religion. We assume that we more or less know what we are talking about when we say "religion"; the argument is about how much freedom religion should be granted. But the concept of religion is itself a hotly contested concept. It is, furthermore, a politically charged concept, not a neutral descriptor. In other words, what counts as religion and what does not in any given context often depends upon and instantiates a certain exercise of power, for good or for ill.[1]

In the context of the current debate over the freedom of the Catholic Church to resist the HHS mandate, I want to explore the usefulness of the concept of religious freedom. In doing so, I will not assume that Ca-

---

1. I make this argument at length in the context of the common contention that "religion" contributes to violence in my book *The Myth of Religious Violence: Secular Ideology and the Roots of Modern Conflict* (New York: Oxford University Press, 2009).

tholicism or Christianity more generally is a religion, and then ask what the government can do to ensure its freedom. I will instead question the assumption that Christianity is a religion to begin with, and examine both the advantages and the problems with claiming religious freedom for the church. I will begin by giving a brief overview of the problem of defining religion in the context of legal battles over religious freedom. I will then explore one case — that of the Pueblo Indians in the 1920s — in which defining one's practices as "religion" and seeking religious freedom had both positive and negative effects. Finally, I will draw some parallels between this case and the U.S. Catholic bishops' position on the HHS mandate, and argue that appeals to religious freedom can be a double-edged sword.

I. Are We Religious?

On the face of it, the question I am raising seems ridiculous. Of course Christianity is a religion. A deeper look at the recent government arguments about the free exercise of religion, however, makes clear that what does and what does not count as religion is at the heart of the matter. The HHS mandate has been framed by its protagonists not as a restriction of religious liberty but as a clarification about what counts as religion and what does not. Churches, synagogues, mosques, etc., are entitled as always to exemption from having to provide insurance coverage for services that violate their principles, based on the concept of free exercise of religion. But schools, hospitals, charities, and other agencies that are affiliated with such congregations have been redefined as not essentially religious, and therefore not exempt from the mandates under the principle of religious freedom, because they do not "serve primarily persons who share the[ir] religious tenets," according to the HHS.[2] As the U.S. Catholic bishops' blog comments, "HHS denies these organizations religious freedom precisely because their purpose is to serve the common good of society."[3] The government's position makes a distinction between church agencies that serve a re-

2. Quoted in "Six Things Everyone Should Know about the HHS Mandate," USCC-Blog, February 6, 2012; http://usccbmedia.blogspot.com/2012/02/six-things-everyone -should-know-about.html?spref=tw.
3. USCCBlog, February 6, 2012.

ligious function and those that serve a social function. The implication is that "religion" is not something that is essentially social.

The Justice Department took a similar position in the landmark case *Hosanna-Tabor v. EEOC*. The Equal Employment Opportunity Commission argued that the plaintiff in the case — a teacher at a Lutheran school — should not be covered by the "ministerial exemption" whereby religious organizations have more freedom to decide who works for them, because the plaintiff taught mostly "secular" subjects, such as math, social studies, art, music, etc., along with religion classes. The government's argument here again makes a sharp distinction between religion and the rest of life, even though the purpose of at least some church-related schools is not simply to tack a little religion onto an otherwise entirely secular curriculum, but to see all of life through a Christian lens. In January 2012 the Supreme Court rejected the EEOC's argument that the ministerial exemption should apply only to those who "perform exclusively religious functions." The Court's unanimous decision stated, "Indeed, we are unsure if any such employees exist. The heads of congregations themselves often have a mix of duties, including secular ones, such as helping to manage the congregation's finances, supervising purely secular personnel, and overseeing the upkeep of facilities."[4] Although the Court seems to believe in the possibility of "purely secular" people, it casts doubt on the idea that "religion" could be kept entirely separate from the rest of life.

These examples indicate that the boundary between religious and secular is not fixed and immutable. This is so because the religious/secular distinction is not engraved in the nature of things, but is a relatively recent invention of the modern West. I hope that the summary of my argument in *The Myth of Religious Violence* that I give in chapter 9 is sufficient to show that accepting the status of Christianity as a religion is contestable and sometimes worth contesting. The point is that religious and secular are constructed categories that are used in different times and places for different purposes, sometimes benign, sometimes not. As a Christian theologian, I want to claim that people of all times and places are subject to an inchoate searching for God. But I agree with constructivists that the categories of religious and secular are invented, constructed categories, not simply part of the way things

4. *Hosanna-Tabor Evangelical Lutheran Church and School v EEOC*, 565 US__(2012), p. 19.

are. And I think, furthermore, that that construction is not neutral, but has often distorted the reality of Christianity in the West.

II. Religious Freedom and the Pueblo

Before I return to the case of Christianity, I want to explore an example from another tradition to illustrate more broadly the ambivalence of accepting the category of religion and the appeal to religious freedom. Tisa Wenger's work on the use of the idea of religious freedom among the Pueblo Indians of New Mexico in the 1920s makes for an interesting comparison with the current debate on religious freedom in Catholic circles. Threatened from without by U.S. government action against traditional Pueblo dances and interference in Pueblo governance structures, elements among the Pueblo appealed to the idea of religious freedom, although the concept "religion" had no parallel in the native language. The idea that there was a Pueblo religion distinguishable from the nonreligious aspects of Pueblo life did not accord with Pueblo experience. Nevertheless, the Pueblo successfully used one of the U.S. government's own guiding principles to preserve traditional practices. As Wenger shows, however, recasting their dances as "religion" also had long-term effects that altered the traditional life of the community that they were trying to defend. Wenger intends her study as a corrective to overly negative accounts that see the category of "religion" as nothing but a tool of colonial dominance over native peoples. By identifying the separation of "religion" from the rest of life — the "secular" world of politics, economics, and so on — with modernity, those who knew no such distinctions were thereby understood by colonial power as "primitive" and in need of modernization. Wenger shows, on the other hand, that the tools of colonial power can be used in tactics of resistance. Nevertheless, as she stresses, "Regardless of its success, and no matter what the intentions of those who employ it, such a strategy of resistance inevitably reshapes the practices it defends."[5]

By the 1920s, the cultural practices of Native Americans had long been under threat from the U.S. government that had "pacified" them.

---

5. Tisa Wenger, "'We Are Guaranteed Freedom': Pueblo Indians and the Category of Religion in the 1920s," *History of Religions* 45, no. 2 (November 2005): 91. Page numbers to this article have been placed in the text.

The Bureau of Indian Affairs' (BIA) Religious Crimes Code of 1883 gave agency superintendents broad authorization to use force against Indian "religious" practices they regarded as immoral or subversive of the U.S. government's authority and "civilizing" policies. In the 1920s BIA commissioner Charles Burke invoked this code in a series of orders aimed at suppressing Indian dancing, which he regarded as generally "useless and harmful performances." Burke's 1923 "Message to All Indians" instructed superintendents to prohibit some dances completely and restrict all others to once a month. Because the dances were seen as interfering with rational and efficient management of the Pueblo's resources, they were to be banned completely during the most important months of agricultural labor. Because they were seen as impeding the improvement and education of the young toward the abandonment of their primitive ways, Burke recommended that no one under the age of fifty be allowed to participate in or attend the dances that were allowed (p. 93). The renewed policy was a verbatim application of recommendations by the ironically named Indian Rights Association, a group of Protestant missionaries and others who saw themselves as progressives concerned with the improvement of Indian life. They defended Indian land rights and sought to eliminate BIA corruption, while simultaneously seeking to move the Indians into the mainstream of American life (pp. 95-96).

In their initial responses to this renewed threat against their way of life, the Pueblo did not use the category of religious freedom. They argued instead that the ban could not possibly apply to their dances, either because their dances were not impediments to their economic self-sufficiency or because their dances were not "religion" at all: they were customs that inculcated respect for ancestors and they were art forms that had intrinsic value as artistic expressions. As the Pueblo Council wrote to Burke in January 1924, "To us, our dances are drama, opera, and poetry." They found it necessary to defend themselves against accusations that their fertility rites were sexually graphic and obscene (pp. 96-97). In the same letter, they used the term "religion" to apply only to the Catholicism that most Pueblos had practiced since they were colonized by the Spanish (pp. 94-95). Starting in April of 1924, however, other outsiders — those from the American Indian Defense Association, who wanted to preserve the native dances as a crucial link to the past — began to urge the Pueblo to appeal to the principle of religious freedom in their fight against the BIA. The All-Pueblo Council subsequently drafted an appeal based on this principle (p. 99).

As the Pueblo traditionalists who wanted to preserve the dances would soon discover, however, the appeal to religious freedom was a double-edged sword that could be used to undermine the Pueblos' traditional customs. Just a few days before the All-Pueblo Council's appeal, a group of Pueblo who identified themselves as "progressives" had met to form a new organization, the Council of Progressive Pueblo Indians. To them, religious freedom meant the right to refuse to participate in the traditional dances. They charged that Pueblo officials had tried "to make slaves of us" by penalizing those who refused to participate in such "secret and unchristian dances" through fines, confiscation of land, and social ostracism. They demanded "religious liberty and a voice in the management of our pueblo affairs which we do not now have on account of our refusal to conform to outgrown customs" (p. 100). These first resolutions were drafted by a white progressive attorney, A. B. Renehan. White assimilationists were instrumental in organizing and supporting the Council of Progressive Pueblo Indians. The Indian Rights Association took up and publicized the progressive Indians' appeal, because it helped bolster their case that Indian dances were regressive and un-American. White assimilationists encouraged the appeal to religious freedom, thus turning the tables on the traditionalists' defense of their dances by the same principle.

One of the effects of the formation of the progressive council — certainly an unintended effect from the point of view of the progressive Pueblos — was to weaken the Pueblo in their disputes over land with white settlers. Whether or not it was unintended by the white progressives is another question; the same A. B. Renehan who drafted the progressive council's resolutions was simultaneously working as an attorney and advocate for non-Indian settlers in land disputes with the Pueblo. As Wenger writes of the Pueblo progressives, "their very existence and their alliance with known settlers' advocates tended to weaken Pueblo unity in the land claims as well as in religious matters" (p. 102). This point was not lost on the All-Pueblo Council, who responded to the progressives in the following terms: "If you were progressive you wouldn't try to destroy your people's unity. . . . As you know, we are all Christians — those few men who proclaim themselves Christian Progressives are no more Christian nor different Christian than we, and we cannot make out how they are more progressive than we, except that they are following after White men who are against us on the land question and that they won't pay their taxes" (p. 100).

For the traditionalist Pueblo, the unity of the people was more important than the individual's right to dissent. The unity of the people was seen as a matter of survival; if each member of the tribe was to go his or her own way, there simply would be no Pueblo people in a matter of a few years. As Wenger writes,

> [M]ost Pueblo people did not think of the dances as part of a defined "religion," a matter of individual conscience that could be separated from the rest of Pueblo life. Instead, these performances served the whole community by bringing rain and a good growing season, and by maintaining the balance and harmony of the whole earth. Each member of the community shared in these benefits. Therefore the tribal leaders had every right to assign, and the governor to enforce, tribal members' participation in the dances. (p. 105)

The conception of "rights" on display here — insofar as the language of rights even applies — differs fundamentally from the progressives' notion of rights as something that inheres in individuals. The danger of assimilation — and therefore the disappearance of the Pueblo as a people — that the traditionalists feared was not simply that individuals would opt out of the dances. Many progressives in fact continued to participate in them. The more fundamental danger was that Pueblo people would come to think of themselves first as generic individuals with rights, and only subsequently as voluntary members of the Pueblo people. Once such a conception took hold, assimilation to the dominant American culture would not be far behind.

The education of youth was a key battleground in this struggle. In April of 1924, Commissioner Burke visited the Taos Pueblo with the interior secretary and threatened action against the Pueblo if two boys were withdrawn from the government day school for over a year of training in Pueblo dances and ceremonies. The Taos council replied that if youth were not trained in the customs of the people, the people as people would die (p. 99). At about the same time, the Indian Rights Association conducted its own investigation at the Taos Pueblo, and asked its governor, Antonio Romero, if he would let his sons be "forced" to participate in "religious ceremonies" if they did not want to. Romero replied that, if his sons were part of one of the special societies responsible for the dances, they would be required to take part, and he further stated that he would insist that his sons join one of these societies because their training was to be valued as much as his own education in English. "He seemed to be saying that if the U.S. government could force children to attend school under compulsory education laws, then Taos Pueblo could also require its children to obtain its own brand of education — one which its people found equally valuable" (p. 104). In other words, what the U.S. government was doing was not essentially different from what the Pueblo were doing. Every people educates its youth in its own way of life. Every people makes that education compulsory, and does not simply allow its young people to opt out. Every people does so not because freedom is an unworthy goal, but because people need to be taught how to be free, and freedom takes very different and culturally specific forms. Every people educates its youth because it believes it has something good to pass on.

The contest over religious freedom was not limited to the question of dancing, but soon spread to the issue of tribal governance. In late 1924, a controversy erupted over the selection of a governor for the Santa Clara Pueblo. Progressives proposed that the next governor be chosen by lot, arguing that it would require "no change in any purely religious custom" (p. 107). The BIA superintendent then got involved, insisting that the traditional form of government of the Pueblo was undemocratic and "contrary to the spirit and practice of the American people" (p. 107). He demanded that the Pueblo hold elections for tribal governor. Traditionalists responded by invoking the principle of religious freedom, claiming that the U.S. Constitution protected their ways of governance because they were "a part of our religion" (p. 107). Both parties appealed to the principle of religious freedom, but what counted as religion and what did not was contested. It is relevant to note that the whole system of governors was itself not a part of ancient Pueblo custom but was an imposition by the Spanish that was intended to strip traditional *caciques* of their political authority and make them into purely "religious" figures; governors would wield civil authority. In practice, the division never worked this way; *caciques* appointed governors, and the *caciques* retained ultimate authority over all aspects of Pueblo life (pp. 107-8). In the 1920s, however, in response to outside pressures, at least some Pueblo people were willing to claim a clear separation of religion from governance in Pueblo life.

In the end, the BIA mandated general elections for tribal governors, a mandate that the various Pueblos seem to have ignored in the 1920s but finally adopted in the 1930s (p. 108). The freedom of each individual to vote was the ground on which the decision was based. As for the issue of dancing, it was resolved on grounds of religious freedom that Pueblo dances could continue, but that individual Pueblo people were free to opt out if they so chose (p. 110). By defining their practices as "religion," the Pueblo were able to defend successfully some of their customs from obliteration by the U.S. government. In so doing, however, they introduced into tribal life elements of individualism and the separation of something called "religion" from the rest of Pueblo life that were foreign to their traditions. They also contributed to the assimilation of the Pueblo to American life, an assimilation not without its benefits, but also not without its dangers, the chief of which was the disappearance of the Pueblo as an identifiably distinct people.

III. Religious Freedom and the Church

Just as the Pueblo were able to defend some of their practices, I am hopeful that the Catholic-led campaign to defend religious freedom will prove a useful tactic in keeping the government from interfering with the life of the churches. I have misgivings about the way the current campaign is sometimes conducted and perceived, especially the way that it often appears tilted toward lending church support to Republican candidates for office, and the way that the focus is almost always on the HHS mandate and not on more egregious violations of freedom, such as the Alabama law against harboring undocumented immigrants that makes it illegal for the church to minister to them.[6] Nevertheless, I let my name be put on one public ecumenical call for religious freedom because I support the demand that the state refrain from coercing the church to violate its principles.[7] The appeal to religious freedom might be an effective tactic in the short term.

Nevertheless, it seems to me that the same ambivalence that dogged the Pueblo efforts to defend their practices also haunts the church's efforts to invoke religious freedom. When the church allows itself to

6. The U.S. Bishops' statement on religious liberty, "Our First, Most Cherished Liberty," refers to the Alabama case. See the document at http://www.usccb.org/issues -and-action/religious-liberty/our-first-most-cherished-liberty.cfm/.

7. The statement is "In Defense of Religious Freedom," March 2012, by Catholics and Evangelicals Together; http://www.firstthings.com/article/2012/02/in-defense-of -religious-freedom.

be defined as a religion, the same individualism, separation of religion from the rest of life, and assimilation to the dominant culture are clear and present dangers. In what follows, I will comment on each of these three dangers.

The Obama administration's position in issuing the HHS mandate is based on the idea that rights inhere in individuals, not groups. In this case, individuals have the right to contraception, sterilization, and abortion, a right that should be recognized by their employers in providing insurance coverage. Religious groups have no right to deny this right to individuals who work for them, even to individuals who claim membership in the sponsoring church. Because religion is inherently a matter of individual preference, religious bodies cannot claim rights. This logic is articulated by the *New York Times* editorial on February 10, 2012, decrying the "phony crisis" over religious freedom. According to the *Times'* editors, "Churches are given complete freedom by the Constitution to preach that birth control is immoral, but they have not been given the right to laws that would deprive their followers or employees of the right to disagree with that teaching. If a religious body does not like a public policy that affects its members, it is free to try to change it, but it cannot simply opt out of society or claim a special exemption from the law."[8] The editorial goes on to refer to Catholic hospitals and universities as the church's "nonreligious arms," since religion is confined to individual belief. The same logic is at play in the Massachusetts federal court decision cited by the bishops in which the Bishops' Migration and Refugee Service was required to provide contraception and abortion services or lose its government contract. The government's position is that individuals have a right to such services, and the church has no right to interfere with that right.[9]

The shift from the medieval ideal of a shared, substantive conception of the good to an individual and formal conception of freedom as the highest good is one of the hallmarks of a modern, liberal society. In his commentary on the *New York Times* editorial cited above, David Schindler has argued that John Locke's conception of rights, on which the Founding Fathers drew, is inherently individualistic. Schindler

8. "The Freedom to Choose Birth Control," *New York Times,* February 10, 2012; http://www.nytimes.com/2012/02/11/opinion/the-freedom-to-choose-birth-control .html.

9. U.S. Conference of Catholic Bishops (USCCB), "Our First, Most Cherished Liberty."

rightly argues "that Catholics make a grave mistake if they approach the current controversy on the assumption that all sides agree in principle about the nature and universality of rights." Liberal conceptions of rights apply to individuals alone, whereas in the Catholic conception the human person is understood as inherently related to God and to other people. As Schindler comments, "[I]f we fail to understand that the present crisis is at root one regarding the nature of the human being, our political strategies, however effective in the short term, will over the long term serve to strengthen the very assumptions that have generated the crisis in the first place."[10]

Brad Gregory has recently traced this shift behind the Enlightenment to the Reformation. As he writes, "Because *individuals* disagreed about the meaning of God's word, *individuals* and not politically favored churches were and had to be the bearers of rights, beginning with the right to religious liberty."[11] The result would eventually be the modern conception of rights as inhering in individuals and the modern conception of religion as a matter of individual personal preference. "Leaving each person free to determine the good based on 'the word of God before him' and 'the mind of Christ within him' would prove to be *at one and the same time* the modern basis for protecting individual human beings against certain forms of coercion by the state, and the unintended road to the elimination of any shared notion of the good."[12] As Gregory notes, the result would be the subjectivization of morality. As he hints as well, the result was also the debilitation of any intermediate associations that stood between the state and the individual, because they were the only bearers of shared notions of the good. As Robert Nisbet remarks, "The real conflict in modern political history has not been, as is so often stated, between State and individual, but between State and social group."[13]

If the bishops want to articulate a corporate right to freedom, the freedom of the church to be itself, they would certainly have ample

10. David L. Schindler, "The Repressive Logic of Liberal Rights: Religious Freedom, Contraceptives, and the "Phony" Argument of the *New York Times*," *Communio* 38 (Winter 2011): 523-47.

11. Brad S. Gregory, *The Unintended Reformation: How a Religious Revolution Secularized Society* (Cambridge: Harvard University Press, 2012), p. 215.

12. Gregory, *The Unintended Reformation*, p. 216.

13. Robert A. Nisbet, *The Quest for Community* (London: Oxford University Press, 1953), p. 109.

theological grounds to do so. As I show in chapter 1, the patristic writers understood human creation in God's image to indicate that all people are created for communion with each other through their communion with God. The image of the body of Christ, so important in the New Testament, ratifies the idea that the church is a corporate personality with a common end, not simply a collection of individuals. But the articulation of a right of religious freedom in America is usually done in a way that appeals not to theology but to putatively secular ideals available in principle to all. The problem is that the dominant secular discourse of rights sees both rights and religious preference as inhering in the individual. This dynamic can be seen clearly in the Supreme Court's resolution to the question of whether or not nontheists can claim conscientious objection to military service, which was open to people on "religious" grounds. Rather than define religion to exclude nontheists, the Court offered the exemption to anyone holding a "sincere and meaningful belief which occupies in the life of its possessor a place parallel to that filled by the God of those admittedly qualifying for the exemption."[14] As legal scholar Marie Failinger comments, "the Court often uses the notion of freedom in a very atomistic way: religious freedom is the right of a person to select his or her religious faith and to choose what it will mean to him or her, whether his or her beliefs are shared by any other person, whether they grow out of any relationship with the external world including a transcendent being, whether they are based on a thoughtful argument or are simply the individual's whim."[15] In this light, the bishops' appeal to James Madison's idea that "the Religion then of every man must be left to the conviction and conscience of every man; and it is the right of every man to exercise it as these may dictate"[16] reinforces the idea that religion is a matter of personal preference. Religious rights, therefore, apply to individuals, not to corporate groups like the church, and the witness of the church as body of Christ is subordinated to the personal beliefs and preferences of individuals.

The second danger inherent in the idea that Christianity is a religion is that religion is defined in liberal society as a matter of beliefs about

14. 380 US 163 (1965), p. 166.
15. Marie A. Failinger, "Wondering after Babel: Power, Freedom, and Ideology in U.S. Supreme Court Interpretations of the Religion Clauses," in *Law and Religion*, ed. Rex J. Ahdar (Aldershot: Ashgate, 2000), p. 94.
16. James Madison, quoted in USCCB, "Our First, Most Cherished Liberty."

the otherworldly and only indirectly applies to the social and political. In Thomas Jefferson's words, belief in one God or twenty neither picks my pocket nor breaks my legs; in other words, religion has no immediate social effect. As I have indicated in my brief genealogy in chapter 9, the very modern Western concept of religion was born out of the desire to identify religion as precisely that which has to do with otherworldly concerns and not with the application of public power in "secular" matters such as politics and economics. The bishops have objected to the government's moves to declare the church's activity nonreligious precisely insofar as it has a social effect. They have also decried "the tendency to reduce the freedom of religion to the mere freedom of worship."[17] At the same time, however, they have continued to insist on the right to be "free in our conscience"[18] and have defined religious freedom as meaning that "all men are to be immune from coercion on the part of individuals or of social groups and of any human power, in such wise that in matters religious no one is to be forced to act in a manner contrary to his own beliefs."[19] The bishops are not wrong to claim the right of conscience and belief to be free of coercion, but insofar as religion is defined in terms of conscience and belief, it is removed from the realm of the bodily, the world of health care and immigration policy and all those activities said to belong to the "secular," nonreligious realm. To resist the confinement of Christianity to concern with the otherworldly, we need a robust defense of the idea that our God is the God of all creation, and that the gospel is concerned with caring for the flourishing of the whole human person, body and soul. We need more than an appeal to freedom of belief and freedom of conscience; we need to question the modern terms under which Christianity is consigned to one side of the religious/secular dichotomy that has been constructed in liberal society. We need to ask, as Robert Shedinger puts it, "whether the concern so often expressed over the politicization of Islam in the contemporary world ought to be replaced by a concern with the 'religionization' of Christianity."[20]

The bishops have chosen to defend the church by using one of the

17. USCCB, "Our First, Most Cherished Liberty."
18. USCCB, "Our First, Most Cherished Liberty."
19. USCCB, "Our First, Most Cherished Liberty." Here the bishops are quoting from *Dignitatis Humanae*, §2.
20. Robert F. Shedinger, *Was Jesus a Muslim? Questioning Categories in the Study of Religion* (Minneapolis: Fortress, 2009), p. 12.

tools provided by American political culture, the concept of religious freedom. Rather than refuse the terms on which the debate is offered, they have sought protection by emphasizing the continuity between Catholic and American ideals. The third danger I see in this strategy is this: in emphasizing continuity, they will cease to challenge the assimilation of Catholicism to an American system that reflexively views Catholicism as a religion and therefore as a matter of personal preference.

In their statement on religious freedom entitled "Our First, Most Cherished Liberty," the bishops do recognize the prospect of unjust laws that Catholics must have the courage to disobey. They also cite Pope Benedict XVI's admonition that the laity should exhibit "a strong critical sense vis-à-vis the dominant culture" in America. The document is nevertheless filled with patriotic language about "our enlightened republic," "the land of the free, and a beacon of hope for the world." The bishops' statement begins, "We are Catholics. We are Americans. We are proud to be both, grateful for the gift of faith which is ours as Christian disciples, and grateful for the gift of liberty which is ours as American citizens. To be Catholic and American should mean not having to choose one over the other."[21] Archbishop Lori's opening homily for the 2013 bishops' Fortnight for Freedom was entitled "Faith Enriches Public Life"; it ends with a rousing "may God bless these United States of America!"[22] The prayer for the protection of religious liberty that was distributed in parishes throughout the country prays that "this great land will always be 'one nation, under God, indivisible, with liberty and justice for all.'" The bishops "exhort" the laypeople "to be both engaged and articulate in insisting that as Catholics and as Americans we do not have to choose between the two."[23]

It is not hard to sympathize with the bishops' attempts to win protection by appealing to the nation's best sense of its own ideals. The problem is that, in minimizing the tension between Catholicism and America, Catholics might too easily assume that Catholicism can be fitted into America as the particular into the universal. In other words, the way that the church and the nation-state have tended to make their peace in modernity is by assuming that a division of labor obtains in

21. USCCB, "Our First, Most Cherished Liberty."

22. Archbishop Lori's Fortnight for Freedom opening homily, http://www.usccb.org/issues-and-action/religious-liberty/fortnight-for-freedom/2013-fortnight-for-freedom-opening-homily-archbishop-william-lori.cfm.

23. From a flyer in the possession of the author.

which the Christian's religious allegiance belongs to God and her political allegiance belongs to the nation. Religious allegiance in a liberal society has increasingly been defined since the mid-twentieth century as subjective, individual, and essentially apolitical, which is precisely the trivialization of Christian faith against which the bishops want to fight.

In 2005, a faithful Catholic schoolteacher in Bridgeport, Connecticut, named Stephen Kobasa was fired in the middle of the semester for removing the American flag from his classroom. He regarded it as a contradiction to the cross of Christ displayed in the same classroom. The local bishop supported the firing, and ignored repeated requests to explain his actions. The bishop's name was William Lori. He has since been promoted to the see of Baltimore, and he chairs the bishops' Ad Hoc Committee on Religious Liberty. This episode illustrates the danger that appealing to American values for protection will lead the church to offer its allegiance to America even when we do have to choose between the two.

IV. Conclusion

In this chapter I have tried to highlight the pitfalls of the church's appeals to religious freedom in the current context. I am not necessarily opposed in all instances to using the appeal to religious freedom as a tactic to win protection for church practices. I am afraid, however, that in the long run accepting the terms on which the debate is offered will offer scant resistance to the reduction of the church to a strictly voluntary association of like-minded people expressing their religious preferences while their public and political allegiance belongs exclusively to the nation-state. A more robust defense of the church's freedom must proclaim the fact that the gospel founds a body, the body of Christ, that deals with the whole person. It is a body, furthermore, that does not always fit neatly with the other types of allegiances to which people offer themselves. In the next and final chapter, I will examine the question of allegiance and the body of Christ through the witness of Dorothy Day.

CHAPTER THIRTEEN

"WE ARE TO BLAME FOR THE WAR":

DOROTHY DAY ON VIOLENCE AND GUILT

IN THE MYSTICAL BODY OF CHRIST

B Y THE TIME the German armed forces breached the frontier with Poland on September 1, 1939, the world had long been on the alert for the outbreak of a "world war" in Europe. The rise of fascism in Italy and the particularly virulent Nazi expansionist ideology had made war increasingly likely in the eyes of the Allied countries. Imagine the surprise of American readers when the *Catholic Worker* newspaper, in its September 1939 edition, located the cause of the war somewhere besides Hitler, somewhere much closer to home: "We Are to Blame for New War in Europe" ran the headline. The accompanying article explained, "The blame rests on the peoples of the entire world, for their materialism, their greed, their idolatrous nationalism, for their refusal to believe in a just peace, for their ruthless subjection of a noble country.... Hitler is incidental; the war must have come sooner or later under the circumstances."[1] Those looking for the reason that the *Catholic Worker* lost nearly 75 percent of its readership during World War II need look no further than this article.

Though the article refers to the peoples of the entire world as "they," the real force of the article comes from the "we" of the title. The non-violence of Dorothy Day and what remained of the Catholic Worker Movement during World War II was based on this conception of "we," that all people are members or potential members of the same body, the mystical body of Christ. To go to war was as unthinkable in this concep-

---

1. "We Are to Blame for New War in Europe," *Catholic Worker,* September 1939, pp. 1, 4.

tion as the hands of a human body taking a saw and cutting off its feet. This aspect of Dorothy Day's thought is well known. What is less well known is the implication of the doctrine of the mystical body for the causes of war. If we are all members of the same body, it is not so easy to separate the guilty from the innocent. The commutability of pain in the body also implies the commutability of guilt, the sharing of blame for the conflict to which Dorothy Day saw the mystical body as the solution. It is precisely for this reason that Day so often prescribed penance as the antidote for war, penance not only for *them,* but also for *us.*

One of the reasons that this theme of shared guilt is so important for understanding Dorothy Day and the Catholic Worker Movement is that it corrects a common stereotype of the movement as a perfectionist and sectarian movement that attempts to hold people to a higher standard than the average person is capable of achieving. The Catholic Worker Movement is often read according to Ernst Troeltsch's typology as a "sect," a gathering of the few who are pure enough to live according to the Sermon on the Mount. In this view, voluntary poverty, sacrificial service to others, and abstaining from violence of all kinds meet the noble ideals of Jesus, but pertain only to a spiritual elite, and so are inspiring but ultimately of little direct historical relevance for living in the real world. If refraining from violence, however, is not an act of perfectionism but an act of penance for one's own guilt and complicity in the world's ills, then nonviolence is not an assertion of one's own virtue but a humble recognition that we are not good enough to use violence rightly.

I will begin by examining some critiques of Christian perfectionism and nonviolence in contemporary Christian ethics. I will then explore the themes of pacifism and the mystical body of Christ in Dorothy Day's writings, and show how penance plays an integral part of life in the body.

I. Pacifism and Perfectionism

One of the standard ways of reading Dorothy Day and the Catholic Worker Movement is to place them in a typology that lauds their purity but questions their ability to face the problems of the world realistically. Famed historian David J. O'Brien's work is typical in this regard. In an article entitled "Join It, Work It, Fight It: American Catholics and the Catholic Way," O'Brien identifies three styles of Catholicism in the

United States that correspond to the trilogy in the title of the article. "Republican" Catholicism seeks to join the system, working within the normal political channels of a pluralistic democracy to promote the common good. "Immigrant" Catholicism sees America as hostile territory and seeks to work the system for its own relative advantage. "Evangelical" Catholicism seeks to judge the United States based directly on the criteria of the gospel, and so to fight the system's many injustices.

For O'Brien, "the Catholic Worker represented the appearance of an evangelical style in American Catholicism."[2] He admires the movement's dynamism, its ability to resist easy accommodation to American power — such as in the republican model — and its movement beyond the narrow self-interest of the immigrant style. Nevertheless, for O'Brien it is the very "perfectionism" and "purist"[3] tendencies he admires that also lead to his critique of the movement as marginal and ineffectual. "The weakness of the evangelical approach is that, by defining issues and responses in Christian terms, its proponents become marginalized in the larger public debate."[4] According to O'Brien, social problems intersect with government policy, and in a pluralistic society one simply cannot make appeals in explicitly Christian terms. "On its own, then, evangelical Catholicism challenges the church, but limits the audience, restricts the language, and shortcircuits a sense of responsibility for the common life, tending toward a perfectionism, even an apocalyptic sectarianism, that questions the legitimacy of all secular institutions, devalues citizenship, and reduces the moral significance of work, politics, and community life."[5] The Catholic Worker Movement can foster small utopian communities of witness to the Sermon on the Mount, but it cannot effectively address common life. For O'Brien, Dorothy Day's appeal to the mystical body of Christ has the opposite effect to that which Day intended: rather than emphasizing responsibility to all, its very perfectionism in fact "short-circuits" that responsibility for the common life. Day's unbending pacifist stand during World War II, for example, only left her and the remnants of her movement isolated from the rest of the church and the nation.

2. David J. O'Brien, "Join It, Work It, Fight It: American Catholics and the Catholic Way," *Commonweal* 116, no. 20 (November 17, 1989): 626.

3. See O'Brien, "Join It," p. 630, where O'Brien refers to "evangelical purists." See also David J. O'Brien, *Public Catholicism* (New York: Macmillan, 1989), p. 246.

4. O'Brien, "Join It," p. 627.

5. O'Brien, "Join It," p. 628.

Throughout O'Brien's article and broader work, "perfectionism," "purism," "utopianism," and, above all, "sectarianism" are opposed to "mediation," "responsibility," and "common life." O'Brien invokes Max Weber's distinction between a "politics of ultimate ends," which he associates with Dorothy Day, and a "politics of responsibility," which he says typifies the republican style.[6] Weber developed the distinction between church and sect in a sociological sense to distinguish between different types of belonging to Christian communities, either by birth (church) or by choice (sect).[7] The church-sect distinction fit into Weber's attempts to explain the supposed rationalization and disenchantment of the previously Christian West. As I discussed in chapter 2, Weber's colleague and friend Ernst Troeltsch famously developed the church-sect distinction such that it tracked the extent to which a Christian group accommodated itself to the norms of mainstream society or maintained a commitment to gospel perfection. "The Church is that type of organization which is overwhelmingly conservative, which to a certain extent accepts the secular order, and dominates the masses; in principle, therefore, it is universal, i.e., it desires to cover the whole life of humanity. The sects, on the other hand, are comparatively small groups; they aspire after personal inward perfection, and they aim at a direct personal fellowship between the members of each group."[8] Sectarian perfection, however, is not the same as the "counsels of perfection" lived out in the medieval church by monks and other religious called to a higher standard. "It is not the heroic special achievement of a special class, restricted by its very nature to particular instances, nor the mortification of the senses in order to further the higher religious life; it is simply detachment from the world, the reduction of worldly pleasure to a minimum, and the highest possible development of fellowship in love."[9] Troeltsch goes on to contrast sectarian asceticism, which is based on primitive Christianity and the Sermon on the Mount, with the asceticism "of the Church and of the contemplative life."[10] Like O'Brien, Troeltsch writes that what

6. O'Brien, "Join It," p. 630.

7. Max Weber, "On Church, Sect, and Mysticism," *Sociological Analysis* 34 (1973): 140-49.

8. Ernst Troeltsch, *The Social Teaching of the Christian Churches,* vol. 1, trans. Olive Wyon (New York: Harper and Row, 1960), p. 331.

9. Troeltsch, *Social Teaching,* p. 340.

10. Troeltsch, *Social Teaching,* p. 340.

sectarians gain in terms of "intensity in Christian life" they lose in terms of the "spirit of universalism."[11]

The charge of narrow sectarianism is the primary lens through which critiques of the followers of Dorothy Day in Christian ethics have been mounted. According to Richard McBrien's entry on "sectarianism" in the *HarperCollins Encyclopedia of Catholicism,* the sectarian spirit is a

> desire to be separated from the larger Christian community by appealing to individualistic aspects of Christianity, stressing the importance of moral purity, and defining true Christianity as incompatible with membership in established Christian churches or with engagement with modern culture. Sectarians tend to reject the value of diversity and define themselves in opposition to others.... A sectarian group is one that is detached from the world and resistant to any involvement in the socio-political problems that exist outside the Church.[12]

According to McBrien, "Although sectarianism is diametrically opposed to Catholicism, a certain sectarian orientation has emerged in recent years in portions of the Catholic peace movement and in some younger Catholic moral theologians influenced by Protestant sectarian ethicists";[13] this is a thinly veiled reference to followers of Dorothy Day and Catholic students of Stanley Hauerwas.

As Benjamin Peters has shown, the intertwined charges of perfectionism, separatism, and sectarianism against the Catholic Worker Movement date back at least to World War II, when Jesuit Joseph Connor critiqued Catholic Worker conscientious objectors as "perfectionists" who demonstrated an "air of exhilarating aloofness and detachment" that smacked of "Albigensian purism." According to Connor, it was morally impermissible for ordinary laypeople to practice the counsels of perfection when they were "morally subject" to the state, which cannot practice those counsels.[14] In the 1980s, Charles Curran and George Weigel made similar charges against

11. Troeltsch, *Social Teaching,* p. 337.

12. Richard P. McBrien, "Sectarianism," in *HarperCollins Encyclopedia of Catholicism* (San Francisco: HarperCollins, 1995), p. 1180.

13. McBrien, "Sectarianism," p. 1180.

14. Joseph J. Connor, S.J., "The Catholic Conscientious Objector," *Ecclesiastical Review* 108 (February 1943): 125-38, cited in Benjamin Peters, "'Apocalyptic Sectarianism': The Theology at Work in Critiques of Catholic Radicals," *Horizons* 39 (Fall 2012): 217-18.

Dorothy Day and the Catholic Worker Movement from opposite ends of the liberal-conservative spectrum. Curran's chapter on the Catholic Worker Movement and Paul Hanly Furfey in his book *American Catholic Social Ethics* concludes that "Traditionally, Christian radicals propose an ecclesiology which is based on the sect — a small group of Christians striving for perfection who are separated from the rest of the world. But Catholic ecclesiology has frequently insisted on its universality,"[15] which means in this regard that Day was, as McBrien put it, "diametrically opposed to Catholicism." Weigel, for his part, appealed to Weber's distinction between an "ethics of responsibility" and an "ethics of absolute ends," contending that "Dorothy Day unhesitatingly chose the latter,"[16] but then made the mistake of trying to apply the "evangelical call to perfection" in the realm of politics.[17] More recently, Kristen Heyer has similarly applied the label "perfectionist" to Day and critiqued her for supposedly setting up a radical discontinuity between nature and grace.[18]

II. The Mystical Body, Violence, and Penance

The charge of perfectionism is often the lens through which Dorothy Day and those who would take her seriously are marginalized in contemporary Catholic social ethics. Is the charge fair? I want to examine Dorothy Day's commitment to nonviolence through a different lens. I hope to show that her pacifism stemmed not from a sectarian perfectionism but rather from a deep sense of the shared guilt of all — including herself and her Catholic Worker community — and the necessity, therefore, of nonviolence as a kind of penance.

Dorothy Day did sometimes refer to the counsels of perfection in opposing the use of violence. In clarifying the movement's refusal to

15. Charles E. Curran, *American Catholic Social Ethics: Twentieth-Century Approaches* (Notre Dame: University of Notre Dame Press, 1982), pp. 159-60.

16. George Weigel, *Tranquillitas Ordinis: The Present Failure and Future Promise of American Catholic Thought on War and Peace* (New York: Oxford University Press, 1987), p. 152.

17. Weigel, *Tranquillitas Ordinis*, pp. 152, 247.

18. Kristen Heyer, *Prophetic and Public: The Social Witness of U.S. Catholicism* (Washington, D.C.: Georgetown University Press, 2006), p. 90, cited in Peters, " 'Apocalyptic Sectarianism,' " p. 212.

support either side in the Spanish Civil War, Day wrote, "It is folly — it seems madness — to say as we do — 'we are opposed to the use of force as a means of settling personal, national, or international disputes.' . . . We feel that if the press and the public throughout the world do not speak in terms of the counsels of perfection, who else will?"[19] Again in June 1940, Day appealed to the counsels of perfection in reaffirming the movement's pacifist stand despite the spread of Nazi aggression in Europe.[20] Here she quotes Father Stratmann, who writes, "More than all, he who opposes war must be inwardly clean. His passion for justice must not be tainted by hidden uncleanness. As long as pacifists are in the minority, let them begin with a steady fight against all that is evil in themselves."[21] In other contexts, Day recommended the counsels of perfection to all, beyond a select few, as part of our general call to holiness,[22] though she acknowledges that "we do not, can not, live up to it."[23] Here, as in other areas, Dorothy Day can be seen as anticipating the Second Vatican Council; the council's emphasis on the laity's call to holiness is a movement away from the kind of two-tiered ethic in which the religious were called to live the counsels of perfection and the laity were seen as held to a lower standard. In its section on the laity, *Lumen*

19. Dorothy Day, "Explains CW Stand on Use of Force," *Catholic Worker,* September 1938, p. 1.

20. Dorothy Day, "Our Stand," *Catholic Worker,* June 1940, p. 4. "We are urging what is a seeming impossibility — a training to the use of non-violent means of opposing injustice, servitude and a deprivation of the means of holding fast to the Faith. It is again the Folly of the Cross. But how else is the Word of God to be kept alive in the world. That Word is Love, and we are bidden to love God and to love one another. It is the whole law, it is all of life. Nothing else matters. Can we do this best in the midst of such horror as has been going on these past months by killing, or by offering our lives for our brothers? It is hard to write so in times like these when millions are doing what they consider their duty, what is 'good' for them to do. But if the Catholic press does not uphold the better way, the counsels of perfection will be lost to the world."

21. Day, "Our Stand," p. 4.

22. See Dorothy Day, "Security," *Catholic Worker,* July-August 1935, p. 4, and Dorothy Day, "Called to Be Saints," *Catholic Worker,* January 1946, p. 2.

23. Dorothy Day, "Poverty and Pacifism," *Catholic Worker,* December 1944, p. 1; "And we must keep this vision in mind, recognize the truth of it, the necessity for it, even though we do not, can not, live up to it. Like perfection. We are ordered to be perfect as our heavenly Father is perfect, and we aim at it, in our intention, though in our execution we may fall short of the mark over and over. St. Paul says, it is by little and by little that we proceed."

Gentium says that all members of the church share the "same vocation to perfection."[24]

What many fail to see is that Day's talk of the counsels of perfection is always set within her broader vision of the mystical body of Christ, which forms the foundational insight at the root of all her reflections on violence, and indeed, all her reflections on any topic. William Miller quotes Day as saying, "The Mystical Body is the doctrine which is behind all our efforts."[25] For Day, justified violence is unthinkable not simply because it is counterproductive or against God's law, but because it represents the members of the same body tearing at one another. But just as all people share one love within this body, by the same token all share the same guilt. The mystical force that binds all people to one another binds our fates together in such a way that no one is free of responsibility for the sin that keeps the body from being what it is called to be.

It is well-known that the mystical body of Christ was the basis on which Day opposed war. In her article "The Mystical Body and Spain," she begins by quoting Pope Saint Clement of Rome: "Why do the Members of Christ tear one another; why do we rise up against our own body in such madness; have we forgotten that we are all members, one of another?"[26] She then appeals to both sides in the Spanish Civil War to stop the killing. Day dismisses consideration of the justice of either side's cause, concluding that there is plenty of right and wrong on both sides. What concerns her is simply the physical act of killing, regardless of the reasons behind it. "Remember only that the Body is being rent asunder, and the only solution is Love."[27] The same appeal to the almost physical reality of the body of Christ underlies Day's approach to World War II and every other war. Her 1942 article "Why Do the Members of Christ Tear One Another?" begins with the same quote from

24. Vatican II, *Dogmatic Constitution on the Church (Lumen Gentium)*, §32: "Therefore, the chosen People of God is one: 'one Lord, one faith, one baptism'; sharing a common dignity as members from their regeneration in Christ, having the same filial grace and the same vocation to perfection; possessing in common one salvation, one hope and one undivided charity"; http://www.vatican.va/archive/hist_councils/ii_vatican _council/documents/vat-ii_const_19641121_lumen-gentium_en.html.

25. Dorothy Day, quoted in William D. Miller, *A Harsh and Dreadful Love: Dorothy Day and the Catholic Worker Movement* (New York: Liveright, 1973).

26. Dorothy Day, "The Mystical Body and Spain," *Catholic Worker*, August 1936, p. 4.

27. Day, "Mystical Body and Spain," p. 4.

Saint Clement and continues by defending the pacifism of the Catholic Worker Movement from charges of cowardice and sentimentality. She invites those who make such charges to live as the Catholic Workers do, in the unheated, vermin-infested slums, with the deranged, drunken, and lice-covered poor.[28] Day's purpose here is not simply to defend the courage of herself and her coworkers, but to make a deeper point about the interconnectedness of suffering in the body of Christ. The Catholic Workers may not be in battle as soldiers are, but they feel the effects of "the monstrous injustice of the class war"[29] that forces people to live in involuntary poverty and squalor. Because we are all members of the same body, we must feel the suffering of others and try to alleviate rather than inflict it. But the alleviation of suffering can never be accomplished from afar; it must always be a participation in suffering, a taking on of suffering. Day turns from talk of this suffering to talk of love. Love must always be the absorption of the suffering of others. As Day writes, "Love is not killing, it is the laying down of one's life for one's friend."[30]

There is more than a hint of expiatory suffering in Day's writings. In "The Incompatibility of Love and Violence," she writes, "We love life, we hunger and thirst for it and only suffering will bring us to life. For this we are put into the world, to love and give up our life for others."[31] The strong identification with Christ implied by the idea of the mystical body indicates a suffering for the sins of others. "For God cannot identify us with His Christ unless He conforms us to His Passion."[32] Day writes during World War II, "You can write and write again, protesting our President's policy of accepting the British blockade. . . . Work and pray, or rather pray that God will show you what to do these dreadful days. These are days when people are flocking to the churches, to the Communion rail. . . . To pray, to work for peace in whatever way you can, to sacrifice and do penance for our sins as a nation, this program is open to all."[33] It is not entirely clear that the church and the Catholic

28. Dorothy Day, "Why Do the Members of Christ Tear One Another?" *Catholic Worker,* February 1942, p. 1.

29. Day, "Why Do the Members?" p. 1.

30. Day, "Why Do the Members?" p. 1.

31. Dorothy Day, "The Incompatibility of Love and Violence," *Catholic Worker,* May 1951, p. 2.

32. Dorothy Day, "Day after Day," *Catholic Worker,* November 1941, p. 1. Here Day is quoting from Zundel's *The Splendor of the Liturgy.*

33. Day, "Day after Day," p. 1.

Workers themselves are fully included in the guilt of the nation; it is not clear, in other words, if they are suffering for their own sins or are suffering for the sins of others. Taken out of context, Day's talk of suffering in response to war can be seen as the expiatory suffering of the pure on behalf of those who wield the sinful instruments of violence.

To read Day in this way, however, one would have to ignore her repeated emphasis, in the context of war, on penance and the guilt shared by herself and by her companions. In her article on the mystical body and Spain, she writes, "Christ offered His death for the sins of the world. So we offer our voluntary and involuntary pains and sufferings for the sins of the world, my own and others."[34] When Day writes in the context of World War II, "We are crushed under the burden of our guilt in starving our brothers in Europe,"[35] one can feel her own anguish directed inward, not outward at others. A month after the attack on Pearl Harbor, she reiterated the movement's pacifist stand, denouncing the war and quoting Father Orchard's call for prayer for an end to the violence. But prayer by itself is not enough. "Let us add, that unless we combine this prayer with almsgiving, in giving to the least of God's children, and fasting in order that we may help feed the hungry, and penance in recognition of our share in the guilt, our prayer may become empty words."[36] In the same vein, Day repeatedly called for acts of penance for the shared guilt of being citizens of the country that used atomic weapons on Japan.[37] In her last major public address, to the Eucharistic Congress on the thirty-first anniversary of the destruction of Hiroshima, she pleaded for the military Mass and all Masses that day to be "an act of penance, begging God to forgive us."[38] "It is a fearful thought, that unless we do penance, we will perish."[39]

Nowhere does Dorothy Day make this emphasis on shared, personal guilt more clear than in her article "Why Do the Members of Christ Tear One Another?" She quotes Father Zossima from Dostoevsky's *Brothers Karamazov,* a novel to which she had frequent recourse and

34. Day, "Mystical Body and Spain," p. 4.

35. Day, "Day after Day," p. 1.

36. Dorothy Day, "Our Country Passes from Undeclared War to Declared War: We Continue Our Christian Pacifist Stand," *Catholic Worker,* January 1942, p. 4.

37. See Dorothy Day, "What Is Happening? Trial Continued until Nov. 16," *Catholic Worker,* November 1955, p. 2.

38. Dorothy Day, "Bread for the Hungry," *Catholic Worker,* September 1976, pp. 1, 5.

39. Day, "Bread for the Hungry," p. 5.

which had a profound effect on her theology of shared salvation and shared guilt:

> "Love one another, Fathers," he said, speaking to his monks. "Love God's people. Because we have come here and shut ourselves within these walls, we are no holier than those that are outside, but on the contrary, from the very fact of coming here, each of us has confessed to himself that he is worse than others, than all men on earth. . . . When he realizes that he is not only worse than others, but that he is responsible to all men and for all and everything, for all human sins, national and individual, only then the aim of our seclusion is attained. For know, dear ones, that every one of us is undoubtedly responsible for all men and everything on earth, not merely through the general sinfulness of creation, but each one personally for all mankind and every individual man. For monks are not a special sort of man, but only what all men ought to be. Only through that knowledge, our heart grows soft with infinite, universal, inexhaustible love. Then every one of you will have the power to win over the whole world by love and to wash away the sins of the world with your tears."[40]

The quote continues on in the same vein. At the end, Dorothy Day adds in her own voice, "I quote this because that accusation 'holier than thou' is also made against us. And we must all admit our guilt, our participation in the social order which has resulted in this monstrous crime of war."[41] She mentions a demented friend who would beat his breast and declare that the war and the revolution were all his fault. "That should be our cry, with every mouthful we eat, 'We are starving Europe!'"[42]

Along with self-condemnation, Day stressed that the condemnation of others was to be avoided, despite the monstrous evils of war that she identified. She admonishes her pacifist readers that "No young man should consider himself superior to his companion who obeys the call to arms."[43] One reason for this, as she makes clear elsewhere, is that there is an element of our choices that is beyond our control, an element

---

40. Fyodor Dostoevsky, as quoted in Day, "Why Do the Members?" p. 7.
41. Day, "Why Do the Members?" p. 7.
42. Day, "Why Do the Members?" p. 7.
43. Quoting Father Stratmann in Day, "Our Stand," p. 4.

of chance — or, better, providence — in where we find ourselves. "While we take this stand we are not condemning those who have seized arms and engaged in war. Who of us as individuals if we were in Spain today, would tell what he would do?"[44] With regard to her "enemies," that is, those who favor and prosecute war, she vows to avoid being "carping in our criticism" and professes, "We love our country and we love our President. We have been the only country in the world where men of all nations have taken refuge from oppression."[45] And she warns against self-righteousness in opposing war: "Remember, too, the publicans can also say, 'Thank God I am not as the Pharisees.' . . . Jesus loved publicans and sinners, He loved His enemies."[46]

Although it is undeniably the case that Day's strong sense of solidarity binding individuals to one another owes much to her background in socialism, it is in the doctrine of the mystical body of Christ that that solidarity reaches its most profound expression, to the point that class antagonism is overcome by a love that assumes that the sins of the antagonist are one's own sins, and the sins of all become radically commutable. As Day professes in *From Union Square to Rome*, "We are bowed down with [Christ] under the weight of not only our own sins but the sins of each other, of the whole world. We are those who are sinned against and those who are sinning. We are identified with Him, one with Him. We are members of His Mystical Body."[47] What makes the assignment of blame to the other — and the claim of purity for oneself or one's "sect" — impossible is the fact that, in the body of Christ, the distinction between the self and the other breaks down. If we are part of the same body, then the sins as well as the merits — both the sufferings and the joys, as Paul tells the Corinthians (I Cor. 12:26) — are shared by all. There is a commutability of sin, such that, as Day says, we are both those who sin and those who are sinned against.

The Eastern ascetic tradition out of which Dostoevsky and his character Father Zossima come contains profound reflections on this commutability of sin. As Orthodox theologian John Zizioulas writes, the Desert Fathers took evil very seriously, constantly doing battle with demons through prayer and fasting. "Yet in a remarkable way they in-

44. Day, "Explains CW Stand," p. 4.
45. Day, "Our Country Passes," p. 1.
46. Day, "Mystical Body and Spain," p. 4.
47. Dorothy Day, *From Union Square to Rome* (New York: Arno Press, 1978), p. 12.

sisted that the Other should be kept from moral judgement and cate-gorization. This they achieved not by disregarding evil but by *trans-ferring it from the Other to the Self.*"⁴⁸ Zizioulas points, for example, to Zosimas, a sixth-century Desert Father, who wrote that the sin of the other should not only be forgiven, but the other should be regarded as a benefactor for making it possible to transfer the blame for the other's sin onto oneself.⁴⁹ If this seems like a violation of justice, of assigning blame to the wrong person, we need to be reminded that all human-ity participates in the Fall. None is without sin, and able to throw the first stone (John 8:7). The kenotic spirituality of the desert ascetics was based on the twin goals of uprooting self-love, which is the root of sin, and taking on the virtues of Christ. In both cases, there is a priority of the other over the self, a kind of self-forgetting that marks the erotic movement of love. Like Christ, one abandons oneself in order to be united to the ultimate Other, who is God the Father.⁵⁰

In this erotic union with the other, the very distinction between self and other is effaced. The establishment of justice — to give each his or her due — becomes of secondary importance, at best. We move beyond the ethical and into the ontological, where all assignment of due and blame is overcome by the sheer injustice of Christ's redemp-tion. It is not only the crucifixion of Christ that is unjust; injustice is overcome precisely by the doing away with justice in the redemption that Christ effects. No one gets what he or she deserves, and that is precisely what is meant by calling the gospel "good news." God's re-demption overcomes the sorting out of the pure from sinners, friends from enemies. Indeed, we can love our enemies because the enemy is us. In declaring her pacifist stand amidst the rage stoked by Pearl Harbor, Day quotes from the Sermon on the Mount: "Love your en-emies, do good to those who hate you, and pray for those who perse-cute and calumniate you, so that you may be children of your Father in heaven, who makes His sun to rise on the good and the evil, and sends rain on the just and unjust."⁵¹ God looks upon the just and the

48. John Zizioulas, *Communion and Otherness* (Edinburgh: T. & T. Clark, 2006), p. 82.
49. Zizioulas, *Communion and Otherness,* p. 83. Though it is generally agreed that Dostoevsky's Father Zossima was modeled on the eighteenth-century Russian bishop Tikhon of Zadonsk, it is possible that Dostoevsky's character was named after the sixth-century ascetic.
50. Zizioulas, *Communion and Otherness,* pp. 83-86.
51. Quoted by Day in "Our Country Passes," p. 1.

unjust with the same love; all are sinners, and all are subject to the same redemption.

For Dorothy Day, the fact that Christ took on humanity as such and redeemed it means that all humanity, without exception, participates in Christ in one way or another. The mystical body of Christ is not the reserve of Christians alone, nor only of the virtuous. The mystical body of Christ is cosmic in scope, and embraces all humanity along with all of creation. It is precisely because of Dorothy Day's profound grasp of the mystical body doctrine that it is so misleading to classify the Catholic Worker Movement as a sect. Daniel DiDomizio's contribution to the volume *A Revolution of the Heart* states: "This personalist, almost anarchist style has bestowed on the Catholic Worker an identity and spirituality similar to that of a sect. Just as members of sectarian groups, Catholic Workers tend to define themselves against the surrounding society."[52] But nothing could be more inclusive than Day's vision of a deep participation in one another in the mystical body of Christ. "We believe that all men are members or potential members of the Mystical Body of Christ. This means Jews, Gentiles, Black and White. This means our enemies as well as our friends. Since there is no time with God, and since we are told that all men are members or potential members of Christ's Mystical Body, that means that now at the present time we must look upon all men with love. We must overcome all evil with good, hatred with love."[53] Day repeatedly used the phrase "members or potential members" as a way of recognizing that in this life not all people consciously acknowledge Christ or act as if they do, but nevertheless all are taken up into Christ's humanity. When viewed *sub specie aeternitatis,* that is, through God's timeless eyes, all human beings must be seen even now as if they were Christ.

This aspect of Dorothy Day's thought is widely recognized. If we see each person as Christ, then we will treat each person with love and hospitality, and certainly not kill the person. Christ is associated with virtue and goodness. But there is another side of Christ's taking on of humanity. This is the Christ of the breadlines, as in Fritz Eichenberg's famous 1939 woodcut. This is the Christ with dirty hair and sunken

52. Daniel DiDomizio, "The Prophetic Spirituality of the Catholic Worker," in *A Revolution of the Heart: Essays on the Catholic Worker,* ed. Patrick G. Coy (Philadelphia: Temple University Press, 1988), p. 232.

53. "Aims and Purposes," *Catholic Worker,* January 1939, p. 7.

eyes, the defeated Christ who stands waiting for a handout of soup and a piece of bread. This is the Christ who has not only been wronged by sin but has also taken sin into himself. This is the Christ who, as Paul says, became "a curse for us" (Gal. 3:13). Although he has not sinned, Christ has somehow taken on sin in order to make the exchange by which "For our sake he made him to be sin who knew no sin, so that in him we might become the righteousness of God" (II Cor. 5:21).[54] The body of Christ, in other words, is not a pure body of virtue that is opposed to a sinful world. It is instead the place where sin is absorbed and healed by the very process of love by which members assume the burdens of each other's sins, both the consequences of those sins and the guilt for them.

III. Conclusion

For Dorothy Day, assuming the guilt of others was not a matter of play-acting, pretending to be guilty while knowing full well that the guilt belonged to those flying the planes that dropped the bombs that blew the limbs off children. Because Dorothy Day's revolution was a personalist revolution, she knew that the solution to violence was rooting out the violence from one's own heart, and the only way to do so was first to recognize that that violence is there, in the heart of each one of us. The personalist revolution was not like the Communist revolution, in which the first step was identifying the class enemy. She thought that ending war was not a matter of killing all the right people. She thought that war would end when individual people simply refused to kill others, not out of a desire to make themselves pure, but from a humble and utterly realistic recognition that they were not good enough to use violence well. Only then could the church, the body of Christ, become not an army inflicting wounds but a field hospital binding them up.

54. For further reflections on the sense in which Christ became sin, see William T. Cavanaugh, *Migrations of the Holy: God, State, and the Political Meaning of the Church* (Grand Rapids: Eerdmans, 2011), chap. 8.

PERMISSIONS

The author and publisher gratefully acknowledge permission to reprint the following essays by William T. Cavanaugh:

"Are Corporations People? The Corporate Form and the Body of Christ," originally published in *Christian Political Witness,* ed. Goerge Kalantzis and Gregory W. Lee. Copyright © 2014 by George Kalantzis and Gregory W. Lee. Used by permission of InterVarsity Press, P.O. Box 1400, Downers Grove, IL 60515, USA. www.ivpress.com.

"Westphalia and Back: Complexifying the Church-World Duality in Catholic Thought," originally published in the *Journal of Moral Theology* 2, no. 2 (June 2013): 1-20.

"Orthodoxy and Heresy in Departments of Economics," originally published in *Christianity and the Disciplines: The Transformation of the University,* ed. Mervyn Davies, Oliver Crisp, Gavin D'Costa, and Peter Hampson (Edinburgh: T. & T. Clark, 2012), 183-201. Used by permission of Bloomsbury Publishing Plc.

"Actually, You *Can't* Be Anything You Want (and It's a Good Thing, Too)," to be published in *At This Time and In This Place,* ed. David S. Cunningham (Oxford: Oxford University Press, 2016). Used by permission of Oxford University Press, USA. www.oup.com.

"What Constantine Has to Teach Us," originally published in *Constantine Revisited: Leithart, Yoder, and the Constantinian Debate,* ed. John D. Roth (Eugene, OR: Wipf & Stock, 2013), 83-99. Used by permission of Wipf and Stock Publishers. www.wipfandstock.com.

"Religious Violence as Modern Myth," originally published in *Political Theology* (2014): 486-502. The online version of this journal can be found here: www.maneyonline.com/pol.

"Political Theology as Threat," originally published in *The Cambridge Companion to Political Theology,* ed. Craig Hovey and Elizabeth Phillips. Copyright © 2015 by Cambridge University Press. Reprinted with the permission of Cambridge University Press.

"Secularization, Violence, and Idolatry," originally published in *Plowshares into Swords?: Reflections on Religion and Violence,* ed. Robert W. Jenson and Eugene Korn (Efrat, Israel: Center for Jewish-Christian Understanding and Cooperation, 2014).

"Are We Free Not to Be a Religion? The Ambivalence of Religious Freedom," originally published in *Pro Ecclesia* 23, no. 1 (Winter 2014): 7-21.

INDEX OF NAMES AND SUBJECTS

119; as liturgical action, 116; as meal, 40; medieval, 114; as sacrifice, 147, 168-69, 173

Failinger, Marie, 245
Fall, the, 89, 151-52, 261
Figgis, John Neville, 49, 138
Francis, Pope, 1-4, 10
Franciscans, 45-46
Freedom, 117; and choice, 77, 82, 83, 87, 106-7; definition of, 89-91, 94; as justification for war, 178, 186, 190, 195-96, 198, 216-20; and markets, 122; and ontology, 19; religious, 10, 37, 234-48; and the secular, 111; of speech, 24; and subsidiarity, 128
Friedman, Milton, 60
Functionalism: critique of, 180-81, 187; and idolatry, 220-24, 231; and politics, 105, 111, 216

Galli, Carlo, 109
Gaudium et Spes, 49-50
Gierke, Otto von, 137-38
Gilbert, Daniel, 85-86, 90-91
Girard, René, 169, 190
Gogarten, Friedrich, 208, 215
Gold, Lorna, 62-63
Goldstein, Rebecca, 202-3
Goodchild, Philip, 68-71
Gregory, Brad, 194, 203, 244
Grumett, David, 114

Hahnenberg, Edward, 76-77
Halbertal, Moshe, 224-25, 230
Hauerwas, Stanley, 99, 158, 209, 253
Hegel, G. W. F., 207, 209
Hehir, Bryan, 130-36
Heyer, Kristen, 254
Hitchens, Christopher, 179, 200, 202, 215
Hobbes, Thomas: and bodies politic, 22; and Carl Schmitt, 215, 217; and the church, 152; and loss of mediation, 109; and religion, 205-12
Hurd, Elizabeth Shakman, 189
Hutcheson, Francis, 80

Idolatry, 208; and economics, 2, 72; and other religions, 9, 205; and secularization, 186, 190, 194, 218, 219-33
Illich, Ivan, 7, 117-20
Incarnation, 210; and corporate belonging, 17, 28; and politics, 100, 103, 108, 115, 117-20
Irenaeus, 163-64
Islam, 89, 111, 178; and politics, 204, 213, 246; and secularization, 223

John Paul II, Pope, 63
Juergensmeyer, Mark, 179, 186-87

Kahn, Paul, 99-100, 104-10, 217-18
Kant, Immanuel, 207
Kantorowicz, Ernst, 21-22, 100-106, 109, 113-16
Kimball, Charles, 177
Klein, Naomi, 28
Kobasa, Stephen, 248

Labor unions, 6, 13, 30, 37-38, 131, 135
Lash, Nicholas, 232
Leamer, Edward, 60
Lee, Gregory, 228-29
Legion of Decency, 38
Leithart, Peter, 8, 157-74
Leo XIII, Pope, 131, 134-37
Leontief, Wassily, 60
Liberalism, 105; and democracy, 142, 197-98; and markets, 23-24, 180; as religion, 180, 221, 233; and violence, 204, 214, 216-17
Lilla, Mark, 9, 104-6, 200-218
Lindblom, Charles, 23, 28
Locke, John: on labor, 80; and religion/politics distinction, 183, 209, 212; on rights, 243; and toleration, 159
Lohfink, Gerhard, 17
Lori, Archbishop William, 247-48
Lubac, Henri de: on the Eucharist, 21-22, 142; on human unity, 16-17; on transcendent/immanent distinction, 7, 100, 113-19
Lubich, Chiara, 126

Luther, Martin, 76-77

MacPherson, C. B., 24-25
Margalit, Avishai, 224-25, 230
Marie de France, 21
markets, 159; in binary with state, 7, 31, 121-28, 134-39; labor, 82; and politics, 14, 22-29; as religion, 66, 68, 71, 221, 223; and values, 63-65; and violence, 143-44, 186, 195, 216, 218
Marty, Martin, 179
Martyrdom, 172
Marvin, Carolyn, 180
Marxism, 55; and primitive accumulation, 81; and reduction of religion, 48, 107; as religion, 111, 180, 216, 221, 230, 233; and revolution, 149
Masuzawa, Tomoko, 184, 212
McCloskey, Deirdre, 72
Mill, John Stuart, 24-25
Murray, John Courtney, 38, 130-31

National Catholic War Council, 37
Nationalism, 115, 189, 207, 213; as idolatry, 249; and mysticism, 22, 28, 101, 142; as religion, 111, 179-80, 192, 216-18, 221, 232-33
Nativism, 37
Nelson, Robert H., 66-68, 232
Neoscholasticism, 38, 113
Nisbet, Robert, 244
Nongbri, Brent, 212, 214
Notre Dame, University of, 55-57, 62, 65
Novak, Michael, 28-29

O'Brien, David J., 250-52
O'Donovan, Oliver, 140, 162-64, 166
Original sin, 67-68, 81

Paul, St., 255n23; and the body of Christ, 16-21, 30, 260; and flesh, 154; and idolatry, 9, 190, 220, 227-30; and pedagogical reading of Scripture, 168, 171; and sin, 160, 263; and the world, 50n23
Perfection, call to, 4, 5, 10, 39, 250-56

Peters, Benjamin, 4-5n9, 253
Peterson, Erik, 108
Pius XI, Pope, 130-31, 135-36
Plato, 15
Polanyi, Karl, 63
Pueblo Indians, 10, 235-42

Radner, Ephraim, 191-99
Reformation, 75-76, 160, 192, 203-4, 244
Religious freedom. *See* Freedom, religious
Rerum Novarum, 124, 134-35
Rosenberg, Alexander, 61
Rosenzweig, Franz, 207-8
Rousseau, Jean-Jacques, 207, 209
Rust, Jennifer, 115-16
Ryan, John A., 37-38

Sacrament, 210; and church, 21, 39-40; and grace, 4n9; and idolatry, 232; and politics, 7, 100, 114-17; and Reformation, 76
Sacrifice, 104, 147, 168-69, 172-74, 217
Salisbury, John of, 21
Schmitt, Carl: and church, 119, 152; and democracy, 113-16; and fiction/reality dichotomy, 7, 100-110; and Hobbes, 215; and political theology, 217
Schwartz, Barry, 7, 83-93
Sectarianism, 3-5; and Catholic Worker Movement, 250-54, 262; and Catholicism, 42-46, 48-49; Troeltsch and, 39-40, 154-55, 250-51
Secularization, 67, 100-101, 202-3, 219-33
Shedinger, Robert, 246
Smith, Adam, 26, 68, 80
Smith, Wilfred Cantwell, 181, 184, 211
Solow, Robert, 56, 72
Stevens, John Paul, 14, 24, 26, 29-30
Subsidiarity, 7, 41, 121, 128-35, 139

Taylor, Charles, 100, 117-19
Thomas Aquinas, Saint, 5n9, 48, 91, 140, 182
Troeltsch, Ernst, 39-40, 44-48, 154, 250, 252-53